Essays on World Education

Essays

on

World

Education:

The Crisis of Supply and Demand

Edited by George Z. F. Bereday

New York
OXFORD UNIVERSITY PRESS
London . Toronto
1969

370
I61e

CONTENTS

Introduction

PART I

v

INTRODUCTION

It has been estimated that one quarter of the world's population will not attend any school in this century. In many of the less developed countries that figure may be 50 per cent. When compared with previous centuries this still represents an advance, but in an age committed to the concept of universal education this is a calamity.

The growing breach between educational supply and demand occurs not only on the crisis level of illiteracy. It is present at all stages of the educational process. For example, when a country attempts to expand primary schools rapidly, a strain is put on its supply of teachers, and the quality of education suffers. Attempts at expansion in secondary schools and colleges are complicated by skirmishes between those devoted to traditional concepts of education and those who long for new curricula. Proponents of established programs offer fare that is sanctioned by tradition, but which is often not easily adaptable to the requirements of modernity. Reformers want flexibility, but the results of experimentation are seldom clear-cut or capable of wide-spread application. The diverse educational enterprises of the world are convulsed by the continued shocks that the demands of the times administer to them. Such expansion as occurs is erratic, and meanwhile millions of children clamor at the closed school gates.

ENLARGING EDUCATIONAL SUPPLY

The essays in this volume are devoted to a consideration, first by substantive topics and then by geographical areas, of the inadequacies of educational supply. They testify to a sense of alarm throughout the world about the lack of sufficient educational opportunities. Countries today feel unprecedented pressure from their citizens to build more schools. The expansion sought is both sidewards and upwards; education for more persons and more education for each person. The recognition grows that the quality of human capital is perhaps the most important determinant of common well-being.

Yet for obvious reasons it is far from certain that the needed increase in educational facilities and opportunities will be fully provided. Our most visible problems are economic. Much has been written about rapid technological change but more work is needed to estimate its impact upon schools. Technology demands that the product of education be flexible enough to shift jobs and domicile in response to demand. Automation increases leisure time, and such a prospect requires research on the relevance of education to the arts and other "ornamental" forms of learning. Distinguished economists have generally confirmed the conviction long held by educators that poor societies become rich only after they invest in education. However, the complicated causal relationship of education to economic growth is not yet fully understood.

Economic development is not the only problem. Forever renewed sources of inspiration are needed to keep the educational process from becoming sluggish. How do we make education uphold and encourage mental powers instead of drowning them? How do we include all mankind in education's reach? How, for example, can we ensure that we get the most out of the highly talented without unbalancing or boring them or over-inflating their egos? How do we continually push up the threshold of academic comprehension of the average and the sub-average who find it difficult to handle abstractions? How do we revolutionize teaching so that the best talents are available at times and places where young persons most need them? How do we maximize the opportunities for large-group instruction and small-group tutoring in the most appropriate ratios and thus boost the quality of education? How do we reform school architecture so that school buildings, like modern museums, uplift one and, like churches, make human imagination soar? How, ultimately, in our educational policies do we balance local, national, and world needs and aspirations?

Such questions are of great consequence to the drive for education and they permeate this book. Solutions are elusive and resolution is often lacking. Somehow investment in the training of the minds of men, the most vital capital at the disposal of society, has never been considered a national priority. Societies do not respond quickly or seriously enough to the rising tide of educational aspirations. In some cases, they are too poor to cope with scarcities which prevent them from meeting even their own modest targets. In other cases they simply lack knowledge of how to cope with the snow-balling pressures upon their social systems.

First there is not enough money for education, even in the advanced countries. Provision of school places always lags behind the need for them. Overcrowded classrooms, overworked teachers, and double sessions are part of school life everywhere. Financing education is an underdeveloped and unimaginative enterprise.

Planning for the intake, training, and multiple destinations of pupils continues to be difficult, even though counting children at birth gives societies at least a seven-year headstart. Human beings are unpredictable, and this, perhaps fortunately, defeats attempts at precise human engineering. As a result of planning, school systems are supposed to tally with the annual manpower requirements of the economy. Instead, the schools either underproduce, and the resulting shortages of manpower drive the labor costs upward and slow down the national development of well-being, or they overproduce, and the intellectual unemployed created by such surpluses become a source of unrest and upheaval. Educational planners are caught in a continuous balancing act to avoid both extremes.

No one likes to pay for what is not a quality product. But research into the nature of the pedagogical process, though expanding, has not really "broken through." Educational programs continue to be predominantly intuitive. To many they appear useless, unrelated to life, or simply boring. Some programs are so theoretical as to be pedantic, while others are so action-oriented as to be narrow of vision. The result in terms of non-performance, discouragement of effort, and frustrated aspirations wrought by curricular deficiencies is immeasurable. Admissions, programs, and examinations discourage those for whom such matters are not habitual. Millions of less privileged children learn to read but emerge non-readers, take examinations after years of schooling but fail, are expected to study but drop out. So much of the scarce educational supply is also a wrong supply.

Another reason for the inadequacy of the supply of educational opportunities is the obsolescence of the systems of educational administration. Too many simply do not respond to pleas for reform. In education as elsewhere wisdom and maturity of judgment have been traditionally assumed to be correlative with age. As a result, positions of educational leadership are everywhere filled by older men. But older men are frequently conservative and tired. The tempo of a technological society demands leaders who are at the peak of their physical and intellectual potential. And educational leadership, because of the Cinderella image of the professional study and position of education, has not been attracting its share of high talent. Hence first-class problems have been met by mediocre solutions. The executive tools used are not brilliant decisions, but exhortation. Crises are often met by interminable speeches, pious generalities, hedging, even mendacity. Action often reduces itself to the appointment of new committees and more talk.

THE DEMAND FOR EDUCATION RECONSIDERED

Confronted by the awesome scarcity of schools and the near impossibility of alleviating it, we have to face also another unsettling argument often put forward by opponents of mass education. Perhaps there is relatively little wrong on the side of supply of educational opportunities; perhaps the size and quality of the demand are unrealistic.

Men demand education for many reasons. They are curious.

They are eager to acquire professional or vocational skills. They are keen to acquire or to maintain the social prestige conferred by education. They want to know the meaning of existence, how things are ordained and how nature can be harnessed. But they also want to know how to get a job and advance in it. The desire for education is partly noble and partly expedient. Though education is advanced in the name of equality, society assumes that more lengthily educated people are in some ways better as a class than their less favored brethren. Perhaps men should not want quite so much education quite so badly, since so many want it for the wrong reasons.

If this is the case, opponents of mass education argue, the demand for educational opportunity, under the impact of which the world's school systems are currently groaning, should be limited. Why should communities set aside more men and money to allow everybody the pursuit of knowledge in and for itself, if instead more action—mining the hills, ploughing the fields, and cleaning up the slums—is most urgently in their interest? Why should vocational skills be taught for glutted or unpredictable markets when apprenticeship and training "on the job" might better regulate what must be learned? Why should so much effort be expended to cater to snobbishness? In theory-building it is always necessary to consider the antithesis before reaching a synthesis. In introducing a book which is totally committed to the opposite view it is necessary to face these disturbing but too often deserved recriminations.

One answer to the opponents of mass education is that whatever his motives, an individual's desire for education cannot be ignored. If societies encourage achievement in order to attain power rather than to serve, glorify making money to attain material satisfaction rather than righteousness, extoll social participation to attain popularity rather than respect, then the infinitely healthier phenomenon of youth in search of schools should never be regarded with hostility. Men are entitled to the use of trained intelligence. If they must hate, let them at least hate intelligently;

if they do evil, let that evil be tempered by reasoning. Robert Ulich of Harvard University used to say that the school is like a policeman who stands at the corner; he is seemingly not doing very much but we could not function without him. Modern schools must guide as well as restrain men but they must never ignore them. In most countries children are being compelled to assimilate some education. We can hope that eventually no one should be denied education of any type at any time if he wishes it. In the crisis of disparity between supply and demand, the demand should be held as given.

The business of integrating young persons into adult societies begins with the fierce attempts to guide, even to force, all children into literacy. It may well end with what Margaret Mead has once called an education which extends "from cradle to grave." In the United States there is some talk at present about assuring the poor a guaranteed income. It is easy to suggest an analogous right, that of guaranteed education. In the appendix to this volume Clark Kerr proposes an "educational bank" for all that would guarantee a number of years of community-financed education. Only some of these years would be used up in adolescence. The balance would be held as credit to be drawn on at any time the individual wishes to avail himself of it. Education must be indebted to Clark Kerr who originated the idea, though we are far away from such an educational panacea. Yet as an ideal the notion is inspiring. The question is not whether we can afford it but whether we can afford to be without it. Mass education should not go down in history as an unfulfilled dream of our age.

✿   ✿   ✿   ✿

These essays were originally presented at the International Conference on World Crisis in Education held October 5-9, 1967, at Williamsburg, Virginia. President Lyndon Johnson called this conference on November 22, 1966, following the enactment of the International Education Act of 1966, "to stimulate deeper mutual understanding among nations of major education problems facing the world." The meetings that resulted were sponsored jointly by the U.S. Department of Health, Education and Welfare and ten United States foundations. Its hosts were John W. Gardner, then the Secretary of Health, Education and Welfare, and James A. Perkins, President of Cornell University. The conference assembled some 150 university people, administrators, and public figures from all over the world and with an interest in world education. Several were invited to submit papers, the revised versions of which form the substance of this book. All participants engaged in work group discussions stimulated by the master document prepared by Philip Coombs and by the papers presented here. The guidelines and recommendations formulated as a result are reproduced in the appendix and may serve as a summary of the context of this volume. Together these materials introduce the reader to the subject matter of the conference and provide a general index to the level of the thinking on the crisis in education which we face today.

In connection with the preparation of the *Essays* one pleasant duty remains to be fulfilled. The editor's thanks are due to Mrs. Shana Conron and Mrs. Janet Abernathy Robertson for exacting editorial work, and to Miss Judith Guerra and Miss Sandra Anthony for typing and collating the manuscript with eagerness and devotion.

New York   G. Z. F. B.

October 1968

Essays on World Education

I

EDUCATIONAL MANAGEMENT AND POLICY-MAKING

ALEXANDER KING

Educational systems throughout the world have until recently
evolved slowly, often from local roots. In many countries, education is strongly decentralized, although there is a general trend
toward central direction by the state. This trend, which ranges
from new nations beginning their educational development to
the United States where federal aid to education has only recently been accepted, is probably inevitable because of increasing
awareness of the relation of education to social and economic
development. It is also encouraged by the growth of urbanism
and by deliberate national policies to provide equal educational
opportunities to all.

GENERAL CHARACTERISTICS

In most countries of the world, education is, after defense, the
biggest single item of national expenditure; it is often the biggest
single sector of the economy. Yet its management is still somewhat primitive and has not been subjected to pressures for higher
productivity and efficient use of resources—manpower and buildings. It is almost the last "major industry" to remain virtually
untouched by the scientific revolution, although the rapid rise
of educational technology is beginning to have an impact.

In most countries of the world, too, the greater part of formal

education is already out of date. It is still more obsolete in relation to the world of the near future into which the children
presently entering the educational system will emerge. The main
aim of educational systems was until recently to improve the
quality of teaching. Now, however, all this has changed. Several
revolutions are taking place simultaneously—in politics, in social
attitudes, in economic development, and through the explosion
of new knowledge. The natural sciences and technology especially are transforming and extending our material environment.
The present world of children at school is thus already quite
different from that in which their teachers were educated; the
world in which they will work and live as adults will be still
more sharply different.

An educational system is no longer expected merely to impart
traditions and skills; it has to prepare for a changing world and
to help individuals adjust to such changes. It is simultaneously
faced with increasing enrollments, rising costs, totally new instructional techniques, new—and as yet insufficiently defined—
social functions, and public discontent.

How, then, is education to increase its relevance? How can its
structures be changed to accommodate larger numbers and more
varied needs? How can its policy-makers foresee the demands of
the not too distant future and lay the basis for occupations and
skills that do not yet exist? How can the management of the
mammoth business of education be made effective? How can
innovation in education be speeded up and made wisely selective to allow for changing demands and to use knowledge from
all sorts of disciplines, even to the extent of "inventing" alternative futures and assessing the relevance of a particular education
to each? These are but a few of the larger problems that educational policy-makers and administrators face today.

Many educational systems have remained somewhat aloof from
other elements of national activity, although this tendency has
been less marked in some countries than in others. This aloofness
derived from the assumption that education had the unique and

relatively simple objective of imparting the knowledge and tradition of a society to succeeding generations. Now education has several objectives. It is still the basic conveyor of knowledge, but in addition it is regarded as an instrument of social policy, as an important object of economic investment, and as a factor affecting consumption. These objectives are not always or easily accepted by educators, who have at times feared they would reduce education to being a mere servant of the economy. Educational planning is becoming, however, much more sophisticated, as education is considered an integral part of national life, influencing and being influenced by other elements of development, including the social and the economic. The ability to relate the educational, the scientific, the industrial, and other components of progress in concept as well as in action has become of paramount importance in social and economic development.

Even a simplified model indicates that an educational system has to respond to four different types of demand: (1) the demand of the individual for the development of his personal potential and for preparation for a career; (2) the demand of the economy, which, as part of national investment, requires a future manpower with highly developed skills relevant to economic needs; (3) the demand of the consumer, which may mount high in an affluent and urban society, for more education as desirable in itself; (4) the demand inherent in social change, extension of equality of opportunity, the function of stabilizing, breaking down, or replacing existing social strata in accordance with politically determined goals.

These demands are, of course, intimately connected, but particular stress on one may give rise to conflict. For example, high consumer demand for education from certain affluent sections of society may, with limited resources, run counter to policies of democratization and to the economic objective of utilizing to an optimum extent the human potential of a country.

It is thus increasingly necessary for educational policy to be a part of over-all national policy, and not a world apart. At different stages of its development a nation's policy may lay quite different stresses on what is required of education, and will determine allocation of resources accordingly. Thus at an early stage it may stress the need for general literacy or for the provision of an elite with vocational and management skills to achieve immediate national economic objectives. At a later stage the establishment of general primary education may be the dominant need, while secondary and higher education must be introduced as they are needed. Such matters require careful consideration, since an educational measure may not be carried out for years, and its effects tend to persist long after the balance of need has shifted. This time lag is the chief difficulty for the planner and policymaker. If measures to correct existing inadequacies are not oriented to the future, educational policy will always be obsolescent.

POLICY AND MANAGEMENT IN EDUCATION

The structure of education varies greatly from country to country. In many it consists of a general framework of policy and objective determined by law, but with implementation and subdecision at a regional, a national or even a parish level. As education expands and becomes more costly, the central government is called upon to take the major share of the financial burden in most cases and hence is more and more able to call the tune, or at least is under the public suspicion of wishing to do so. The complexities of running the socio-economic enterprise called education come to necessitate a corresponding structure.

The major trend is thus toward professional policy-making at all levels of education. Even uncontroversial proposals to modify schools or colleges do much more than cost money: they may determine the quality and the quantity of the educational product for fifty years or more and influence not only educational policy but manpower policy and national policy in general. In educationally decentralized countries rather little is known about how educational decisions are made—about who decides and under what pressures and with what convictions. We cannot be sure that those governing the schools really know enough about national goals to make local decisions that will further those goals. There follows a series of embarrassing questions about the competence of local school boards and governors, even those who are politically orthodox and deeply devoted. Can a large and part-time management really have the depth of knowledge, the skill, and the time to make wise decisions on which so much will depend for so long a time? The present administrative structure of education in every country was set up at a time of simpler alternatives and of different political criteria. In terms of efficiency and resources alone the previous mechanism is unworkable or, at best, creaks along maintained by continuous and unsystematic repairs and has little vision of future needs. On the other hand, placing all decisions in the hands of a powerful central bureaucracy poses new dangers.

Any one of the three features already mentioned necessitate a proper administrative overhaul of the system: (1) the vast expansion of enrollment; (2) the inevitable leveling off of budgets as expansion continues; (3) the need to build into the system, mechanisms for prevision and continuous innovation.

THE PLANNING OF EDUCATION

If education is regarded as a major national investment in social and economic progress, its constituent elements must be selected and managed at least as seriously as are more concrete investment items.

One of the most striking approaches to the problem has been the concept of educational planning, which has grown rapidly during the last decade. This is not the occasion to enumerate the various attempts to establish plans for future educational growth, but we should mention that these attempts have at times appeared to be contradictory or fractional. For example, in developing countries a manpower approach has often seemed most reasonable, while in more developed societies consumer demand projections have proved more useful. As planning methods become more refined, the contradiction of such approaches tends to disappear. Much of the impetus for educational planning has come from international sources: for example, Harbison's contributions to the Ashby report on Nigerian education;[1] the success of the United Nations Educational, Scientific, and Cultural Organization in securing world wide support for integrated programs relying on education as a mainspring; the stimulus and assistance given by the International Institute for Educational Planning (attached to UNESCO); the initiative the Organization for Economic Cooperation and Development (OECD) took in pioneering the manpower approach, especially through its Mediterranean Regional Project which has provided guidelines of development for the education of six countries of the European Mediterranean. As a result of the OECD's activities, the European ministers of education agreed unanimously to regard education as an investment as well as a consumption item and to set up educational investment planning units in their ministries. This resolution has been largely implemented.

Although educational planning was hardly discussed five years ago, it is now developing much faster and is finding more ready acceptance than economic planning. It suffers, however, from approaches borrowed in too facile a manner from economic planning. In the economic field the central preoccupation is the development of a plan within whose framework private firms and national corporations can take their investment decisions and rely on the mechanisms of the market to ensure efficiency and the growth of the system. In education there is no corresponding internal corrective to assure efficiency. Public authorities, whether

1. Frederick Harbison, "High-Level Manpower for Nigeria's Future," in Report of the Commission on Post-School Certificate and Higher Education in Nigeria, *Investment in Education* (Nigeria: Federal Ministry of Education, 1960).

central or local, have therefore a much more direct responsibility for the implementation of educational investment and innovation decisions. This means that educational policy and planning are much more dependent on the explicit formulation of policy objectives and goals and on a deep understanding of the interaction among the different elements of the educational system.

The establishment of a detailed and quantitative basis for the planning of education is certainly one of the initial steps in providing for a more rational process of educational decision-making and of management improvement. Hence an important postulate is that each country that has yet not done so should create within its educational ministry, and preferably in contact with the economic-planning authorities, an educational investment-planning unit to work out guidelines of educational development consistent with the attainment of general national goals.

Effective educational planning depends on reliable statistics based on clearly formulated definitions. These need not be elaborate, but their quality must be high. A recent OECD publication, *Mathematical Models in Educational Planning*, gives an indication of the type of data required.[2]

For the purpose of planning education, each country should endeavor to provide a simple but clear statistical basis. Ideally this basis should be agreed upon internationally so as to make possible comparison between countries.

EDUCATION AS A SYSTEM

Just as education as a whole too often has been considered somewhat apart from other national activities, each of the various stages of education—primary, secondary, technical, higher, and postgraduate—has been regarded in isolation. This is highly improper, because rapid developments in one stage have a major influence, immediate or delayed, on the others. Furthermore, it

2. Organization for Economic Cooperation and Development, *Mathematical Models in Educational Planning* (Paris: OECD, Directorate for Scientific Affairs, 1967).

is impossible to maintain such isolation in view of the present preoccupation with the interconnection between education and society.

There is, in fact, much to be said for regarding education as a system: a subsystem within the national system, interacting with social, economic, scientific, cultural, or financial subsystems, responding to impacts from and giving impulses to these, and at the same time interacting more remotely with the educational subsystems of other countries. Within education itself, the existence of interactions, feedback loops, and so forth is becoming ever more obvious. Rapid expansion of secondary school intake, for example, has a delayed but probably calculable effect on higher education and at the same time requires a new type of coupling with the primary education circuit, which can be regarded no longer as an end in itself. Again the proliferating needs of society and the economy are generating new demands on higher education, which require extension and diversification and feed back to secondary education by specifying alternative paths of individual instruction to be articulated with the offerings of the universities.

Such a view of education, developed on the basis of sound statistics, can make possible the construction of models capable of demonstrating the existing and probable future flows within the system and of yielding valuable information to decision-makers on the probable consequences of various alternative assumptions and policies.

The development of mathematical model building is only beginning, but already some areas have been identified where useful applications should be possible. The most obvious concerns the *flows of students* into, within, and out of the educational system. Study is already in progress in a number of countries to: (1) predict student enrollment at each level and type of education; (2) predict the percentages of enrollment in each professional category and the impact of these educational outputs on the future economy; (3) predict future teacher supply; (4) provide a framework for measuring the social demand for education, and analyze the factors influencing student choice; (5) examine the effects of major policy decisions on student numbers and output; and (6) identify in advance, and hence attempt to eliminate, imbalances in the educational system which may have undesirable social and economic effects.

A second and important application of mathematical models will be in the efficient *allocation of financial and other resources* among competing claims within the educational system. In this type of input/output analysis clear formulations are essential. Inputs are defined as capital and operating expenditures for facilities and equipment as well as teacher outputs by qualification; outputs are defined in terms of different terminal qualifications.

Further help to educational managers can come from new techniques of systems analysis and operational research used to secure *efficient utilization of resources*: to obtain maximum output or optimum combinations of outputs from each separate input or from different combinations of these.

THE NEW RESEARCH

Such approaches hold great promise for the efficient management of the complex educational machine, but they are only emerging from the research stage, and their methods are far from fully developed. They are striking examples of the new type of research which is beginning to feed results into educational development. Education as an activity is somewhat analogous to engineering or medicine, in that it is developed by contributions from a whole spectrum of different disciplines. It is now clear that the great changes to be expected in the nature of education and in our understanding of the learning process will likewise come from research in many separate fields as well as from interdisciplinary attack on particular problems. We are just at the beginning of the process that is likely to revolutionize the structure, nature, technology, management, and efficiency of education. It is important that top management in education should be continuously and intelligently aware of this movement and make arrangements not only to sponsor basic and applied research for its own immediate needs, but also to make rapid and effective use of the flow of new knowledge, from whatever country of origin or scientific discipline. Education will need much more experimentation and the creation of pilot projects as in the development stage of engineering or of clinical research in medicine.

Some idea of the range of research considered relevant to educational development is given in the program of the Policy Research Center of the United States Office of Education. It includes contributions from economic, behavioral, biological, and physical sciences as well as from technology. It includes the need to foresee the emergence of new trades, professions, and occupations, and the influence of urban development, of live language instruction via satellite communication links, of new architectural technologies, of biophysical and biochemical advances, of man-machine symbiosis, of behavioral neurophysiology, and so forth. Such matters are of immediate concern to the educational authorities of a few highly industrialized societies, but they are the beginning of a general impact on education from the diverse disciplines of learning, which is likely to change profoundly the nature of the school, the learning process, and the structure of education. Decision-makers in education must arrange to be kept informed of the progress of this work.

REVIEW AND EVALUATION OF SCHOOL SYSTEMS

Although the educational systems of the world's nations have evolved from local traditions and in response to different environmental causes, there is nevertheless a great similarity among nations in the problems presented by the expansion of education and its relation to social and economic goals. The exchange of experience between nations is highly desirable at this time of rapid change, when the relative success or failure of particular experiments or institutional approaches in one nation can be of great profit to others. The need is not for superficial comparisons between systems, but for deep and uninhibited discussion and mutual criticism.

To meet this need, OECD has instituted a series of examinations whereby over a period of a few years the trends, experiments, policy changes, and problems of each member nation are investigated in the presence of the other nations. The review of a particular country may take about a year to prepare. A *rapporteur* appointed by the international organization spends considerable time in the country in question preparing a background report which is largely descriptive but gives the essential quantitative data and attempts to formulate the main problems. When this report is ready, a group of two to five senior examiners, chosen for their eminence and for their competence on particular facets of the review, visit the country under examination. They discuss matters with the minister of education, officials, research leaders, planning economists, university presidents, and others and make their own judgment about the development of the national educational system and the adequacy of available means to surmount its main problems. The examiners then write a report enumerating a number of areas in which they intend to ask questions.

The final stage of the review—the confrontation—takes place at the headquarters of OECD, where a group of senior representatives of the country under examination, at times led by the minister of education, are questioned for one or two days by the examiners in the presence of senior representatives of education from all the other countries. After appropriate editing, the examiners' report, the background report, and the main lines of the confrontation are published.

This procedure has a number of advantages. First, it means that over a given period the committee and secretariat at

OECD have a detailed and intimate knowledge of the structures, achievements, and problems of each country, which provides a realistic basis for the programs of the organization. Secondly, it is an important means of communicating live experience from one country to others and suggests new approaches which can be picked up by others and modified to suit national traditions and institutions. Finally, for the country under examination it is a salutory experience which forces a clear formulation of problems and trends, much like what the investigations of a firm of management consultants may achieve in a large industrial enterprise. Similar reviews are undertaken of the science, manpower, and economic policies of OECD countries.

This technique of review has much to offer in other parts of the world as a mechanism of mutual aid and exchange of experience.

POLICIES AND MECHANISMS FOR CONTINUOUS INNOVATION

If education is to be developed as an essential part of the social and economic fabric of nations, its response to outside needs must become much more rapid than it is now, and innovation will have to be carefully selected and planned, to allow both for the changing requirements of society and for the internal possibilities of improvement presented by new knowledge. The development of analytical, managerial, and evaluation techniques outlined above will enable problems of change to be more clearly foreseen, effectively analyzed, and better controlled but will not by itself ensure the necessary change. Mechanisms must be established for the wise selection and introduction of change, for experiment, and for changing attitudes. New educational technology—for example, novel curricula, experimental structures— is not likely to be effectively assimilated unless teachers and pupils have positive attitudes of participation, and unless teacher training colleges inculcate openmindedness and a willingness to experiment.

It will be necessary, therefore, for the responsible authorities to establish both policies and mechanisms for innovation. An interesting example of such action can be seen in Sweden, which has accepted the concept of "rolling reform."

Much of the preparation for innovation must come through research—for example, in the reform of curricula. It must be understood, however, that development in education, as in other social fields, is more complex than in natural science and technology. The link between new knowledge and new practice in a system as complex and socially sensitive as education cannot be achieved without a significant amount of experimentation within the system itself, involving all the partners—teachers, pupils, parents, and those who decide about the investment of new educational resources. If anything is known of the psychology and sociology of change, it is that participation in the preparation for change is indispensable to the acceptance of change. It is, therefore, necessary to incorporate into the educational system a much wider range of experimental innovations, which would be related to new knowledge and evaluated by the educational community; if successful, an innovation could be assimilated gradually into general practice. Such pilot work is in any case essential to ensure the validity of any change before it is generally applied. Some countries, such as France, have created experimental schools where such pilot experiments can be carried out. Widespread interest in new curricula for mathematics and the natural sciences, necessitating experimental courses, has prepared many countries for this approach.

It is generally recommended, therefore, that each ministry of education create a center of educational innovation to advise the minister and his senior officials on the need for change and on the selection of experiments, to undertake pilot work, and generally to establish conditions that will enable education to respond to social and economic circumstances.

In addition to national machinery, educational institutions will be required to adjust systematically to changes in curricula, teaching methods, and organization. Part of the present resistance to change arises from the absence of recognized procedures for its systematic introduction within schools and colleges; the result is that most changes are made in "crisis" situations or appear as a threat. It may be necessary to establish various consultative arrangements in the schools for this purpose, to reward teachers for pioneering or experimental work, to institute more systematic retraining schemes, and to mount evaluation procedures for institutional performance by outside groups equivalent to consultants in industry.

THE TRAINING OF EDUCATIONAL ADMINISTRATORS

The activities mentioned above—whether in research, planning, or practical experimentation—will lead to a growing body of new knowledge and techniques concerning the promotion and management of changes in complex and expanding educational systems and to a corresponding transformation in the principles of educational policy and the administration of management parallel to the development of industry and defense over the last fifty years. They will certainly tend toward centralization if the fruits of new knowledge are to be harvested, but they must also safeguard regional and local needs and interests.

The explosive growth of research and experiment in education has not yet been matched by a sophisticated administration, and few opportunities exist for leading policy-makers and the pioneers of educational research to put their ideas into practice. This lack constitutes a major obstacle to educational development.

The problem of innovation is particularly difficult to tackle owing to the long educational cycle. The task here is to see that decisions are taken in relation to the needs of society at the time they will become fully operative and not merely, as is now generally the case, to meet problems of the moment or of the past; otherwise, education will always trail behind the real needs of the individual and his society. The establishment of mechanisms for continuous innovation will impinge on the planning function and probably in most cases will be combined with it. This is necessary, but not sufficient, because the psychological and sociological aspects of innovation are probably more important and certainly more subtle than those of planning in general. All measures toward change that do not evoke response in the teachers are likely to fail. It is essential to attract to teaching and to the management of education openminded and flexible people, who are trained to balance tradition and stability with innovation and experiment. With this aim, each minister of education might appoint a personal adviser on innovation, who would inform him of the opportunities for and also of the dangers inherent in particular innovations, would sift out the essentials in the new educational research, would identify obstacles to change, and would be constantly preoccupied with the problem of relating education to society and the economy. Such an adviser would have a relationship to the minister or chief executive of the ministry similar to that of operational research workers to the military commanders during the Second World War. He would have no direct responsibility for making decisions but would contribute greatly to them by furnishing facts and making clear the opportunities, dangers, and future trends.

It has been impossible to discuss here many other important problems facing the educational administrator of the future. One problem will certainly be how to increase the efficiency of the system in the face of growing costs and budgets that are leveling off. It will be essential to make more effective use of funds, of buildings, and of teachers' time. On the capital cost side, it has already been amply demonstrated that building costs can be considerably decreased with, at the same time, substantial functional improvement in school and university buildings.

A further and somewhat different problem concerns university administration, which in many countries requires basic reform. It is no longer possible, for example, for a university rector to be effective if elected for a very short period and on the basis only of his academic eminence without reference to his skill in administration and policy-making. University administration will also have to be strengthened and will have to adopt new methods if it is to meet the problems of expansion and of increasing cooperation with industry and society. Again, there is the problem of continuing education throughout life to enable men to retrain for changing skills and occupations as technology alters the economy; this problem will present many difficulties to the formal education system, which will have to be tackled in cooperation with industry. More fundamental, young people at school and at the university must be provided with the necessary intellectual tools for further development and with the capacity to learn throughout life. This involves a basic change from the concept of the formal stage of education as a single endowment for life to the concept of it as an initial impulse to be reinforced subtly and frequently throughout a career.

EDUCATIONAL RESOURCES
AND PRODUCTIVITY

FRIEDRICH EDDING

The need for more and better education seems unlimited. Ignorance, narrowness of outlook, inability to cope with personal and social problems, among other symptoms of insufficient education, are dominant features of contemporary life. This is true even of the most advanced nations. As societies develop and become more complex and more artificial, their need for widespread, intensive, and continued education increases. Survival, internal balance, and economic growth depend on it. In addition, education increases the appetite for education as a means to enjoy life and to participate in cultural riches.

But the resources available for education are certainly not unlimited. The proportion of national income spent on education has risen sharply in many countries during the past years. Now resistance is visibly growing against the continued expansion of public spending on education through increased taxation or at the expense of other sectors. The propensity, on the other hand, to spend directly for education out of private income and to forego other expenditures is generally not developing fast enough to compensate for the restrictive tendencies in public spending.

Are there ways to overcome this resistance or reluctance? Research has provided us in recent years with much circumstantial evidence that education is not only a general cultural need and desirable for its own sake but also a productive enterprise, which

—in a world allowing substitution—might be credited with high marginal returns, or is absolutely necessary for economic growth. This research should be intensified, and its results given wide publicity, in order to promote a better understanding of the importance of public finance for education. Similarly, private spending on education may be encouraged by demonstration of its great and lasting possible benefits to the individual and to individual firms, and by better information based on intensive and up-to-date research into specific situations.

On the basis of flexible projections, models, and budget programs the interdependence and relative utility of various possible allocations of resources may be shown in order to force parliaments and other decision-makers to see specific budget proposals in the context of over-all planning for the development of human resources and other long-range societal needs. Since it is impossible to calculate and compare marginal returns to be expected from investments in education and other public activities, arguments of plausibility are bound to play an important role here. But those responsible for allocation decisions at least want to know what, with some degree of probability, will happen as a consequence of their decisions and what the alternatives are. In individual situations it is often possible and useful to describe in detail the merits and demerits of various alternative courses of allocation policies. In many cases it can be shown that certain uses of resources, with properly planned education, promise to contribute little to over-all development or may even have a negative influence.

Since education is viewed more and more as a lifelong process of learning accompanied by, or embedded in, gainful occupation, a larger part of the financing than heretofore may be shifted from the public treasuries to individual firms or to special funds furnished by firms. In France, for instance, a scheme to finance apprenticeship by special levies from industry has been functioning well for many years. The Industrial Training Act of 1964 introduced in Great Britain another scheme of this type. Educational costs financed in this or similar forms directly by industry, as a rule, will be expressed in the prices of the goods these industries produce. In a way, therefore, this method of financing education is simply another way of collecting from private households and of restricting other uses of individual incomes. But in comparison with direct taxation it has definite advantages and can be regarded as a particularly promising possibility for expanding the resources available for education.[1]

Transfer from one region, state, or district to another for the purpose of financing education is a common and normal procedure for financial equalization among parts of a nation that have developed differently. There are good arguments in favor of expanding this practice and extending it to the relations between richer and poorer nations. In fact, financial assistance earmarked for education to developing nations has been increasing considerably in recent years. It may increase further as the dangers of the widening gap between poor and rich countries and the key role of education in efforts to close this gap are more widely recognized.[2]

PRODUCTIVITY CONCEPTS IN EDUCATION

Some of the recent writings about the investment character of education have been wrongly interpreted as guaranteeing that any expenditure on education is highly profitable. This is, of course, a dangerous assumption. A continued increase in the resources available for education can be expected only if consistent efforts are made to improve the productivity of education: that is, the relation of efforts for education (or inputs) to its results (or outputs). The input/output relation in education is,

1. See also the scheme described in Selma Mushkin, "Resource Requirements and Educational Obsolescence," in E. A. Robinson and J. E. Vaizey, eds., *The Economics of Education* (London: Macmillan, 1966), pp. 463–478.

2. Lucille Reifmann, ed., *Financing of Education for Economic Growth* (Paris: OECD, 1966).

however, essentially different from that in industry. Students are not materials to be processed or assembled. Education generally does not cater to a market. The labor market offers a price for only a part of all the qualities possibly resulting from education. Some of these qualities are economically priceless, but they may have a high social value for a decision-maker and may be weighed by him as values among other desirable values against estimated costs. Because of these inevitable value judgments the input/output relation in education generally eludes all attempts at exact measurement.

But even those who put such a high value on the results of education that they can be quite certain it cannot be had in any cheap way[3] must agree that it does not make sense to increase indiscriminately the efforts for education. There must be some ways to improve the relation between means and ends even in a field where measurement is so difficult. How this can be done depends on the point of view and the scope of the planning. We have to distinguish between the relation of means to ends inside an educational system, on the one side, and the totality of relations between educational efforts and society outside educational institutions. We shall, therefore, define the productivity of education as a complex having two components that are not always in harmony: namely, internal efficiency and external efficiency.

The concept of internal efficiency requires some assumptions about the objectives or measurable achievements of an educational system. The objective may be to produce a number of graduates who have attained certain well-defined standards of knowledge and abilities. The ratio of graduates from a course to the number of those who entered the course may be another specification of the objective. It is also possible to assess and compare the achievement of a class in a certain subject category at the beginning and at the end of a period of learning and to consider the difference in average achievement as the result. In

3. See Raymond E. Callahan, *Education and the Cult of Efficiency* (Ann Arbor: University of Michigan Press, 1964).

each case the results or objectives are related to the measurable efforts needed to achieve them: for example, teachers' time, students' time, use of facilities and other resources. These inputs can be measured as expenditures or costs. (The term "cost" is used if, for instance, an estimate of the income a student foregoes or of imputed rent is included in the money expression of inputs.) The expenditure or cost of a certain course of learning can then be related to the attainment or objective. This relation is an expression of the internal efficiency of education: the effort needed to reach certain attainments in a period of organized learning or the attainment achievable with a certain effort.

The internal efficiency of education has so far been calculated mainly as *cost per graduate* of a course. To lower these costs means an increase of efficiency, and vice versa. This is a useful concept as far as it goes. For efficiency measurements it is certainly more useful than the calculation and comparison of cost per student per year as long as the costs of the year are not shown in relation to the achievements in this year. The costs per student per year in a certain type of education may be much higher in one country than in another, but the cost per graduate may be lower in the country spending more per year. The reason can be that the latter country is paying high salaries to teachers, has a low student/teacher ratio, and is giving much financial aid to students in order to free them from material worries. As a result the average student may graduate within half the time needed by the average student in the country showing low yearly costs per student.

This example—based on reality—emphasizes that cost comparisons of educational courses can become meaningful in considering efficiency if— and only in so far as—the results can be measured. The methods used to measure means and ends are far from perfect.[4] How to account for dropouts, for instance,

4. See Edding, *Methods of Analyzing Educational Outlay* (Paris: UNESCO, 1966), and Everett Franklin Lindquist, ed., *Educational Measurement* (6th printing; Washington: American Council on Education, 1966).

is an unsolved problem. Are the costs incurred by dropouts just wasted, or can it be assumed that there are lasting educational advantages even if a student does not reach the end of his course? Can the percentage of dropouts be used as a measuring weight to correct the output measured in numbers of graduates, and if so, how could this be done? In higher education further complications arise because education is one function; the others are research and public services. The costs per graduate, then, often include considerable noneducational expenses. More doubts are raised by the attempts to assess and compare the efficiency of courses using different methods and incurring different costs. One is forced as a rule to make liberal use of the *ceteris paribus* assumption.

But are methods and costs of education the most important determinants of its results? What about the various influences outside the classroom, the social background and the motivation of students and teachers?[5] In many cases negative environmental influences tend to outweigh gains in formal education. Then the question arises whether to continue increases in conventional educational efforts or to shift the emphasis to improving the environment.

Other unsolved problems lie in the difficulties of measuring achievements other than knowledge and vocational skills. Yields of education rarely considered in examinations are, for instance, knowledge of how to learn and eagerness to continue learning; ability to cooperate, to take the initiative, to make decisions under conditions of uncertainty; and virtues like tolerance, honesty, self-control, and creativity. These are possibly the most important results of education, but they are harder to measure than the performances usually judged and marked in certificates. Planning for efficiency in education is in danger of being misled by the usual methods of measuring results, which sometimes tend to measure relatively non-essential qualities. This is often

5. See Bergen Richard Bugelski, *The Psychology of Learning Applied to Teaching* (New York: Bobbs-Merrill, 1964).

true also if the needed "products" of education are measured on the basis of manpower forecasts.

This suggests the limits of the internal efficiency concept in assessing the productivity of education. Institutions of organized learning can theoretically be viewed as autonomous units, secluded from outside influences and requirements of social utility. If the objectives they have set themselves are attained at comparatively low cost, they may claim to be efficient. In fact, however, these institutions might perhaps appear totally unproductive evaluated on the basis of societal needs.

In tradition-bound societies and social groups a fixed canon of educational ends made it possible to assume harmony between the internal efficiency and the external utility of education. Today this situation no longer exists. Continuous change of values, knowledge, social structures, manpower needs, and many other components of culture is the most characteristic feature of developing societies. Not only development but fast development is nowadays the generally recognized goal. Societies demand that education be geared to this goal. As a result the demand for stable interdependence between education and society has given way to the demand for interdependence of dynamic development.

It follows that now the ends and means of education have to be constantly adjusted in order to achieve internal efficiency in view of changing external needs. These needs are generally not those presently observed but are assumed for some time in the future. This poses some difficult problems. How can we know about the needs for private and societal life in the future? How can we plan for an educational productivity that means present internal efficiency geared to future external efficiency? Much of the recent research into methods for planning education is centered around these questions. The results so far are not satisfying. All the simple approaches recommended not so long ago under the labels "manpower approach," "returns approach," "correlations approach" have been discovered to be dubious as theory and often almost useless practically for the decision-maker. More and more factors formerly considered to be explanatory variables in the analysis of past developments and as parameters in planning education are now seen as policy variables in a wide field of interdependencies. For instance, not so long ago the ability to absorb and profit from secondary and higher education appeared to be restricted by natural inheritance to a relatively small group in any population. Nowadays this ability appears to be less limited. It is seen rather as a product of social conditions, aspirations, and learning opportunities offered. The manpower structure, formerly regarded as determining the amount and kind of education needed, is now viewed as an object and a result of societal planning, including the planning of education. Similar changes of view can be observed with regard to population, degree of urbanization, income, and many other factors commonly used in planning models.

It follows that the questions raised concerning planning for educational productivity cannot be answered with one formula applied with the help of a computer in all countries and situations. At present we do not have a theory of planning or a method that can tell the decision-maker which measures of educational planning will ensure optimum productivity in the double sense outlined above. Research can only help the decision-maker become aware of the dynamic complexity of his object. It can, for instance, caution against fixed targets of long-term plans. It can recommend some approaches and means, which in all probability will improve the productivity of educational efforts.

UTILIZATION OF EDUCATIONAL RESOURCES

The first condition for educational productivity is the conviction among politicians, administrators, teachers, students, parents, and the public that it is necessary and desirable. This productivity presupposes a general motivation for achievement, modernization, and rational action. It means very often a break with deep-rooted traditional attitudes and with the inertia characteristic of many of the groups and institutions whose cooperation is needed. It means in particular that education must not be allowed to remain or to become a secluded province. It should participate in activities for societal development and should attract the participation of noneducators in teaching and learning.

If resources are to be put to their best use, the broad ends for which they are to be used must be clear. Political consensus is necessary on the general goals of education—for instance, on the priority to be given the principle of equal opportunity or on the relative weight to be given to cognitive growth in proportion to moral and social virtues. Should specialized vocational education or general education be dominant? Some basic political decisions on curriculum and structure of education are a precondition for productivity-oriented planning.

In order to enable politicians to reach wise decisions and to ensure current evaluation of the measures implemented, planning institutions are necessary. They have to initiate and evaluate statistics and research, give a clear analysis of the situation and the results of projections, show the consequences of alternative courses, and ensure internal consistency of educational plans and also consistency with general social and economic developments. Further, they must try to combine the forecasts of the social demand for education, enrollments, and manpower needs with the knowledge gained from returns analysis and with the financial possibilities in a given period of time.[6] Clearly none of these approaches by itself can guarantee optimization of productivity. Neither can a combination do it. But that does not mean that continued work on these lines could not considerably improve the situation of the decision-maker.

Rationality is the general condition for productivity-oriented planning. But this does not mean that figures and mathematics

6. George Z. F. Bereday and Joseph A. Lauwerys, eds., *Educational Planning; The World Year Book of Education: 1967*, (New York: Harcourt, Brace and World, and London: Evans Bros., 1967), and Mark Blaug, "Approaches to Educational Planning," *Economic Journal*, 77 (June 1967), pp. 262–287.

are needed for every aspect of the planning process. To ensure a strong positive motivation of all participants in the learning process, for instance, seems to be an important task in efficiency planning. Motivation has many sources in the individual and social background of students and teachers. These sources can be explored, and possibilities to optimize the process of learning under various conditions can be studied. Empirical research in this field is somewhat undeveloped but deserves high priority. Some general conditions of efficiency in teaching and learning, however, can now be pointed out as promising, without waiting for the results of future research. One of these conditions is motivation.

It can be said that pressure and punishment as means of motivation have steadily lost supporters, whereas incentives of various kinds have gained in general recognition. It is an incentive if students and teachers feel that their work is regarded as complementary to, and at least equal in importance to, work in factories and offices. It is a disincentive if students are made to believe that real life begins after the period of learning, and if teachers for the same reason have low social prestige. It is an incentive if every student knows that he has a real chance of obtaining the highest degrees, and if every teacher can see a possible way to the upper ranks of his profession. It is a disincentive if students work under handicaps of social background and financial restraint, and if teachers have no real chance to achieve top positions.

An important means of improving motivation is the organization of learning as short steps in a lifelong process, thereby providing the possibility of alternating between learning by systematic study and learning by doing. The amount of knowledge has been growing and continues to grow faster and faster. But the old pattern of thinking is still widespread and influential, so that most of the knowledge available has to be crammed into the brains of young people before they start their active life. Prolonged continuous learning periods between five and thirty years of age are often the consequence. Enormous wastage is caused by this procedure. Many students lose interest, achieve poor results, or dropout. To concentrate the curriculum on a few subjects at a time; to break up the long courses into short periods, each resulting in a certificate; to make it a rule that intervals of learning by doing follow each course of systematic learning; to ensure that everybody has a real chance to continue courses of systematic learning throughout his active life: these seem to be the most promising ways to increase motivation and, thereby, the productivity of education.

In such a scheme the student will always see the next goal as a possible reward of his work clear before him. He will gain by concentrating in each learning period on a few subjects, and he will return from the intervals of gainful work with a fresh interest stimulated by practical experience. Decisions for vocational specialization will be made "near the market" and therefore will, on the whole, be more appropriate. Such decisions made many years before entering the labor market are often bound to lead to frustration, because the qualities demanded in practical work are unknown and also often change so fast that manpower forecasts and vocational guidance are valid only for short periods.

To the student of the sociology of education these proposals should sound familiar. Indeed, they are an extension of the argument that certain groups are not motivated to enter courses of higher education, because they are not accustomed to middle class values and the acceptance of deferred gratification. Reforms on these lines, therefore, would help to overcome the social distance between underprivileged groups and the middle class establishment.

How education is enjoyed depends not only on the curriculum and organization but also on the training and motivation of the teachers. Boredom caused by teachers' ignorance of the fundamental rules of learning psychology and didactics means a waste of resources. It is widely believed that any person with knowledge of a subject can teach persons of lesser knowledge. In fact, a good teacher needs wide competence in didactics and educational psychology as well as in the subject. In addition, in the near future teachers will have to know how to use new techniques, such as language laboratories and programmed instruction. It takes many years of learning to gain this complex knowledge and the ability to apply and transfer it efficiently. On the other hand, a teacher should start work in the classroom early. Therefore it seems necessary to reorganize the teacher's career into a succession of steps of learning by doing and learning by study, at the same time allowing for promotion with growing competence. The career of the teacher at present too often ends at an age when in other occupations there are still many chances open for promotion. Without appropriate incentives most people tend to fall back on a kind of routine. But teaching is a science as well as an art and requires a strong interest, dedication, and continuous learning.[7]

It may be argued that such large numbers of teachers are needed that it is practically impossible to give all of them the opportunity for very long systematic studies. In fact, the need is for enough to reach full competence so that all members of the teaching profession have the prospect and the incentive of a career that in principle never ends. Fully qualified teachers should work as masters surrounded by apprentice teachers and assisting personnel in complementary functions at various levels of competence. Such division of labor can prevent wastage of teaching ability in supervisory and clerical work and can improve the motivation of personnel at all levels.

Motivation is to be considered along with rationality in many methods of productivity-oriented planning. In order to have a maximum of rationality it may seem necessary, for instance, to have a highly centralized educational system and to give the state a monopoly to run and finance educational institutions.

7. Bruce J. Biddle and William J. Ellena, eds., *Contemporary Research on Teacher Effectiveness* (New York: Holt, Rinehart and Winston, 1964).

The evidence now available, however, casts strong doubts on such a course of planning and action. It appears, on the contrary, that optimum productivity is to be gained by finding a balance between centralization and decentralization according to national conditions. A framework of laws and directives ensuring a reasonable degree of uniformity, geographical mobility, and equal opportunity throughout a country will be necessary everywhere. But one should not overlook the motivation for initiative, competition, and continuous improvement in the use of resources resulting from delegating responsibility to local authorities, headmasters, teachers, and other educational personnel. Productive innovation may be expected more often in a system of widely distributed responsibilities than in a highly centralized one.[8]

New techniques offer great possibilities for increases in productivity. Programmed instruction in books and on tapes as well as instruction by television can improve considerably the cost/benefit relation in learning, provided these new techniques are developed on a large scale. Heavy investment in research and development is one condition; production and sale in big numbers, another. Here again there is the danger of too much uniformity and too little chance for individual responsibility and personal give-and-take. But to know of this danger may help to avoid it.

A similar problem arises in the field of educational building. New techniques permit the prefabrication and large-scale production of all the parts of buildings according to their functions. Rationality seems to require a central organization of plants producing these parts and providing a service for assemblage on the local sites. The cost digression would be enormous, even more so if the size of schools were increased as far as the techniques of building and the transport system permit. But would the communities, the teachers, and the students happily go along

8. H. Thomas James, J. Alan Thomas, and Harold J. Dyck, *Wealth, Expenditure and Decision-Making for Education* (School of Education, Stanford University, 1963; mimeographed).

with such a development? There is hardly any doubt that here, too, are limits to the implementation of possible techniques and cost savings. Again it is a question of balancing the advantages of standardization against the merits of giving wide scope to local atmosphere, preferences, and willingness to contribute.[9]

The British system of minimum standards and cost limits for school buildings offers an example of how centralization and decentralization can be combined with good results. The Ministry of Education in London introduced such a system in 1949, with the result that there was a 30 per cent decrease in the cost of a pupil place, in spite of greatly increasing average building costs. On the whole, there was more praise than criticism of this system. The central ministry has been restricting its directives to some broadly defined minimum necessities of security, hygiene, and teaching space, on the one side, and to fixing the upper limit of the cost per pupil place. These limits were chosen according to the results of experiments and analyses and were changed from time to time according to general price developments. The local authorities, parents, teachers, and architects were left wide latitude to prove their ingenuity in building a good school which would be to their taste as well as functionally appropriate. Anybody traveling in Britain will find that on the whole they did the job well and are satisfied. Nobody can complain about too much uniformity, and the costs per unit are still so low that educational and financial planners in many countries envy Britain in this respect.

Rationalization by using old and new ways of analysis, experimentation, and planning and by introducing new techniques is certainly necessary in order to increase the productivity of education. But rationalization that neglects the sources and powers of motivation would be detrimental. This chapter has outlined a few possibilities for ensuring a favorable balance between centrality and uniformity, on the one hand, and individual initiative,

9. See Guy Oddie, *School Building Resources and Their Effective Use* (Paris: OECD, 1966).

on the other. There is some evidence that a proper balance between these possibilities will not only result in a fuller use of educational resources but also help to increase the total resources available for this purpose. Favorable cost/benefit relations will make the educational enterprise attractive for public and private investors. Private households, individual firms, organizations, and local authorities are likely to spend more for this purpose if they participate in the responsibility instead of only following central directives.

ACCELERATING THE INNOVATION PROCESS IN EDUCATION

LADISLAV CERYCH

It is by now commonplace to describe educational systems as "the most conservative industries," the least innovating of all sectors of social activity, and to regard this characteristic as a major contributing factor to the present critical situation of the world's schools and universities.

Whether these notions are strictly correct remains to be seen. Certainly other aspects of human endeavor need innovation at least as much as does education: for example, several of the existing legal systems, public administration in many countries, and most areas of the life in big cities almost everywhere. However, it cannot be denied that education is one of the domains where the innovation process is extremely slow, particularly when it is compared with health, defense, transport, and probably all industrial production.

It may be useful at this point to define the process of innovation. Most of the literature on the subject calls innovation itself the origin of the process and the acceptance of this innovation by the members of the system concerned the end of the process.

In education, as in other fields, the major source of innovation as such—that is, of new solutions to educational problems—is undoubtedly research (whether conducted within or outside the educational system). But while certain industries devote to research 10 per cent or even more of their gross income, and

34

developed countries use 1.5 to 4 per cent of their gross national product on research in general, only a fraction of 1 per cent of the total expenditure on education goes into educational research.[1]

This lack of educational research is related to what may be an even greater weakness: the difficulty of having innovations adopted and generalized. An increase in educational research expenditure can be of real use only if institutional mechanisms are provided to increase the possibility that innovations will be not only generated but also adopted by the system on a more or less spontaneous and in any case continuous basis.

INSTITUTIONAL BARRIERS TO EDUCATIONAL INNOVATION

It is evidently inadequate to state that educational systems are too conservative, or that educational innovation is one of the most urgent needs. We must first attempt to explain this situation. The lack of innovation in education may well be a "natural condition," while an innovating educational system or organization may be "not quite normal." The present discussion takes this assumption as its initial hypothesis. To use an analogy from medicine, innovation may to some extent be a foreign body to education and may be rejected by it as "genetically incompatible" in the same way that blood of a given group is not assimilated by a patient of a different group.

The primary function of most educational systems has always been socialization: that is, the transmission of existing values; in Talcott Parson's words, a "pattern maintenance function." In this respect, therefore, innovation in education implies a certain disfunction, which the system as such will by definition resist.

Such resistance can be similarly explained if education is considered from the point of view of organizational theory. As an organization—or an integrated set of organizations—an educa-

1. In the United States, which is most probably well ahead of all other nations in this respect, $98,000,000 were spent in 1965 on educational research—that is, 0.22 per cent of the total educational expenditure. But this figure is more than twice the 1960 rate ($33,000,000, or 0.12 per cent). In Sweden the rate was 0.10 per cent in 1964–1965.

tional system seeks a "satisfying solution rather than an optimum one," and it stops its "search behavior" once a pattern is found that is considered "reasonably good" or "acceptable."[2]

How can the innovation process be made "genetically compatible" with the existing organizational and institutional patterns of educational systems? A useful approach to this question will be offered by an analysis of a certain number of variables that, by all available evidence, influence the rate of innovation adoption. Six of these variables, as defined by E. M. Rogers, can be mentioned:[3]

1. The *relative advantage* of an innovation: that is, the degree to which it is considered an improvement on the ideas and solutions it supersedes.

2. Its *compatibility*: that is, the degree to which it is consistent with the existing values of the prospective adopters.

3. Its *divisibility*: that is, the degree to which it can be tried out on a limited basis, and thus to which its utility can be demonstrated before generalization.

4. Its *complexity*: that is, the degree to which it is relatively difficult to understand and use.

5. Its *communicability*: that is, the degree to which its results can be easily demonstrated to all those concerned, and to which knowledge of it can be easily passed from one member of the system to another.[4]

6. Of a slightly different nature but related to the preceding is a sixth variable, the type of *decision-making process* on which the rejection or the adoption of an innovation depends.

No doubt other variables could be discerned, or those mentioned could be more or less redefined. This conceptual frame-

2. H. A. Simon, *Administrative Behavior* (New York: Macmillan, 1945).

3. E. M. Rogers, *The Communication of Innovations: Strategies for Change in a Complex Institution* (Paper presented to the National Conference on Curricular and Instructional Innovation of Large Colleges and Universities, East Lansing, Michigan, November 1966).

4. *Ibid*; Rogers stressed only the first part of this proposition.

work, however, seems sufficiently broad and allows, in any case, a rapid definition of some general reasons for the slowness of the innovation process within existing education systems.

1. *The relative advantages of educational innovations* over past solutions almost by definition cannot be perceived rapidly. Education is in the main a long-term process; usually years must pass before the results of a new teaching method, a new curriculum, and, even more, a new educational structure can be considered fool-proof. A notable exception to this rule is the training and re-training for specific skills required by industry, the armed forces, and other employers. This perhaps is one of the reasons that many educational innovations have been adopted by them earlier than by the formal school system.

2. *The problem of the compatibility* of innovations with the prevailing values of a given educational system constitutes probably the most notorious barrier to their diffusion and adoption. Not only formal values, however, are involved: informal values as well as status considerations, role expectations, and the whole role structure are relevant in this connection. Educational television may be resisted because it is believed to diminish the importance of personal contact between teacher and pupil (formal value of the system), or because it weakens the exclusive position of the teacher (role expectation). The suppression of certain examinations may be opposed as a threat to the existing educational standards. Similarly motivated resistance to innovations exists, of course, not only in education but in all kinds of organizations. Education's complexity and the vague and diffuse nature of its goals, its manifest and latent functions, its role structure, and its external as well as internal linkages are such, however, that the issue of compatibility of a given innovation with declared values of the system can be raised at practically any opportunity—and certainly more readily than in the case of a hospital, a prison, or a business corporation where both formal and informal values can, in spite of everything, be defined much more precisely.

3. The degree to which innovations in education can be tested

on a limited basis (*their divisibility*) appears at first relatively extensive. Do not the thousands of schools and classes existing in each system represent a most appropriate framework for launching innovating experiments, with the possible negative consequences restricted to a minimum? Does education not benefit here from conditions as favorable as, for example, those applying to agriculture, where a new corn can be tried out easily but convincingly on just one or a few small fields?

Only partly so. It is true that the fragmented nature of an educational system allows a great deal of experimentation. Indeed, many past and recent innovations have eventually been generalized because of their successful introduction in pilot schools, classes, or courses; and several of the great university reforms have been implemented in a whole nation only because one institution has first set an example (thus Humboldt's ideas spread over Germany following their "trial run" at the University of Berlin).

However, the very divisibility of innovation in education raises a serious problem. The success of an innovation in an experimental school or college is not necessarily considered a valid justification for its general adoption. There are always grounds for doubting that an experimental school has taken into account all the "normal condtions" of the system, that it is representative, and consequently that the results of the experiment provide conclusive evidence for its generalization. It may, for example, be argued that the teachers or pupils involved were above the national average, or that the apparently excellent results of a new teaching method may have certain aftereffects or latent consequences which will be discernible only when the innovation has been implemented under "normal conditions" for a considerable time. In short, the argument about the difficulty of experimenting in social sciences is widely used against the credibility of a positive outcome of a pilot project in education.

4. Are innovations in education more *difficult to understand* and to use than those in other areas of social activity? In this respect a distinction must be made between innovations in the

organization of education and those in the technology of education in the more narrow sense of the word. In the first case it can safely be said that the existing systems are in almost all countries so complicated and unclear—being the product of a centuries-long evolution and of thousands of influences, which have led to continuous additions and a host of both functional and unfunctional linkages—that organizational innovations can normally tend only toward simplification and clarification of the organization chart. As such they should be easily grasped by the users, and their adoption should be generally favored. In practice, however, this advantage is often blurred by the fact that new organizational schemes do not simply replace old arrangements; they are added to or superimposed on existing structures, with the result that the new pattern is even more complicated than the old one; and the innovations are blamed for the additional confusion.

As far as purely technological innovations are concerned, the degree to which they can be easily understood and used varies from case to case. There seems to be no reason why educational innovations should be at a greater disadvantage than innovations in other fields. However, it must be remembered that what often appears to be, and technically is, simple becomes considerably more involved in the context of an education process. Thus, for instance, in television not only does a knob have to be turned, but teachers must be specially trained to use the new medium efficiently and as an integrated part of their courses. Many of the limited results of technological innovations of this kind in the past can be explained by their inadequate integration in the teaching process and by the fact that they have been treated as technical gadgets only.

5. The problem of the *communicability of educational innovations* can be considered from two points of view: as a problem of visibility and as a problem of channels. Innovations in education are certainly less visible than those in business and industry. Whereas public opinion is informed almost instantaneously of the development of a new type of textile fiber, even a very suc-

cessful new method of language teaching is for a long time known only in restricted circles. This means that the diffusion process in education is long not only because of various individual and social resistances, but also because a great number of those on whom implementation depends simply ignore the existence of a new way of solving a particular task. Agriculture was for a long time—and in many countries still is—in a similar situation; only through a network of extension services, courses for adults, and the effectiveness of certain demonstration farms has the trend been reversed. Such a process is not yet generalized in education, although it has started in a few countries.

The reasons for this poor visibility of educational innovation are no doubt numerous. They are related partly to the nature of the traditional role behavior of participants in educational organizations (many teachers are not as interested in new ways of teaching as modern farmers are in new ways of farming) and partly to the type and density of the communications channels (this is closely connected with the last variable mentioned: the decision-making process on which education innovation depends).

To use Rogers's typology again, innovation decisions can be classified under two broad headings: individual and authority decisions. Individual decisions—which Rogers subdivides into optional, contingent, and collective—have the common characteristic of being made by consensus: independently by an individual in the first and second case, and by some group decision in the third. An authority decision implies that an innovation is imposed upon individuals by someone in a superior position.

Research is not yet sufficiently advanced to show whether some of the decision-making processes above encourage, or retard, more than others the adoption of educational innovations; but it is certain that these processes play an important role in innovation diffusion. At first it would seem that authority decisions contribute to a faster rate of innovation adoption. Yet "authority decisions are more likely to be circumvented and may eventually lead to a high rate of discontinuance of the innovation. Where changes depend upon compliance under public surveillance, they are not likely to remain established once the surveillance is removed. Though contingent and collective decisions are made much more slowly, because groups are involved, they are more likely to result in lasting change because of the higher degree of individual participation and commitment."[5]

And, indeed, some studies show that submission to a central authority does not necessarily favor the rate of adoption of innovation.

Table 1 indicates that innovations were much more readily accepted in independent than in centrally controlled schools; whereas the latter excelled in bureaucratic virtues like tenure, pensions, and highly specialized services.

TABLE 1.   SCHOOL PRACTICES IN 16 INDEPENDENT AND 16 CENTRALLY CONTROLLED SCHOOLS IN THE UNITED STATES.[6]

School practices	Independent schools	Centrally controlled schools
Movable classroom furniture used	11	0
Teacher experimentation encouraged by superintendency	12	6
Course of study developed cooperatively by local teachers	14	2
Adequate provision for vocational education	6	16
Provision for pupils with special disabilities	8	16
Adequate tenure provisions	2	16
Total schools studied	16	16

5. *Ibid.*, p. 7.
6. A. H. Barton, *Organizational Measurement and Its Bearings on the Study of College Environments* (New York: College Entrance Examination Board, 1961), p. 26.

ELEMENTS OF A STRATEGY

The foregoing analysis should not be interpreted as a pessimistic view of the possibilities of innovation in education. It can, however, lead to the conclusion that the need is for, not just more technological or organizational devices—innovations per se—but for institutional conditions favoring the innovation process as a whole.

Obviously innovation must be generated and potentially available in the first place. This, as already stressed, requires educational research and appropriate units within the educational system capable of undertaking it on a continuous basis and on a sufficiently large scale. In spite of what has already been said about the still highly insufficient over-all research effort in education, much has happened in this respect during the past years in several countries. Not only have numerous educational research and evaluation centers been created or developed, but many have been integrated into educational organizations or systems. In a sense this implies a significant departure from the norm that educational systems are seeking a "satisfying solution rather than an optimum one." Educational organizations or whole systems are beginning to apply an organizational device long common in industry: research and development divisions "deliberately constructed to enable the organization to continue research activity even when most of the organization's members are quite satisfied . . . ; they tend to define for the organization successively higher levels of satisfaction, by raising the standards of what is considered all right. In this way organizations have been able to build in mechanisms to make themselves rationally dissatisfied and to continue to search for improvement."[7]

A whole series of practical examples can be quoted. In Sweden four teacher-training institutes are provided with research departments which directly serve the National Board of Education and the "rolling reform" principle on which the present system is based. In Germany the Institut für Bildungsforschung in der

7. A. Etzioni, *Modern Organization* (New York: Prentice-Hall, 1964).

Max-Planck Gesellschaft acts as a central research institute for all the German *Länder*. In France the newly created university institutes of technology (IUT) have been provided with a special center in charge of research and evaluation of their work and operation. In the United Kingdom an almost formally organized research network is beginning to operate under the Schools Council.[8] In the United States, under Title III of the Elementary and Secondary Education Act of 1965, a network of research and development centers has been set up, and in 1967, $175,000,000 (almost double the total United States educational expenditure in 1965 for "new ideas in education") has been appropriated. This last scheme, known as PACE (Projects to Advance Creativity in Education), goes beyond the mere development of educational research in attempting to stimulate and capture the innovating forces at large.

As individual organizations the educational research centers, institutes, or departments of many American and Canadian universities no doubt provide the best examples of this new role and emphasis on educational research; the major novelty is not that more Ph.D. theses are written on subjects dealing with education, but that this increased research effort is an institutional part of a mechanism "deliberately constructed to enable the organization to be rationally dissatisfied and continue in search of improvement."[9] It is significant that several of the new universities, even in countries with systems resistant to innovation, have taken the lead in establishing educational research departments or centers—for example, the University of Konstanz in Germany.

Often the new units originate in scientific self-evaluation, which in itself is significant for the present trend. Indeed, for a long time self-evaluation was resisted by educational establish-

8. For further details on these and other research organizations in Western Europe, see OECD, *Curriculum Improvement and Educational Development* (Paris, 1966), as well as OECD's country reports on educational planning.

9. Etzioni, *op. cit.*, p. 31.

ments in general and by universities in particular: self-satisfaction represented their most natural condition. If today the reverse is becoming more common—on the level both of individual organizations and of systems[10]—this means that an important institutional obstacle to the innovation process is being removed.

But the main thesis of this discussion must be repeated here: an increase in the educational research and evaluation effort and the establishment of the necessary organizational facilities (leading to educational innovation as such) is only the first step in the innovation process; it does not automatically imply an increased rate of innovation adoption. Unlike research divisions in industry, none of the educational research units mentioned above is powerful enough to overcome by itself the barriers that educational systems, by their intrinsic nature, impose upon the diffusion of innovation. Furthermore, it is not at all certain that these institutional, impersonal barriers are not, in the last analysis, much stronger than the individual or group resistances commonly considered the major cause of the slowness of innovation in education. Strong support for such an assumption—at least in the United States—is provided by a recent (1966) Gallup Poll measuring parents' and school board members' reactions to innovation.[11]

Both groups were asked to evaluate thirteen educational innovations covering items such as programmed instruction, team teaching, and shortened summer vacations. Nine innovations were favored by 59 to 96 per cent of those questioned; only four innovations were opposed by the majority of the two groups. A commentator on the results of the poll could therefore quite

10. One of the best-known cases of self-evaluation on the level of a nation is probably the Robbins Report in the United Kingdom. But even in countries where such evaluations have not been made under the sponsorship, and by the decision, of formal authorities, they have been made, often quite vigorously, under the auspices of less formal bodies. A good example is the 1966 congress of French university professors in Caen.

11. This poll was sponsored by the Institute for the Development of Educational Activities of the Kettering Foundation; see "School Boards Tell Gallup Poll: We want to Innovate," *Nations Schools*, 79, no. 2, February 1967, p. 59.

appropriately conclude that, "They are ready for more new practices than the schools are giving them."[12]

To assess at least some elements of an over-all innovation strategy, we can again refer to the variables above and show, by practical examples, how they can be manipulated in order to create conditions favoring the innovation process as a whole.

Not all these variables can of course be manipulated easily, and some may be almost impossible to influence in the short run. Thus, it will probably always be difficult to perceive rapidly the *relative advantage* of certain educational innovations over ideas and solutions that they supersede. This is particularly true of organizational innovations, possibly less so of innovations in teaching methods. In many countries, but not in all, the former can be introduced more or less rapidly only by the creation of new institution. This implies an important assumption: namely, that in certain countries or in education systems of a certain type, innovations are more easily diffused and adopted in swarms than in isolation. Even if research in depth has not yet provided sufficient evidence for this assumption, it can be justified by numerous practical experiences of which the best examples are precisely many of the new and very innovating schools which, existing in the middle of highly traditional systems, have introduced simultaneously new organizational structures, new administration procedures, and new teaching methods and media.

The *compatibility variable* seems both difficult and relatively easy to manipulate. The difficulty is unavoidable: the prevailing value structure that an innovation has to confront cannot be changed rapidly. Thus, if compatibility is to be achieved, more or less important compromises have to be made to implement an innovation. This happens not only in education: modern train engines often continue to be served by two men although one would be sufficient; the social consequences of the technical improvement had to be avoided in order to use the new engine at all. Similarly, an educational innovation may be deprived of

12.   "Parents Are Ready," *The Instructor*, October 1966, pp. 149, 154.

parts of its meaning in order to make it compatible with existing values and traditions. If institutional autonomy remains an absolute and sacrosanct principle, a new interorganizational coordination device may have little impact; conversely, if centralization has to be in all circumstances respected, institutional autonomy must remain a fiction even if it is considered a new formal goal.

Nevertheless, the compatibility of an innovation with prevailing values often can be achieved relatively easily by an appropriate interpretation of its nature and consequences. If educational television or programmed learning are opposed just because, presumably, they diminish the role of teachers, it must be shown that the contrary is true.

The only strategy in this case seems to be an increased public relations effort, concerning not only the efficiency of the innovation but the values it might prejudice. The only other alternative is a more or less radical change of the values that resist innovation diffusion—a necessarily slow process in all but exceptional circumstances. Even phenomena such as wars or the acquisition of national independence have often not been sufficient to produce the required breakthrough. Although the political and social values of many European countries changed profoundly in the immediate postwar years, nothing comparable happened to their educational values. On the other hand, the compatibility argument can easily be overstressed or used as a simple excuse. The Gallup Poll mentioned earlier indicated clearly that attachment to some of the traditional values might not be as strong as it was believed to be.

The strategy for the *divisibility* requirement of educational innovations appears obvious, at least theoretically: experimental projects must be conceived so that account is taken of the "normal conditions" of the system. A good example seems to be the League of Cooperating Schools set up in the framework of the Institute for Development of Educational Activities (IDEA) sponsored by the Kettering Foundation. This scheme, which aims at becoming a vast laboratory for educational research and innovation, covers twenty schools in Southern California, good and poor ones, representing virtually all population groups, all kinds of school building, and all types of educational problem found in the United States. An important experiment with educational television undertaken in Niger tries to deal with school conditions as they prevail in the country: ill-qualified teachers, rudimentary building facilities, and so on. In Norway a state board for experiments in schools has been created; it covers not just a few isolated projects but one-third of all schools in the country and nearly all aspects of educational development. The latter scheme may possibly indicate the direction in which an answer lies to the problems of "normal conditions" of experiments in education and of the "credibility" of their results.

As to the *complexity* of educational innovations, the only strategy requirement that can be formulated here is a simple consequence of the conclusion drawn above: innovations should, as far as possible, simplify the existing patterns of education and not be mere additions to existing solutions. Introducing comprehensive secondary schools and maintaining, in one form or another, the multiplicity of traditional types has in several instances been a safe way to limit the chances of general adoption of and popular support for the new formula. On the other hand, schemes such as the recent reorganization of technical education in Great Britain (the creation of a network of polytechnics following the transformation of colleges of advanced technology into full universities), which imply an integrated and a simplifying approach and not just a simple addition of a few institutions, seem a priori to be much more promising.

With regard to the *visibility* of educational innovations, the possibilities of an effective strategy are probably considerable. The analogy with agricultural expansion appears to have particular relevance in this respect, and two significant examples from the United States may be cited: on the one hand, the Institute for Development of Educational Activities and, on the other, the

Regional Education Laboratories set up under the Elementary and Secondary School Act of 1965. Both schemes use, or intend to use, techniques clearly inspired by the agricultural extension services, which proved so successful in the past. IDEA has organized, within its Innovation Dissemination Division, a demonstration schools project as a means of assisting the country's most innovating schools by facilitating their communications with each other, by supporting program improvement in the schools, and by encouraging the systematic evaluation and dissemination of promising educational practices. Some fifty innovating schools which have committed themselves to a wide program of improvement are taking part in the project. The aim is to give these schools (with the help of a materials dissemination center) a high degree of visibility and thereby to promote change.

The Regional Education Laboratories are involved in a variety of programs, ranging from demonstrating various approaches to the teaching of reading to the establishment of regional educational plans. They, too, try not only to test innovations but to spread them as widely as possible throughout public and private schools, higher education, and local state boards of education, all of which are in a sense participants in the scheme.

More or less similar projects are, of course, undertaken in other countries by various international organizations. They all tend to intensify the innovation diffusion process by creating new channels of communication—an indispensable condition for increasing the rate of innovation adoption.

Most of the practical examples of new approaches to innovation in education described above are too recent to allow any kind of real evaluation. Some of them are already considered failures. For example, the Regional Education Laboratories in the United States were denied, temporarily, further federal funds because results after the first year appeared insufficient; the School Councils in Britain were criticized for having no coherent policy; and in general many of the new innovation-promoting institutions are believed to lack clarity of purpose, to suffer from structural weaknesses, to engage in overlapping activities, and to fail to attract talented and qualified leadership and/or manpower. Whether these criticisms are justified is beside the point here, but it would be surprising if the new trend should come about smoothly and without a great deal of trial and error. This would in fact mean that educational systems and organizations are not complex, that they are not intrinsically resistant to innovation, and that we have a more or less perfect understanding of their mechanisms. Clearly the contrary of all this is true; and discouragement at this stage would appear, therefore, to be an abdication in face of what might be one of the greatest challenges of our time.

One aspect of the criticism concerning the new schemes should, however, be stressed in conclusion: namely, the lack of qualified people to run the different innovation agencies. It must be asked whether this weakness does not reflect a more profound phenomenon, which in itself represents another important factor contributing to the slowness of the innovation process in education: the fact that education has not attracted as many people who by their nature and attitudes are innovators, as have industry, science, and the arts. This is not to suggest that the elite of contemporary societies have especially shirked education in favor of other fields of activity, leaving the less qualified in charge of schools, universities, and educational administrations; it simply means that fewer of the "innovation oriented" among the elite have entered or stayed in education than have entered other fields. Evidence for this thesis is not easy to provide, and it is difficult to present a completely convincing explanation of why this should be so; a commonsense answer is all we can rely on.

If educational systems or organizations are relatively unfavorable to innovation diffusion, there is no reason that "natural innovators" should be attracted to it, or even that they should not be repelled by it. Thus is created a vicious circle: the absence of a sufficient number of innovators reinforces the already institutionally conservative nature of education, which in turn continues to weaken its attractiveness to innovators, and so on. Unless the circle can be broken. There are strong reasons to believe that this is now happening; not just because innovation is the new "in" word among educators, but because so much innovation is actually being attempted in all fields of education and in almost all countries of the world, even if a great deal of it has not yet come to fruition.

Eric Ashby said recently that in the development of universities—and the same goes for all education—there are, as in biological evolution, periods of mutation and hybridization when suddenly, after a long stagnation, new forms appear.[13] All the available signs indicate that we may well be on the threshold of such a period.

13. Eric Ashby (Queens Lecture, University of Bochum, May 22, 1967).

DEMOCRATIZATION OF
EDUCATIONAL OPPORTUNITY

FRANK BOWLES

The current educational crisis has been defined as the inability of educational systems to keep pace with their environment. A significant aspect of the problem is, then, the relation of educational systems to attempts at democratizing education. This chapter poses three questions bearing on this relation:

1. How successful have the efforts been to democratize educational opportunities?
2. How successful have the efforts been to democratize societies through education?
3. What further steps are needed to achieve the foregoing social objectives?

"Democratization" in reference to education is the process of assuring equality of opportunity for educational achievement throughout a given society. According to this definition democratization is not confined just to assuring equality of schooling. This is attainable by standardizing the schools, a condition that now exists in most countries. Standardization, however, does not equalize opportunities for achievement unless the pupils are also standardized. If they are not, a variety of opportunities must be created. The democratization of education is much like the democratization of the franchise. The opportunity to be educated, like the opportunity to vote, becomes a right that may or may not be exercised. When exercised, the act may be done well or badly. What counts is that the right be established.

ELITIST SYSTEMS

The nature and the acknowledgment of this right must be understood, because no known system inherently or automatically assures equality of educational opportunity throughout a nation. Conversely, many systems that have stood for years as models for successful education—that is, education that supported the national interests—have been restrictive in the extreme. When the English, French, and German systems, for example, served as world models, they were not democratized in any sense of the word. They were starkly elitist in nature, and through their imitators they became models for systems of elitist education which exist throughout the world.

To say that an educational system has been elitist is not necessarily to condemn it. Historically, elitist systems served well in countries where educational demands were simple and easily classified. In such countries a small group of university graduates supplied professional services and made whatever national and professional management decisions were needed. Administrative chores were left to less well-educated, but well-trained, functionaries, and no attention was paid to the apprentice system which trained workers and craftsmen or to the functional illiteracy of the peasantry. Such a system was not costly; it suited a stable society and in fact contributed to its stability. Under favorable conditions it provided a measure of opportunity for the talented and brilliant from whatever class, so that there were always men in public life who had risen from low estate.

Regardless of how unsatisfactory such systems might have been to social theorists or to proletarian families denied access to elite schools, they became ill suited for national purposes only when creeping industrialization produced three quite separate results. First, incomes were raised for all occupations (except subsistence agriculture), and this brought advanced education into public view as a part of a general rise in aspirations. Second, industrialization created a demand for trained workers which the elitist systems could not meet. Third, it brought to the fore the inadequacy of the elite part of the educational system as a preparation for the management of industrialization.

These developments did not invalidate the existing systems; they merely established a case for change. In most countries the ground for change could be seen about twenty years before any action was taken—which is to say, shortly after the close of World War II. In many instances there would probably still be no action had not the old systems begun to break down under pressures they could not control. Overcrowded secondary schools, high rates of failure in examinations at the end of secondary school, and high dropout rates combined to transfer the question of enlarged educational opportunity from education to politics and to establish a political mandate for educational expansion.

CURRENT STATUS OF DEMOCRATIZATION

Educational expansion, however, is not the same as democratization. Expansion may simply mean that all parts of the educational system must be enlarged to accommodate all possible pupils and to produce specific types of trained manpower. Democratization is a larger idea, based on a belief that in individuals at all social levels there are untapped potentials for development which are not reached by the conventional educational system. To tap the potentials requires new insights and new institutions. Democratization, then, instead of being simply more of the same, is a new order of applied educational thought, just as democracy itself was a new order of applied political thought in the eighteenth century. Democratization involves a large-scale effort to reach and to understand the riddles of individual and group differences and then to ensure that, besides achieving the common learning of the time—a task that every system must accept—all students are permitted, if they choose, to develop their own competences and achieve their own individualities.

These are the ideal goals of democratization, and no school system, however dedicated, can fulfill all of them. Nevertheless they must be present in some form before the concept of democratization can be introduced.

These comments on the nature of democratization make it possible to recast and to clarify the three basic questions posed earlier:

1. To what extent have national governments accepted an obligation to assure equality of educational opportunity to all sectors of their societies, and how successful have their efforts been?

2. When provisions for equality of opportunity for educational achievement have been established within a society, to what extent has this influenced the general democratization of that society?

3. What further steps are needed in the development of education in order to achieve a general democratization of societies, and how are they to be achieved?

Thus framed, the first question is fairly simple to answer. Democratization has been tried, either experimentally or operationally, in a surprisingly large number of places. For example, five European countries have initiated educational change on a scale that can be called democratization. The English moves, beginning in the main with the Education Act of 1944 and still continuing, are well known and have been extensively documented by a series of fine public reports. Swedish reform leading to a broad democratization at all levels of education is well under way, now that the long research evaluating the established system, combined with a careful estimate of future educational needs, has been completed.

French democratization has removed many of the long established barriers and the failure points where marginal students were diverted into terminal programs. In addition, new programs at the secondary and higher levels and particularly in technical fields have been opened to care for the swelling demand. An emphasis on guidance and orientation for each student marks a new order of concern for the individual.

In Italy a highly significant experiment in democratization was the development of Telescuola, which used television as the instructional vehicle to carry the regular middle school program into areas never before reached. The experiment showed that effective instruction by television was expensive and highly sophisticated; but it also demonstrated television's flexibility and capacity to overcome problems of substandard teacher preparation, facilities, and learning materials.

Russian education merits being called democratized, not only because it has expanded greatly over half a century, but rather because it offers further opportunity to those who seek it and encouragement and reward to those who will follow it. This is an essential feature of any educational democratization. A large-scale introduction of Western democratization would, in fact, create serious problems in the Russian system. By giving students a wider choice in career decision, it would almost certainly place a serious burden on the already heavily loaded higher secondary schools, higher technical programs, and universities.

It seems fair to say that democratization of education in other European countries is somewhere in the discussion stage. This means, at least, that educational problems have emerged in the form of swelling enrollments, teacher shortages, manpower shortages in technical fields, and other now well-known patterns, and that the traditional methods of dealing with them by changing rules and restrictions have not helped. The idea of reform through democratization has been proposed as an alternative solution and is now battling its main opposition, which comes from within the field of education itself: the universities and ministries of education which so far are stronger than the social reformers. It also seems fair to say that the whole problem will not be dealt with until it becomes a political issue—a development that is not within the foreseeable future.

In North America the United States undertook its first major democratization in the 1930's, broadening the secondary curriculum and launching a vast expansion in facilities. Recently it was realized that this effort had reached only a small percentage of Negro students, so that a major effort in this field is under way. Still another democratization is being undertaken in the United States at the level of post-secondary education, with the rapid development of tax-supported community colleges.

Elsewhere in North America, in Canada and Mexico, democratization has made substantial headway in the sense that it is publicly discussed as a political as well as an educational concern. Considerable liberalization has taken place in both countries, and more is in prospect.

The Caribbean has its affinities to North America and to Europe. In Puerto Rico the American pattern has been applied widely and is still being expanded. Other islands, with limited resources, are now occupied mainly with expanding elementary education and developing a genuine structure of secondary education. Little is known about the educational developments of Cuba, except that they have been important and, within the prevailing social doctrine, strongly democratized.

In Central and South America there is sporadic discussion of democratization, but there are no known experiments outside of some radio and television efforts, and no change is foreseeable. The universities, the ministries, and the entire professional class are opposed, in the main, to any expansion of education, both for reasons of cost and for the dangers they fear to the class structure. In Venezuela, Colombia, Chile, and Brazil educational action groups are forming to work for the extension of education, and some actions have followed their efforts.

In Asia and Africa the entire thesis of democratization was severely set back by the decisions taken about fifteen years ago to build European-style universities as a preparatory step to breaking colonial ties. Such universities, of course, required European-style secondary schools. The curricular and enrollment restrictions, on the one hand, and the cost of the establishments, on the other, have made it impossible to consider democratization at any level of education, unless it is done as an internationally supported experiment—an idea that has so far not been considered seriously.

There are exceptions, however. In the case of African and Asian countries of the Middle East, close contacts with industrialized countries and in some cases their own large revenues have made educational developments a current and continuing political concern. The results have been interesting. There has been a forced draft development of educational systems in the wealthier countries such as Kuwait and Saudi Arabia, but on the conventional model. Though richer, they have been much like the institutional structures that already exist in other Middle Eastern countries. In general, therefore, it can be said that education in the Middle East is democratized only in the sense that it offers more opportunity than it did a generation ago. It is not at all democratized from the standpoint of striving to fit education to needs, capabilities, and realities.

In addition, much of the education in the area—particularly higher education—suffers from an illusion that does not distinguish between hope, form, and substance. There are too many cases in the Middle East of universities without teachers, libraries without books, laboratories without equipment, and degrees without meaning. It makes for a picture of educational inflation similar to economic inflation. All young people are forced to remain in the educational system as long as possible, since there are no jobs for any but university graduates. The entrances to and exits from the university system accordingly become so clogged that the government has to manage both university admission and graduate placement by assignment from a central statistical bureau. In the process a good degree is lost in a sea of meaningless ones, so that Gresham's Law is proved again in another medium of exchange. In the end the schools and universities are flooded with students, and the whole moral structure of education collapses as the professors multiply their jobs without expanding their teaching, and the students pass into unacknowledged abandonment of their studies.

In Asia the idea of democratization has also taken root in Japan, partially perhaps because of the American domination of the Japanese system during the crucial postwar years. Its best feature has been a great extension of opportunity for secondary education, including imaginative use of radio and correspondence courses for students unable to continue formal schooling. Its worst feature is a complicated structure of higher education, which is difficult to enter but quite undemanding once students have penetrated it. Inevitably further democratization of Japanese education will have to wait until the university system can put its house in order.

Elsewhere in Southeast Asia and India democratization is likely to be an empty word. Problems of education in many countries begin with the practice of parents paying teachers for extra instruction—a form of bribery. The problems continue to include shortages of teachers and money and a marked degree of corruption affecting appointments, textbooks, and examinations. These are major handicaps to democratization, even though all systems do not suffer from all of them.

Finally, in Oceania, Australia, and New Zealand have evolved systems that are on the way to democratization in much the same pattern as the American, even though their break with traditional restrictions on higher education has yet to come. We must also mention the television-controlled school system on American Samoa which, like Italy's *Telescuola*, has shown that television instruction can produce a higher average impact in a shorter time over a number of widely separated schools than any other known combination of instruction and supervision.

The conclusion to be reached from this quick survey is that the process of educational democratization is tied to industrialization, but it should be added that there is no inherent reason for this connection. Two nineteenth-century examples of democratization, both on a limited scale but nevertheless effective, were the Danish folk high schools and the American land grant colleges: both were tied to an agricultural economy. The fact nonetheless remains that present preoccupations are with industrialization, and that democratization of education will take place in relation to industrialization.

CONDITIONS OF DEMOCRATIZATION

This phenomenon, in turn, works in its own way to limit the movement toward democratization, because there are many nations whose governing groups see no early prospect of industrialization and actively resist democratization as unnecessary and probably dangerous. This is understandable. Democratization is a high productivity form of education which maximizes the abilities of all students, and which, in the end, increases the proportion of skilled and qualified people within the population. Countries that do not have high industrial productivity do not require high productivity from their educational systems; and until they can build their industrial potential, they also cannot afford it. If they could afford it, they might well prefer full employment at a low educational level to unemployment or underemployment at a high educational level.

Hence, in areas where industrialization has not yet arrived as a major force, the democratization of education remains essentially a philosophical concept, discussed, praised, but not applied.

The amplified answer then to the first question is this: efforts to democratize educational opportunities have been successful in nations where the process of industrialization has created a need for educational expansion, and where there is a broad political base which gives the electorate the opportunity to record its educational demands through political channels. In countries where one but not both of these conditions exists, partial moves have been made toward democratization. In countries where neither condition exists, there is little recognition of the problems of democratization.

The second question concerns the relation between opportunity for educational achievement and the general democratization of a society. This calls for a judgment; and it is a difficult judgment to make, partially because it is not easy to identify clear acts of democratization of education which can be linked in a cause-and-effect relation to clear signs of social democratization. However, one case seems strong enough to merit presentation here.

This case is the evolution of American public attitudes toward movements for Negro rights. The history begins with Marcus Garvey and his United Negro Improvement Association, founded in 1917. This remarkable enterprise, beginning as a one-man inspiration, attracted a vast Negro following and raised more money than observers at the time believed possible. It employed all the paraphernalia of organization—parades, rallies, publicity—and formed business enterprises to be conducted by Negroes for Negroes. The white community was first amused, then—as the power of the movement became evident—alarmed. The movement came to a sad end. The money raised disappeared, much of it into high advisory fees and ill-advised projects of white businessmen who were too profitably involved. Their part in possible fraud was never investigated, but Garvey went to jail with a shockingly severe sentence, and the association vanished, almost forgotten.

Forty years later a new Negro rights movement was launched. It was vocal and powerful, and it did not fear a confrontation with the holders of power. Far stronger than the Garvey move-ment—and by the standards that had been applied to Garvey, far more threatening to the white governing class—it was never-theless treated very differently. It attracted legislative and judicial support. It received full press coverage—much of it sympathetic. Even more important, it has achieved great public understanding and acceptance. It has had, and will have, its ups and downs, but its great achievements to date far exceed any reasonable expectation of ten years ago.

The purpose in presenting this historical parallel is, of course, to draw a contrast between a condition of rejection and virtual suppression in 1917 and acceptance and even support in 1957, and to seek reasons for the difference. The reasons certainly are complex, but one factor is clear. In 1917 the education of a twenty-year-old American, according to the draft statistics, was below the eighth-grade level. The mean education of male Negroes was certainly far below that, since in the states of the deep South where the majority of Negroes then lived, there were no public schools they could attend; and indeed, conditions were not much better in northern cities, as the early Negro migrants learned. Viewed in educational terms, therefore, the Garvey movement can be described as an effort by some millions of Negro functional illiterates to achieve status in a white-dominated society where the intellectual norm was tied to the completion of elementary or preadolescent education.

Forty years later the national educational mean had risen by a full four years to, or beyond, the completion of high school, largely as a result of the intensive democratization of secondary education during the 1930's. The Negro mean had also risen, not so far or so fast, but at least above the literacy level, with the important corollary that a sizable group of well-educated Negroes had also developed.

There can be no question that the relatively high level of Ameri-can educational achievement is a major factor in the successes of the present Negro rights movement. This does not exclude the importance of other factors. In a fundamental sense, however, the movement is a triumph of tolerance. The base for the tolerance is still not broad enough to assure ease of relations between the races. Indeed, the recent riots have made it plain that mutual tolerance between diverse groups cannot be achieved until equality of education between them has also been achieved. But at least a beginning has been made.

Other examples exist of the relation between educational and social democratization. The English experience, since the Education Act of 1944, can be examined profitably in order to measure the intellectual and social distance between that act and the more recent Robbins Report. The educational reform now developing in Sweden is itself the product of a social climate created by a long-standing public policy of educational opportunity. The present-day German arguments for educational reform reflect the problems involved in taking the first steps to change a traditional system.

The foregoing cases justify the assumption that over a period of time democratization of education leads to changes in social attitudes throughout a nation. The most immediate changes take place with respect to the continued expansion of provisions for education; and when new opportunities are introduced anywhere in an educational system, they must surely produce demand for new opportunities at other levels.

The enlargement of these educational changes into social change takes longer, and its form is less predictable. There is support for believing that the change will be in the direction of greater awareness of social issues, greater tolerance among groups in the society, and public support for meaningful social action. Certainly such changes have taken place in nations that have undertaken educational democratization. Yet in accepting this view, we must be careful not to be misled by our hopes to confuse cause and effect. Perhaps democratization can only begin where social attitudes have already begun to shift, and is therefore itself only a symptom of political and social democratization.

Or, on the other hand, perhaps it is the trigger that sets off the chain reaction.

The only objective answer one can give to the second question is that opportunity for educational achievement is positively related to the achievement of democracy in a society.

The third question—what else is needed to achieve the social objectives of democratized educational opportunities and democratized societies?—must be answered in terms of educational steps. The use of the word "steps," however, poses a difficulty in itself, for no given series of actions leads to assured democratization. Rather, there is a series of problems to be solved. The steps, and the time sequence in which they are taken, are controlled by local circumstances.

The first problem, which all educational systems face, is modernization, which is not the same as democratization. A great deal of modernization can take place in a highly authoritarian educational system without any basic philosophical change. Conversely, democratization does not necessarily lead immediately toward modernization. The paths may eventually lead to the same goal, but the goal may be far away. However, semantics aside, modernization involves at least three basic tasks.

1. The Expansion of the Common Learning

The main task of the schools for at least another generation is to achieve an expansion of the common learning. The assumptions concerning the basic stock of knowledge and skills which every person should possess have been static for a long time, while industry and government have busied themselves with changing the world in which we live. A student today could follow the curriculum of the 1920's with no noticeable discomfort, except for a few obvious anachronisms. But he could not survive as a self-supporting mechanism outside of school if it were not for the additional, out-of-school learning, which is his most important possession.

The time required to impart the common learning was established in the nineteenth century as four years and has been
gradually increased to eight years during this century. It would
be fair to estimate that it should increase by another 50 per cent
before the century ends. In some countries this would carry it
to twelve years; in some, to fourteen or even sixteen.

2. The Organization of Specialization

Traditional systems have concerned themselves mainly with
the major professions and have left specialization of all kinds to
apprentice training at various levels and through various institutions. But this method of providing specialists no longer suffices.
For one thing, the number of specialists now required is much
too large to be trained by the slow apprentice system. For
another, the idea of specialist training as a by-product of professional practice or production is no longer workable. In fact, it
may well be that the professional himself does not know many
of the techniques on which he now depends for indispensable
support. Further, the specialist must often be trained in techniques that he himself will introduce in the field. These are
techniques that come out of on-going research and can only be
adapted and applied in schools.

The need for a new method of producing specialized manpower is obvious enough, but it is not clear where in the system
the task is to be assigned. If it is assumed that the span of time
for imparting the common learning must be lengthened to at
least twelve years, then it is clear that specialists will for the
most part be trained within higher education. Certainly the
movement is in that direction, but the management of the operation is uncertain. European and European-organized universities
are not well suited for specialist production. Their cycles are long,
their teaching staffs are small, their pace is leisurely. A specialist
in training requires a well-defined program, careful supervision,
ample practice time, and clearly defined standards to establish

his qualifications. At present many nations are dealing with these needs by means of ad hoc programs and institutions. But as the number of institutions multiplies, some organizing principle must be established to manage them, or chaos will set in. It does not perhaps matter greatly who takes the responsibility in a given country, but someone must take it.

3. The Support and Application of Research

The third major task is to support and apply research as a part of educational development. This may seem a truism, but teachers, administrators, and scholars know well that the research activity in most countries is far below what is needed, and that the application of research findings as a part of day-to-day instruction lags behind even the production. The problem is even more difficult than this statement implies, for experience is clear that research begets research, and that diminishing research leads to no research. In the same sense, research-based teaching leads to research, and tradition-based teaching leads back to tradition. The tasks of modernization, it is clear, involve both organization and expansion. They are the first steps in meeting the current educational crisis.

In addition to modernization, a problem arises from the implications of democratization. Democratization is essentially a commitment to individuality. As already suggested, it does not and cannot work by standardization. Rather, it depends on reaching and developing the interest, the talent, and the aspiration of each student. This means that democratization is deeply concerned with environment and must be prepared to modify it where and when such action assists in the process of individual development. This may involve reaching into the home of the preschool child, perhaps via television. It may—it should—involve forming new types of school environment. It may involve forming new educational environments for continuing education.

These are all major undertakings, and it is easy to foresee that they could easily become authoritarian in their development and administration. The key to the problem lies in understanding that democratization cannot be imposed by authority. It must be freely accepted, or it will fail at the crucial point.

Another problem of democratization is that it calls for educational strength. A weak educational system does not command teachers who are educated to understand the purpose or meaning of democratization. It does not have the resources to reach all who seek education, and it cannot meet the demands of the pupils it has. A weak system that adopts the forms of democratization without their substance is inviting the disaster of educational inflation. The transformation of a weak system into one strong enough to achieve democratization is long and costly. It involves a general lengthening of the educational span for all students, the expansion of programs, new types of training for teachers and administrators, new facilities, new learning materials, and new services. In such a transformation the fiscal problems alone are large; and beyond them the problems of commitment of the educational profession itself and the achievement of broad understanding of the process are long and difficult.

Yet another problem of democratization lies in its immediate consequences. The opening of new educational opportunities inevitably involves new programs and institutions. Some of these will be of relatively low standard, and some will fail. At the same time the new opportunities will raise the levels of aspiration among students, and demands for new opportunities will come faster than they can be provided. The educational system will be attacked from without and within because of these differences, and the traditional system that has been put aside will become the symbol of abandoned excellence.

There is no easy way to deal with these matters. Experience in America and England suggests that basic adjustments to democratization require a full generation, and that each set of adjustments sets up problems that require another full generation. It is doubtful that any nation embarking on the process can shorten the time greatly.

Knowing these problems, and suspecting that others may be hidden beneath them, we come finally to the question of whether the path of democratization will lead us to resolution of the current crisis. There is no one answer to this question. For some countries it may well be that modernization—in the terms already suggested—and maintenance of a traditional system may be the best immediate solution. For others, the trials of democratization will be signposts along the only possible way to solution. Those who have already committed themselves to democratization know already that the choice, once truly made, is irreversible.

SCHOOL STRUCTURE AND THE UTILIZATION OF TALENT

TORSTEN HUSÉN

In the developing and the developed countries alike, two major forces lie behind attempts to reform the school structure, particularly of secondary education. One is the democratization of secondary and higher education in order to broaden opportunities for young people from all walks of life and especially for talented students from the lower social classes. The other is the need to provide an expanding economy with a sufficient supply of trained manpower at various qualification levels. In rapidly expanding economies—the United States, many European countries, and Japan are examples—the major problem facing educational planners is the need to structure the educational system so as to provide mass education beginning with the secondary level, but followed rapidly at the university level. What this entails is a mobilization of the "reserves of talent," wherever they might be found.[1]

The implications of democratization and the use of the "reserve of talent" must be viewed in the light of research on the relation between the use of talent and the way the school system is structured. The main problems to be considered are the kind of built-in barriers that prevent the optimal utilization of talent, and how these barriers function. Research in the international sphere and in Sweden will be used in the examination of those problems.

1. A. H. Halsey, ed., *Ability and Educational Opportunity* (Paris: OECD, 1961).

One point is worth making here. An optimal output of investment in education will not be achieved merely by removing barriers that prevent able students from getting as much education as they can reasonably absorb. More specifically, it will not be achieved merely by changing the structure of the school system or by devising student aid programs that would remove economic barriers.

An imaginary experiment may help explain why. Let us assume that an emerging country had not previously been able to provide all its children with even an elementary education. Let us assume further that this condition underwent a dramatic change. The emerging country received assistance in the form of resources —teachers, school buildings, and instructional aids—by which it not only could give a secondary education to all children but could provide a sizable proportion of them access to an academic program. What could we expect to happen? Among other things, dropouts would most likely occur at a tremendous rate, because students and parents alike would see little promise of occupational opportunities in this type of education. Thus the lack of economic relevancy would result in a lack of student motivation.

One cannot view the school structure and/or the curriculum as if they operated in a socio-economic vacuum—a conception held by many educators, particularly in the academic secondary schools in Europe and their counterparts in former colonial areas. Even if educational development is less rapid than economic development, there must be a close relation between them. The socio-economic background of students and their motivation to carry on in school account for much more of the cross-cultural (and even more of the within-country) variation in the outcomes of school learning than purely pedagogical factors, such as number of hours of instruction, teacher competence, and size of class.

TOWARD A UNIFIED SCHOOL TRACK

There are good grounds for saying that during the last decade in most developed countries, a cardinal problem of school policy has been to organize an educational system that abolishes or diminishes the dualism or parallelism between prolonged elementary school education on the one hand and selective academic secondary education on the other.[2] Economic expansion has made it necessary to prolong basic education for all young people, regardless of whether in a compulsory elementary school or in a secondary academic school.

The school structure in Europe, and in countries that have tried to imitate European systems, has been molded by certain historical and social forces that have created the parallel or dualistic system. There is no need to describe that system in detail, since its nature is well known. The question now is whether West European countries—faced by the demand for trained manpower, by a higher "consumption of education," and by soaring secondary school enrollment—can structure secondary education in ways that will satisfy both elitist preparation for university studies and prestigious careers and the demand for universal education at the secondary level. The question, moreover, is even more urgent because the rapidly growing need for trained manpower and the increasing "consumption of education," reflected in the so-called educational explosion, conflict with a school organization and a curriculum designed for a static economy and a society characterized by a rather rigid social structure.

Until recently both the occupational status structure and the social class system in many economically developed countries could be symbolized by a pyramid. In all sections of the economy the base of the pyramid was formed by a mass of unskilled or semiskilled manual workers. Most of these had a modest formal education provided by a compulsory elementary school. The next level consisted mainly of white collar workers, such as clerical and sales workers, supervisors of industry, and nurses. The formal education required in most cases exceeded elementary school by a few years, in many cases by some kind of middle

2. T. Husén, "An International Perspective on the Academic Secondary School," *The High School in an Inter-Dependent World* (Edmonton: Department of Secondary Education, University of Alberta, 1965).

school (*Mittlere Reife, cours complémentaires*), with graduation at fifteen or sixteen—a schooling that did not qualify for university entrance. The middle schools either were separate establishments or consisted of the lower section of the pre-university school and/or the university. Individuals with these qualifications provided recruits for the subprofessional group.

In developed countries with highly advanced economies, the qualification and social status structure of the occupational universe now increasingly resembles the shape of an egg. At the bottom of the status hierarchy is a diminishing number of occupations that require a modest amount of formal schooling and vocational training over a considerable time. In the middle a rapidly increasing number of occupations require formal education to the age of sixteen to eighteen after which a specialized vocational training is being sought. At the top, finally, the number of persons with higher educational and professional occupations also increases rapidly.

The school structure in most European countries and in former colonial areas has until now reflected the occupational status structure of a static society. Until the nineteenth century, formal schooling was principally provided for the professionals. The program was academic, consisting of liberal arts with an emphasis on classical languages. Enrollment was limited mainly to young people from the upper social strata. This was true even if the schools to a modest extent served as agents of social mobility by recruiting from lower strata. When elementary education, consisting mainly of the three R's, was made compulsory in the nineteenth century in many of today's economically developed countries, it was designed for the masses and not for those who had previously entered the learned academic school. As a rule, therefore, several grades in the compulsory school ran parallel to the pre-university school. In some cases the parallel was complete: that is, children from privileged homes were sent to private preparatory schools. Currently the parallel in countries like France, England, and Germany has occurred mainly from the age of ten or eleven and up. Thus in West Germany children generally transferred from the fourth grade of the elementary school (*Volksschule*) to the academic secondary school (the nine-year *Gymnasium*). In England and France they transferred after five years in the elementary school—that is, at eleven—to grammar school. Schools of this type resist the "explosion" at the secondary level and have been characterized by competitive entrance and selectivity examinations, grade-repeating, and dropout. Indeed, the growing consumption of education has made these schools more and more competitive. Thus, in England and Germany until recently only about one-fifth of an age group have been admitted to the academic secondary school. A considerable proportion of these students are screened out during the course and do not graduate. Grade-repeating or dropout in the Federal Republic of Germany is so frequent that less than 20 per cent of those admitted to the *Gymnasium* graduate. In England, according to a Ministry of Education report, almost 40 per cent of those admitted to the grammar school fail—that is, drop out or lack sufficient scores on the General Certificate of Education (G.C.E.) examination.[3] A follow-up study of a year's intake in the Swedish *Realskola* (middle school) showed that about 50 per cent failed to graduate in time, and that about one-third repeated at least one grade.[4]

Dropout and grade-repeating in England tend to be related to the social background of students. Thus, among the best third of the students admitted to the grammar school by the 11+ examinations, there were approximately four times as many failures among students whose fathers were workers as among those whose fathers were professionals or executives. Similar findings are reported in Sweden.[5]

3. British Ministry of Education, *Early Leaving* (London: H.M.S.O., 1954).

4. T. Husén and G. Boalt, *Educational Research and Educational Change—The Case of Sweden* (Stockholm: Almqvist and Wiksell, and New York: John Wiley, 1968).

5. T. Husén, "The Relation Between Selectivity and Social Class in Secondary Education," *Educational Sciences*, Vol. I, no. 1, February 1966, pp. 17–29.

In theory the selective schools are supposed to admit and promote their students on the basis of "genuine ability" and not because of social background or place of residence. Thus, to the extent that tuition is free, "equality of opportunity" is supposed to operate with full force even in a highly selective and competitive system. Everybody with the same amount of ability has the same chance to succeed by "free competition." What criteria of ability, then, are usually employed? They are mostly school marks, examination scores, and "intelligence" and achievement test scores, used separately or in combination. These criteria, however, are not independent of social background. A comprehensive body of research has shown that all criteria of selection are more or less loaded with social factors, such as parental education or occupational status and geographical accessibility of the schools.[6] There is ample evidence that the selection procedures for academic secondary and higher education, as well as the screening of students during the course, contain built-in handicaps for children from less privileged social backgrounds. If the effective utilization of the pool of talent is a prime concern not only for the individual but also for the economy at large, a school structure that does not promote the abilities of all its students would have to be reformed.

Comparisons of the merits and drawbacks of selective and comprehensive systems have as a rule been confined to the end-products—such as the average performance of the students in a graduating class. Even these assessments have been purely subjective, as cross-sectional empirical data have not been available. Meanwhile critics of the comprehensive system who point to the high average quality of the graduates of the selective academic schools, overlook certain important elements in the picture. For example, when European and American undergraduates are compared according to intellectual standards, only about 5 to 10 per cent of the age group in Europe is compared with about 30 to 40 per cent in the United States—a dubious

6. *Ibid.*

methodological procedure. Furthermore, the price that is paid in loss of talent in selective systems is considerable, particularly due to grade-repeating and dropout. In a competitive system with formal equality of opportunity, wide latitude is allowed to social factors, such as parental education and social aspirations. Both in Sweden[7] and in England[8] the relation between social class and educational selection has been carefully studied. Even with formal equality of opportunity the social background of the student plays a surprisingly important role.[9]

SOCIAL BIAS IN SCHOOL PROMOTION

The earlier the selection is made—that is, the earlier parents must decide whether a child should go on in the elementary school or compete for entrance to the secondary school—the more strongly can the social factors be expected to operate. A child of ten or eleven cannot reasonably be expected to be involved in his future educational and vocational career to the same extent as a young person of fifteen or sixteen. Therefore, one thing can be expected in countries where transfer to secondary (selective) education takes place at an early age: the social class structure of enrollment would differ more from the social composition of the general population than in countries where transfer takes place later, or where the compulsory school system is comprehensive—that is, provides all children in a certain area with all kinds of education under one roof.

In the International Project for the Evaluation of Educational Achievement (EEA), samples of two target populations in twelve countries were tested by internationally devised mathematics tests.[10] Stratified random samples were drawn of thirteen-year-old students, irrespective of where they were in the school

7. G. Boalt, *Skolutbidning och skolresultat for barn ur olika samhalls-grupper i Stockholm* (Stockholm: Norstedts, 1947).

8. J. Floud *et al.*, *Social Class and Educational Opportunity* (London: Heinemann, 1956).

9. T. Husén, *op. cit.* pp. 17–29.

10. T. Husén *et al.*, *International Study of Achievement in Mathematics: A Comparison of Twelve Countries* (Stockholm: Almqvist and Wiksell, and New York: John Wiley, 1967).

system, in all the countries and also of students from the grade where the majority of the thirteen-year-olds were found. Furthermore, students in the last grade of the pre-university school were sampled—for example, those who were about to take the *Abitur* in the Federal Republic of Germany, or the sixth-formers in England who were about to sit for the G.C.E., A-level. The students, their mathematics teachers, and school principals had to complete questionnaires covering the students' social backgrounds, the teachers' competence, school facilities, instruction, etc. The students were given an opinionaire to assess their attitudes toward mathematics. They were also asked to indicate both the education and the occupation of their fathers and mothers. The occupations were coded in nine groups. Group 1 consisted of higher professional and technical occupations. Group 9 comprised unskilled manual workers (excluding agriculture, forestry, and fishing, which were in group 8). Group 0 included those unclassifiable.

The percentage of students in each occupational category for the two populations—the thirteen-year-olds (1a) and the terminal students in the pre-university school in the math-science and non-math-sience programs respectively (3a and 3b)—are given in Table 2. Australia and Israel have been omitted, since population 3b was not tested in these two countries. Because all students at the age of thirteen are in full-time school, the occupational structure of population 1a (the thirteen-year-olds) can be regarded as the best available national estimate of the occupational distribution of each country. The percentage of occupations belonging to a given group or combination of groups can therefore be used as a base. In comparing population 1a with 3a + 3b, an index of social bias can be derived by dividing the percentage of a given occupational group of terminal students by that of population 1a: this gives the percentage of children of a certain parental background who reach the last grade of the pre-university school. The ratio has been multiplied by 100.

The occupational groups in Table 2 have been combined in Table 3 to correspond to the usual division into upper, middle, and lower classes. Thus, groups 1 and 2 comprise the upper;

TABLE 2.   PERCENTAGE OF STUDENTS IN EACH OCCUPATIONAL CATEGORY

Country	Population	\multicolumn{10}{c}{Occupational Category}										Total	Total Number
		1	2	3	4	5	6	7	8	9	0		
Belgium	1a	4	4	9	12	5	18	40	0	9	0	100%	1656
	3a	10	7	16	15	5	19	25	0	7	1	100	516
	3b	17	8	11	14	6	23	17	0	3	1	100	993
England	1a	4	1	8	9	2	8	62	2	1	3	100	2899
	3a	15	12	21	13	2	15	20	1	1	0	100	960
	3b	20	15	19	14	2	10	17	1	1	1	100	1763
Finland	1a	5	4	14	5	25	2	40	1	4	0	100	743
	3a	12	14	22	3	26	1	17	0	4	1	100	367
	3b	6	17	15	7	23	1	27	0	3	1	100	395
France	1a	2	2	11	9	5	7	53	1	4	4	100	2292
	3a	17	6	19	17	4	7	18	1	1	3	100	213
	3b	14	6	26	9	5	9	25	1	1	3	100	187
Germany	1a	4	5	8	9	5	14	42	1	5	3	100	4318
	3a	33	19	15	5	4	17	6	0	0	1	100	636
	3b	37	17	10	9	5	14	5	0	0	3	100	622

TABLE 2. PERCENTAGE OF STUDENTS IN EACH OCCUPATIONAL CATEGORY (Con't.)

Country													Total	N
Holland	1a	4	7	8	6	11	13	43	5	2	1	100	423
	3a	16	20	17	9	7	17	12	2	0	0	100	116
	3b	32	18	14	8	4	10	14	0	0	0	100	50
Japan	1a	3	10	6	16	24	10	24	2	2	3	100	1969
	3a	8	25	6	19	15	10	10	1	1	5	100	772
	3b	4	16	5	21	25	12	13	0	1	3	100	4209
Scotland	1a	5	2	8	4	3	6	61	2	4	5	100	4972
	3a	21	8	21	10	3	10	24	1	2	1	100	1401
	3b	13	9	13	9	3	10	33	3	3	4	100	2037
Sweden	1a	3	5	13	7	16	4	43	4	3	3	100	2458
	3a	17	12	22	12	6	5	21	1	1	3	100	748
	3b	15	11	23	10	4	7	19	1	2	6	100	207
United States of America	1a	8	7	10	6	5	12	43	2	1	6	100	5806
	3a	15	4	17	8	12	14	27	0	3	0	100	1525
	3b	10	6	13	7	6	8	43	0	2	5	100	1920
All Countries	1a	5	4	9	8	8	9	48	2	3	4	100	26021
	3a	15	13	16	11	7	12	21	1	2	2	100	8814
	3b	12	12	11	14	12	12	22	1	1	3	100	12381

groups 3, 4, and 6 the middle; and groups 7 and 9 the lower class. In order to account for differences between countries in the distribution of urban and rural inhabitants, groups 5 and 8 (farm proprietors and farm laborers) have been kept separate.

In the first column of Table 3, eight countries have been ranked according to the percentage of the total age group in the last grade of the pre-university school. The next three columns give the retentivity indices for students from the upper, middle, and

TABLE 3. RELATION BETWEEN RETENTIVITY AND SOCIAL BIAS AT THE PRE-UNIVERSITY LEVEL

Country	(1) Per cent of total age cohort in pre-university year	(2) Per cent of sample schools which are comprehensive	(3) Professionals, high technical executives (groups 1 and 2)	(4) Middle class subprofessionals, clerks, working proprietors, etc. (groups 3, 4, and 6)	(5) Farm proprietors and farm laborers (groups 5 and 8)	(6) Working class skilled, semiskilled, and unskilled groups (7 and 9)
U.S.A.	70	94	117	120	129	85
Japan	57	100	204	114	79	48
Sweden	23	79	344	169	30	48
Scotland	18	45	364	200	100	48
Finland	14	0	272	117	94	58
Belgium	13	0	263	126	110	51
England	12	20	620	184	75	31
Germany	11	0	589	113	45	12
Rank correlation with column 1		0.86	−0.76	−0.05	0.36	0.62

lower classes, as categorized above. The rank-order correlations between retentivity in terms of the proportion of the age group retained until the pre-university year, on the one hand, and the proportion of students coming from upper or lower class homes, on the other, are high, being —.78 and +.78, respectively. Thus, one is justified in making the generalization that the more retentive the school system is, the less selective it is from the social point of view.

There is a striking difference between countries with a dualistic school system, where the students are competitively selected for academic secondary education at the ages of ten to twelve, and countries, such as the United States, Sweden, and Japan, where the students are kept within the same type of school until they are fifteen to eighteen. The selective systems have a strong preponderance of upper class students in the last grade of the pre-university school.

A second way of calculating the amount of social bias operating in a school system is to compare the proportions in low status categories to those in high status categories at the thirteen-year-old level with the proportions of the same categories in the the pre-university year. (The distribution of fathers' occupations for all thirteen-year-olds is then regarded as typical of the school-going population.) We have chosen groups 1 and 2 (higher technical personnel, professionals, administrators, executives, and working proprietors, large and medium scale) to represent the "high" categories, and group 7 (manual workers, skilled and semiskilled) and group 9 (unskilled manual workers, excluding agriculture, forestry, and fishing) to represent the "low" categories.[11]

11. The following represents the initial calculation for each country; the letters a through f represent the appropriate percentages:

	Groups 1 and 2	Groups 7 and 9
Population 1a	a	b
Population 3a	c	d
Population 3b	e	f

The index of bias for population 3a is then $\dfrac{bc}{ad}$ and for population 3b $\dfrac{bc}{af}$.

The indices are given in Table 4. The larger the index, the more biased is that population toward higher occupational categories. Tables 3 and 4 suggest a strong correlation between retentivity in general, on the one hand (in terms of the proportion of an age group enrolled in the last grade of the pre-university school), and the social class composition of the enrollment, on the other. Thus, a social bias seems to be inherent in the less retentive—that is, selective—systems. This, in its turn, implies a lower degree of utilization of academic talent. Obviously very few working class students get through to the pre-university year in Germany, where the bias is higher than in any other country.[12] In the United States, where about 75 per cent of an age group graduate from secondary school, the bias is very low.

The rank order of social bias according to Table 4 for each of the national populations (with the least biased ranked 1) has been correlated with the percentage of an age group in the math-science and the non-math-science programs, respectively.

TABLE 4. SOCIAL BIAS IN PRE-UNIVERSITY ENROLLMENT

	3a Math-Science Students	3b Non-Math-Science Students
Australia	4.7	—
Belgium	3.6	7.3
England	16.2	24.5
Finland	6.0	3.7
France	17.3	—
Germany	45.3	56.4
Holland	12.3	—
Israel	3.6	—
Japan	6.0	2.9
Scotland	10.4	5.7
Sweden	2.1	7.0
U.S.A.	1.9	1.0

12. Cf. R. Dahrendorf, *Arbeiterkinder an deutschen Universitäten* (Tübingen: Mohr, 1965).

As can be seen from Table 5, the lower the percentage of an age group in the pre-university year, the greater the social bias.

It would also be interesting to investigate how far social bias is correlated with the age when the decisive selection for the academic schools takes place. As we indicated above, it is reasonable to expect that students of ten to twelve years of age could not be as committed to their future educations and

TABLE 5.   RANKS-ORDER CORRELATION BETWEEN SOCIAL
           BIAS AND PERCENTAGE OF AGE GROUP IN
           PRE-UNIVERSITY YEAR

(a)	Math-Science Program	0.66
(b)	Non-Math-Science Program	0.78

vocations as those of sixteen to eighteen. This, then, implies that systems with an early selection for academic secondary education would show a higher degree of social bias than systems where students are on the whole kept together in the same program until the age of fifteen or later.

Table 6 presents the rank-order correlation between social bias according to indices in Table 4 and age of selection for secondary academic education. The Federal Republic of Germany has the earliest selection, at the age of ten. Then come England, Finland, and France with selection at age eleven; Scotland, Australia, Belgium, Israel, Japan, and Holland select at twelve; Sweden at sixteen; and the United States at seventeen to eighteen. As can be seen in Table 6, social bias is significantly tied to age of selection: the earlier it takes place, the stronger the bias.

TABLE 6.   RANK-ORDER CORRELATION BETWEEN SOCIAL
           BIAS AND POINT IN SCHOOL CAREER WHEN
           SELECTION OCCURS

(a)	Math-Science Program	−0.72
(b)	Non-Math-Science Program	−0.51

Another set of related problems studied in the International Project for the Evaluation of Educational Achievement pertained to the following, more general questions: What is the relative "productivity" of the comprehensive or retentive system and of the selective system? How far is it possible to foster an elite within a comprehensive system where the students are kept together under the same roof and/or, in some instances, in the same classroom for their entire mandatory school career?

It would be necessary to examine the results at the pre-university level and in some instances at the intermediate level in order to pass judgment on the productivity of the respective systems. Let us look at the achievement at the pre-university level, and confine our comparisons to those who study mathematics as a main subject—the "fruits" of the educational system.

According to Chart 1, the average mathematics score among United States high school graduates taking mathematics is far below, for instance, that of sixth-form pupils in England or *Abiturienten* in the Federal Republic of Germany. We have, however, to take into account the fact that in the United States about 18 per cent of the age group of seventeen to eighteen are taking mathematics and science in the graduating class, compared with only 4 to 5 per cent of the age in England or Germany. In light of this fact, the problem can be restated more fruitfully: How far has it been possible within a comprehensive system like the American to produce an elite comparable in size and quality to the one produced within a European selective system? One way of answering this question is to compare equal proportions of the age groups in the respective countries. The dotted line in Chart 1 gives the average performance of the mathematics pupils in the twelve countries, with Israel and England at the top and Australia and the United States at the bottom. The score of United States pupils, on the average, is less than half the score of pupils in several European countries. But let us compare the average score of the top 4 per cent of the corresponding age group, a proportion selected because it represents the lowest relative number of pupils taking mathematics in any country, namely Belgium. Such a comparison is represented by the solid line. The range between countries is in this case much more narrow than for the entire group of terminal mathematicians. The United States' top 4 per cent score about the same as most comparable European groups. Two countries with a comprehensive system up to the age of fifteen or sixteen, namely Japan and Sweden, score highest of all. On the basis of the distribution of scores among all the terminal mathematics pupils in all the countries, international standards in terms of so-called percentile scores can be obtained. Chart 2 gives the percentage of the total age group within each country which has reached the standard achieved by the upper tenth of all the terminal mathematics pupils across countries. None of the comprehensive and/or highly retentive systems are among the five countries at the bottom; whereas two, Japan and Sweden, together with England, are at the top.

The explanation for these findings seems to be this. The comprehensive and/or retentive system provides a broader range of opportunities and a better utilization of talent. Systems with an early selection to academic secondary education show a stronger bias in favor of upper and middle class students at the pre-university level than do systems that are more comprehensive and retentive and more flexible in that the final choice between a pre-university and a vocational program is made at the age of fifteen to seventeen instead of at the age of ten to twelve.

As we indicated earlier, the productivity of a school system should not be assessed only by the quality of its final products— that is, the students who are qualifying for university entrance. And we have also noted that there is no point in evaluating the relative efficiency of the respective systems by the mean performances of their terminal pupils, for that is to compare widely varying proportions of age groups and to leave out those who either are excluded from secondary education or do not survive it. Certainly the "total yield" of an educational system cannot be assessed solely by the quality of its pre-university students, since their proportion varies considerably among countries. We are therefore entitled to put the question in this way: How many

Chart 1. Mean Mathematics Test Score (1) for the Total Sample and (2) for Equal Proportions of the Age Group in Each Country for Terminal Mathematics Populations.[13]

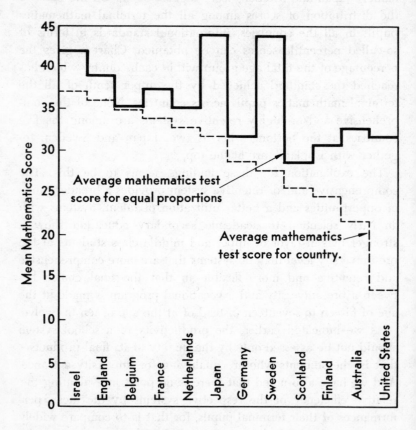

13. T. Husén, *et al., International Study of Achievement in Mathematics* (Stockholm: Almqvist and Wiksell and New York: John Wiley, 1967).

Chart 2. Percentage of Age Group Reaching Upper Tenth of Terminal Mathematics Pupils of International Standards.[14]

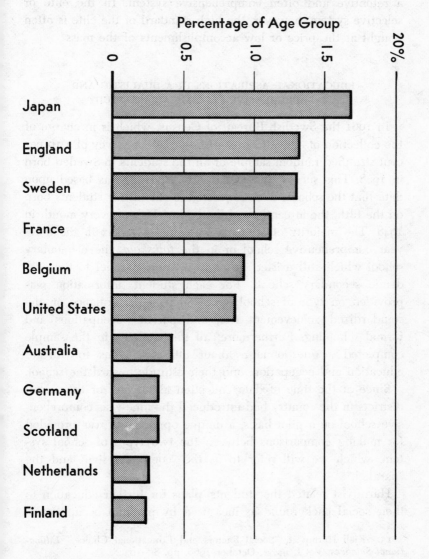

14. *Ibid.*

are brought how far? We have presented evidence that an elite comparable to that of an "elite system" can be cultivated within a retentive and often comprehensive system. In the elite or selective system, however, the high standard of the elite is often bought at the price of low accomplishments of the mass.

EDUCATIONAL ASPIRATIONS IN A DUALISTIC AND A COMPREHENSIVE SYSTEM: A CASE STUDY

In 1961 the Swedish Bureau of Census, which is in charge of the collection of educational statistics, made a survey of a 10 per cent stratified random sample of all the students in Sweden born in 1948. This survey, planned by Härnqvist,[15] was based upon data that the schools were requested to submit for students born on the fifth, the fifteenth, and the twenty-fifth of every month in 1948. The majority of students were in Grade six in the nine-year comprehensive school or in the *folkskola*, the elementary school which still existed in many districts parallel to the academic secondary schools. For each student, information was provided on type of school, grade, marks, performance on the standardized achievement test, and parents' occupations and formal schooling. Furthermore, all the students in the sample completed a questionnaire about interests, plans for further education and occupation, and their attitude toward the school.

Since at the time of data collection about half of the school districts in the country had introduced the nine-year comprehensive school on a pilot basis, a unique opportunity was provided for making comparisons between the two types of school system, which we will refer to as the "comprehensive" and the "parallel."

Härnqvist related the students' plans for further education to their social background as measured by parental occupation.[16]

15. Kjell Härnqvist, "Social Factors and Educational Choice," *Educational Sciences*, Vol I, no. 2, October 1966, pp. 87–103.
16. *Ibid.*

The proportion of students who intended to embark upon an academic program was of special interest in relating educational plans to social background in the comprehensive and parallel school districts.

An "academic" choice in the parallel districts was obvious: it meant transfer from the elementary to the traditional academic secondary school before completion of the former. The academic choice was not equally obvious in the comprehensive school, where at that time (before the 1962 Education Act) it meant two foreign languages, English and German, in grade seven and as a rule a transfer to a class within the grade where "the academics" were brought together. Future educational aspirations were assessed by asking the students whether they had plans to sit for the matriculation examination (*studentexamen*), which at the age of nineteen to twenty would qualify them for university entry.

The students were divided in five categories according to parental occupation. The categories were:

A. Professional (occupations required professional university degree), teachers (both elementary and secondary), officers in the armed forces, executives, proprietors (of large enterprises);
B. White collar occupations requiring formal education up to matriculation, proprietors (of small or medium enterprises);
C. White collar occupations requiring formal schooling only through elementary school;
D. Farmers (owners or tenants of farm enterprises);
E. Manual workers;
F. No information.

The percentage of students who chose the academic program after grade six in comprehensive and parallel districts respectively were:

	Comprehensive	Parallel	Difference
Girls	66	51	15
Boys	58	42	16
Difference	8	9	

In the first place, it should be noted that the higher frequency of girls choosing the academic program than boys runs contrary to previous experiences. The switch from a "male-dominated" academic secondary school to a "female-dominated" one cannot be accounted for in this case only by a change in attitudes toward higher education among girls. Since girls tend to perform better in foreign languages, which play an important role in the Swedish secondary school curriculum, it could be expected that compared with boys, they would more easily agree to take more language instruction than they were compelled to take.

The interesting comparison in this connection, however, is the one between comprehensive and parallel districts. Academic choices are made 15 to 16 per cent more often in the comprehensive districts.

The problem, then, is to interpret this difference. Is it due mainly to the school structure per se or to something else? Has the introduction of the comprehensive, "elective" system stimulated further studies to a larger extent than the parallel "selective" one has?

We cannot, however, contend that grade seven as organized in the traditional secondary academic school (*Realskola*) was comparable to the two-language classes in the same grade in the comprehensive school. Furthermore, we do not know whether the comprehensive districts are comparable to the parallel districts in socio-economic structure. It might well be that comprehensive districts are more urbanized and modern, with more favorable attitudes toward academic education. The two districts have therefore been compared by socio-economic groups in Table 7.

TABLE 7.   DISTRIBUTION OF SOCIO-ECONOMIC GROUPS IN
THE TWO TYPES OF SCHOOL DISTRICT

	Comprehensive	Parallel
A. Professional, etc.	6.5	4.2
B. Higher white collar, etc.	11.8	8.5
C. Lower white collar jobs, etc.	21.7	19.6
D. Farmers	7.0	16.5
E. Manual workers	48.3	46.9
F. No information	4.7	4.3
Total	100.0	100.0

Table 7 shows that the parallel districts are less urbanized, with about half as many farmers as the comprehensive districts. Thus, the differences in socio-economic structure seem to be *one* explanation for the higher frequency of academic choices in the comprehensive districts. The question is, then, whether this is the whole explanation. We can get an answer to that question by comparing the two districts by academic choices within occupational groups, as in Table 8.

TABLE 8.   PERCENTAGE OF ACADEMIC CHOICES AT THE
END OF GRADE SIX BY SOCIAL BACKGROUND
AND TYPE OF SCHOOL DISTRICT

Socio-Economic Group	Boys		Girls		For All Types of School
	Comp.	Par.	Comp.	Par.	
Professionals, etc.	92	87	94	92	91
Higher white collar, etc.	85	72	91	83	82
Lower white collar, etc.	68	54	72	65	63
Farmers	43	26	72	41	38
Manual workers	45	32	53	40	41
No information	59	38	62	45	47
All groups	58	42	66	51	52

When socio-economic background is kept under control, academic choices are throughout more frequent in the comprehensive districts. The differences within the subgroups are smaller than those between the total groups. However, particularly in regard to students from farms, the differences between the two districts are striking; this confirms the contention that comprehensive education considerably broadens the opportunities for children from rural areas.

But the objection remains that the willingness to pursue an academic program cannot be measured by the choice of the two-language program in grade seven. The intention to transfer to the *Realskola* cannot be compared with the choice of a two-language program in the comprehensive school. We shall therefore have to test the hypothesis about the effect of the comprehensive school on the attitude toward further academic education by means of other data in the questionnaire. The students were asked whether they planned to matriculate—that is, sit for the examination in grade twelve or thirteen which qualifies them for university entrance. The percentages of those who answered "yes" were:

	BOYS			GIRLS	
Comprehensive	*Parallel*		*Comprehensive*	*Parallel*
27	15		28	17

A considerably higher proportion of students in the comprehensive districts planned on matriculation. The extent to which this difference is due to differences in socio-economic structure between the two districts is indicated in Table 9. The difference is marked among students whose parents are white collar workers, farmers, and manual workers, twice as many of whom plan to matriculate as do the corresponding groups in the parallel district.

TABLE 9. PERCENTAGE OF STUDENTS ASPIRING TO QUALIFY
FOR MATRICULATION

Socio-Economic Group	Boys		Girls		Total
	Comp.	Par.	Comp.	Par.	
Professionals, etc.	79	58	73	65	68
Higher white collar	50	41	51	48	47
Lower white collar	32	20	33	20	25
Farmers	12	5	18	8	8
Manual workers	13	8	16	9	11
No information	31	11	30	11	18
All groups	27	15	28	17	20

CONCLUSION

Well into the twentieth century the secondary schools in most countries, both industrialized and nonindustrialized, were supposed to prepare a social and, in part, intellectual elite for the professions and for the social role played by a leading section of the community. Scientific progress, the transformations that technology has brought to industry, business, and our daily lives, and the expansions of trade and communications have, during the last few decades, increased tremendously the need for well-educated and trained manpower. Capable hands are in short supply, and the economy expects the educational system to tap more efficiently the available talent. A growing proportion of teenagers are in full-time school. New forms of education at this age level have been developed. Thus, schools offering curricula in engineering, social studies, and modern languages coexist with schools offering the classical pre-university program. As a consequence of broadened recruitment and curricula, there is a tendency toward less selectivity. Where the problem used to be primarily one of picking and choosing, we are now more concerned with allocating students to fields of study most suited to them. The guidance function has become increasingly important. Programs of general education are devised so as to put off as long as possible a definitive choice of career. The former opposition between general education and vocational education and training is being assuaged. In regard to organization, curricula, and staffing, the present trend in countries with rather developed school systems is to integrate the different school types that formerly ran parallel at the secondary level. A flexible school system, where a definitive choice between various educational paths is postponed as long as possible, can take care of talent from all walks of life more readily than a rigid system with an early selection, which to a large extent depends upon social background.

SCHOOL SYSTEMS AND MASS DEMAND:
A COMPARATIVE OVERVIEW[1]

GEORGE Z. F. BEREDAY

Those who believe that the development of education at the present time is in a state of crisis base their arguments on the widening gap between the rapidly changing social demands for education and the power of the schools to adapt to those changes. Attempts to change the systems of education as such do little to solve the problems of such crises. Systems of education are by definition agents of conservation and stability. Most human systems are designed not to promote but to retard change. In this way man safeguards himself from becoming a victim of his world. We recognize the very fast rate at which technology is capable of advancing life, and we also know that the slowest agent in the forward motion is man himself. Since he is the initiator and the ultimate beneficiary of the advances of civilization, it makes sense that those advances should be geared to his pace. Man builds systems, consciously or unconsciously, to protect himself from too rapid destruction of the way of life to which he has become accustomed. Although no well-meaning person can accept the failures to teach literacy and the bitter frustrations of the educational ambitions of so many people, the point this chapter attempts to make is that those who seek remedies

1. An earlier version of this chapter was published as "School Systems and the Enrollment Crisis: A Comparative Overview," in *Comparative Education Review*, Vol. XII, no. 2, June 1968, pp. 126–138.

in the reform of school systems deal with the tail ends of change rather than with its sources.

Insofar as there is a crisis in education, it cannot be alleviated simply by restructuring systems of education. A reorganization of the systems follows at its own pace—a much slower pace and often a reluctant one—other changes in society. Westerners accept the proposition that education should adapt to and should further the social and technological advances that other institutions are making. If Easterners or Arabs or Africans search within their own traditions, they might be less ready to agree that the business of forming persons for life has, or should have, very much to do with the material consequences of living. But even Westerners cannot ignore the evidence furnished by the history of several educational systems, which suggests that successful rapid reforms of schools are extremely unlikely. Historically, successful rebuilding or refurbishing of educational structures has been possible only through war or as a result of war or similar cataclysms. Americans can occupy a Japan or a West Germany and can try to convert the shape of the schools according to their own pattern or wishes. A military hero turned dictator—such as Kemal Ataturk in Turkey or, to an extent, Charles de Gaulle in France—can restructure forcibly the school track of his country. A group of strong leaders in the Soviet Union or in Meiji Japan can force educational reforms to modernize their school systems, only after they succeed first in restructuring virtually everything else.

The very mention of these examples, however, suggests how limited the success of school reorganization can be even under these extreme conditions. Thirty years after modernization of the Arabic script, continuous reforms of curricula in elementary schools and the *lise*, and efforts to involve the army in training illiterate conscripts and using military cadets as rural teachers, the face of Turkish education is still the face of education in an undeveloped country. Twenty years after the proposals to reform French education and ten years after their enactment, the French educational system continues to function or malfunction pretty much as it did before. The bitterness and disappointments attendant upon the failures of the Americans to influence the Germans or the Japanese are too well known to bear restatement. In the Soviet Union and in Japan the reforms of the schools have been accompanied by brillant statesmanship. But even there, as books by Timasheff and Doré, for instance, testify, *plus ça change, plus c'est la même chose.*[2] The new school systems have managed to resemble, or on occasions to revert to, the slowly moving traditional patterns.

School systems, therefore, should be regarded as the given, though it would be nice if this were not so. Let us say that the schools of the sons must in at least half of the cases resemble the schools of their fathers. An effective change of educational patterns can be accomplished only by evolution over three generations. Efforts to harness education in the service of development cannot afford to ignore these persistent social laws.

The point of this chapter, then, must be that the remedies for the world crisis in education do not lie in changing the structure of the systems. Reforms of structure, if well thought out and pushed, may improve the flow of pupils and streamline the curricula; but they cannot solve the problem of educational underproduction. Underproduction occurs because school systems exist. By definition they are restrictive and repressive in character. Maybe that is the way things should be, but this state of things does not favor revolution. A revolution can only burst forth if, instead of restructuring school systems, we decide to undo them.

STATIC FEATURES OF SCHOOL SYSTEMS

What is meant by a school system can be explained very easily by comparing the flow of pupils to a trapezoid. School systems possess a broad, increasingly universal base of entrance and,

2. Nicholas S. Timasheff, *The Great Retreat* (New York: E. P. Dutton & Co., 1946); Ronald P. Doré, *Education in Tokugawa Japan* (Berkeley: University of California Press, 1965).

invariably, a much narrower, restrictive line at final exit and graduation. What varies from country to country is the lengths of the base and the top and their ratio to each other. A few fortunate industrial systems have achieved a base of entrance which takes in almost 100 per cent of the pupils in relevant age groups. None has achieved an exit through which more than 50 per cent of the age group pass as university graduates. Efforts have been made all over to increase the quantity, to press for the total opening of the entrance base, for an extension and elevation of the exit gate, and for the improvement of the size of that gate relative to the base. Fitted into the over-all trapezoid are other trapezoids corresponding to the chronological age and to the social and educational advancement of the pupils. Most systems possess the primary, secondary, and higher education layers. Some are so well developed that they break into six layers: preschool, primary, junior-secondary, senior-secondary, postsecondary, and postgraduate. The rules of growth within each of the levels conform to the rules postulated for the system as a whole. All subsystems attempt to expand the entrance and exit to each level and to improve the size of the exit relative to that of the entrance. But distinctions persist. The primary level of education is intended or happens to provide minimum education and literacy for ordinary people; secondary education enables the middle class to pursue the occupations and to enjoy the status of clerks and technicians; the university level prepares leaders of society for the highest professional positions. Even when only two distinct social groups face each other in the population, as in the Soviet Union where people are either the managers or the managed, the three levels inside the education trapezoid are repeated, and they determine the flow of pupils upward.

Moreover, in the second and third horizontal level it becomes increasingly apparent that there are three ways of dealing with the flow of pupils, particularly their graduation. Implicit in the old notion of the educational flow is the first and oldest solution. This is best called the dual system. In it a small minority of suitable people are taken upward to graduation, usually in general education but also in specific professional subjects, to man positions of leadership in society. The rest of the school population, perhaps less well endowed or less fortunate, are "lost on the way." These people are funneled into a variety of less skilled or nonskilled occupations. At best they receive the type of sound general preparation provided, for example, by the nine-year German *Volksschule*. At worst they are dispersed without any schooling or with one or two years of perfunctory education, such as that provided by a large group of primary schools in Brazil.

In direct contrast to this dual system is the modern ideal of total mass education for all youth up to graduation level. This system, of which perhaps Japan is at present the best example (the United States and the Soviet Union are two other examples), envisages an exit level for all students that means universal general education. It also means that the teaching of an array of professional skills is woven into the general training or attached fanlike to it. Everyone entering this school system is guaranteed at least equivalent, if not equal, education at an identical level. The notion of college education for all, reiterated by men such as Earl McGrath,[3] expresses the hope that such a system is feasible.

The third vertical solution, inherent in the development of contemporary schools, is the tripartite system, which possesses features of both the others. One group of people goes through from entrance to graduation destined for positions of leadership. Another group, at the other end of the spectrum, is abruptly or gradually phased out of the system. Between the two is a third, buffer group, as in Germany's movement to build up the second road to the university (*Zweiter Weg*) and in several Western European countries in the middle school movement (*scuola media, Mittelschule*, Leicestershire plan). In the Soviet Union

3. Earl McGrath, *Universal Higher Education* (New York: McGraw-Hill, 1966).

this group is represented by the second-level technicians, whose training is backed up by the excellent *technicums*. The college entrance ambitions of the best Secondary Modern schools of England are another example of aspirations toward such a group. An effort here is to build up a compensatory, rather than an equivalent, school ladder ending perhaps in college, but in a non-elite college of a land grant, ag-tech type.

In summation, throughout the world, educational systems, including higher education, have common features. First, the number of pupils at entrance is larger than the number at final graduation. Second, the flow upward is regulated, and in some cases impeded, by horizontal barriers of required age and attainment. Third, the upward movement of pupils develops according to three patterns: (a) dual division of very high and very low educational attainment; (b) tripartite division of very high, medium, and very low attainment; (c) an open system of equivalent though varied levels of attainment for all. This latest stage exists more on blueprints than in fact; though several systems, Sweden and New Zealand for instance, have now joined the major pioneers of mass education.

DYNAMIC FEATURES OF SCHOOL SYSTEMS

To these three static features of school systems can now be added three dynamic ones. First, the major effort of the system makers has been devoted, not to changing the structure of the system, but to expanding the intake and the output. Second, all other efforts are made primarily to improve the mechanics of upward promotion. Finally, the ideal of perfect upward promotion according to ability is retarded by tradition. As a matter of fact, now the question is being raised whether an elite that is intellectual rather than aristocratic and economic is an improvement on the old status quo.

The first essential fact about the dynamics of school systems as outlined above is that their shape has not been changing rapidly.

The efforts of reformers are directed primarily toward expanding quantity. The walls of the trapezoid are forever pushed outward, but the structure remains the same. There is pressure all through the system, perhaps more at entrance than in the middle or at the exit because universal literacy is more appealing as an ideal than a high rate of graduation (the latter is resisted in the name of high standards and of the traditional selective process). In some countries the base and the top expand at the same rate. In a few rare countries the trapezoid becomes taller, as the graduations race ahead of admissions. In most cases it becomes flatter as expansion of intake into primary schools is not matched by expansion of output. The tremendous pressure for expansion of quantity is sometimes limited by finances, sometimes by lack of teachers, sometimes by fear of diminished quality. At other times the pressure is allowed to "break through," and vast numbers of new places are hastily provided to meet political demands or economic needs. All this has done little to change the shape of the structure. The trapezoid remains. That means entrance and graduation restrictions, either educational or economic, are placed in the way of many. At present the number of those who are in some way frustrated is growing so large that we have a world crisis in education.

To combat real or implied injustice in the selectivity involved, all efforts for reform, other than those directed at increasing quantity, have only been concerned with improving "articulation" within the system. Since some students must be chosen and others rejected, the major concern has been to ensure that the process be "just." In predemocratic societies the opportunity to enter or to exit may have had nothing to do with possessing the most suitable skills or attaining a certain educational level. When there was more than enough talent to go around, automatic selection on the basis of bloodlines or wealth provided enough people of better than average quality to fill the available vacancies. There was no need to search through the "talent pool" and to provide a systematic ladder of upward educational promotion for all. Accordingly entrance to a higher level of education could be secured without attendance at and graduation from lower levels of education. Entrance to secondary school in England and France, for instance, could be won without study in the primary schools. Private tutoring or private preparatory schools could be relied upon as substitutes. The same applied to entrance to the universities. From Germany to Japan entrance to universities was earned by examinations and not necessarily by attendance at lower levels of education.

Predemocratic schools were built on a system that might be described as discontinuous. Democratic societies have attempted to build, instead, systems that are continuous. The educational trapezoids everywhere provide for an orderly and unbroken progression upward through successive filters of educational evaluation and selection. Entrance from outside at any level other than the lowest, if grudgingly permitted at all, is stringently regulated. The energy of the system is consumed in endeavors to maintain smooth flow and good selection. Parents and teachers tremble until their charges "get through," since educational failure at one level usually precludes all chances of entering the levels above.

These efforts resemble in its pure form Jefferson's plan for education in Virginia: the essence of it was that primary education would reach all children at a certain age, that the best children in each locality would be selected for study in the regional secondary schools, and that the best of these would be in turn selected to graduate from the state university. The ideal of articulated systems is that educational selection should be always according to merit. The school is to be the scene of a cumulative upward surge. The process is to hoist up the best to become leaders in society.

Michael Young's *The Rise of the Meritocracy* has cast doubt upon the effectiveness of this type of selection.[4] Several objections

4. Michael Young, *The Rise of the Meritocracy* (New York: Random House, 1959).

have been, and are being, made to the articulated system of educational promotion, in addition to Young's warning that government by the cleverest tends to degenerate into a totalitarian state run by a hereditary aristocracy. Even when an educational system can stay justly selective from generation to generation, it will be governed by the children of the well-to-do, who persistently score better at examinations even when such examinations are not intentionally skewed in their favor. These environmental inequities are compounded by the imperfections of the selective procedures—that is to say, by the waste of talent resulting from the loss of those rejected by error. All rejections, just or unjust, result, in any case, in aggravating social frustrations. Society pays a heavy price for depriving its children of hope and self-esteem. It causes alienation from intellectual life, criminality, and cynicism instead of citizenship.

This price may be appropriate in order to promote high educational standards and the emergence of the best people as leaders. For our purpose it is enough to say that efforts at perfect articulation significantly slow the growth of school systems in quantity of intake. When school entrance and graduation are barred by all sorts of restrictions, the effort to maintain them, to contain the fury of the rejects and their parents, and to do the countless things involved in processing the flow lowers everybody's potential, let alone the determination to do something for all children. Maintaining the educational trapezoid, however generously open it may be, directly inhibits the offer of adequate school places "according to need."

Furthermore, in industrial societies the numbers of educated elite required and the demand for high-level skills of all workers have been increasing so rapidly that there seems little to be gained from gearing school systems only to selection of the best. It seems that all over the world, societies will have to rely instead on the average person to perform well as a leader. Political democracies in particular depend in some measure on leaders who are temporarily most popular rather than permanently most able. The task of a democracy is "how to make the second best good enough" to govern. It is in recognition of this need that great efforts to articulate upward larger numbers have been and are being made. There are indications from all sides that these efforts, though successful and worth while, have not been enough.

All societies pay a price for having any school system. By definition, systems mean rigidity, vested interests, impediments. We now know that mental growth is continuous, but our schools continue to be closed for a total of three months a year. We know that the after-lunch hours are times of drowsiness, but schools merrily offer classes, only to stop when things perk up toward the cocktail hour. The Berlitz total immersion courses, and Ford Foundation-sponsored experiments in Indiana, show that fluency in a foreign language can be attained within one to nine weeks. We continue to offer three hours weekly for six years, at the end of which our pupils know nothing. We proclaim as saints those who have had religious revelation, and we respect the Zen Buddhists who have attained satori, but we fearfully shrink from consciousness-expanding drugs and hesitate to research or even speculate on their potential for improving academic comprehension. We now know that the scatter of human ability is a continuum from the very few highly talented through the masses of the average to the very few seriously handicapped. But we continue to talk with brilliant semantic absurdity about the bright and the slow (not bright and dim or fast and slow), as if there were two opposed groups of students in the schools.

TOWARD AN EDUCATIONAL "UN-SYSTEM"

It seems that what is needed in an age of unprecedented demands for education is not a system but an "un-system." To cope with the multiple demands made on the schools, multiple and flexible ways of admitting people into and graduating them from educational courses must be made available. Entrance at various levels of education should no longer be barred by requirements for previous cumulative qualifications. We should deliberately foster a kind of educational chaos, on the premises, long unrecognized, that school programs are primarily "exposure" to learning, and that "effectiveness" of learning is another matter about which relatively little is still known. The work of established school systems will, indeed, continue at a pace and with a rationale of its own. A mopping-up operation to take care of those left over must supplement, if not supplant, them.

Several comparative examples of discontinuous school programs are worthy of study; they suggest at least the pilot approaches that could be made to the greatest educational shortcomings.

(1) American Elective Secondary School

The American high school, though a continuous day school, bears in school programs the precedents for discontinuous education. Practices vary from state to state; but, generally speaking, common subjects prevail in the grade schools in which one teacher is in charge of each classroom. The three grades of junior high school provide a gradual switch from common to elective subjects, and senior high school is almost completely selective, with individual teachers in charge of specific subjects of instruction. Broadly speaking, subjects are grouped around academic, commercial, vocational, and general specializations. Only credits in English and local history are a requirement for graduation in some states. In New York State a high-level Regent examination regulates college-bound graduations from high school. Promotion from grade to grade is usually according to chronological age, with a minimum held back for academic reasons. Though formidable to administer and vulnerable to low standards, the American school system is potentially the most suitable provider of flexible, ad hoc, and discontinuous education tied to children's interests and to the needs of the moment. It has sometimes been called cafeteria-style education. It could be just that in the best, as well as in the worst, sense of the word. It could permit each person to enter and exit the education track at a place of his choosing and to take whatever courses he and his advisers deem most relevant.

(2) Evening and Supplementary Education—Workers' Education Association and Further Education in England

A similar pattern of *smörgasbord* education has been established in evening and part-time education system for adults and adolescents. The best examples of such facilities are the Workers' Educational Association in England and the English Further Education system. The Workers Educational Association has an ancient tradition and operates now predominantly as a university extension system. There is one full-time college (Ruskin College) at Oxford. Several hundred classes are provided by local education authorities and can lead to the acquisition of secondary school qualifications. The programs strongly emphasize liberal arts, music, political science, sociology, and science. There are relatively few vocational courses. There are short courses of a few lectures as well as larger courses and tutorial meetings lasting up to one year. Further Education by contrast has been envisaged by the 1944 Education Act as a supplement to education of adolescents between the ages of fifteen or sixteen and eighteen. The major portion of Further Education is on a part-time, one-day-a-week basis and as such is similar to the training offered in German and Scandinavian schools. There is an increasing number of more extensive educational provisions and full-time colleges leading up to such institutions as the National College of Horology and the National Foundry College. Further Education and adult education provides a prototype for part-time and evening educational offerings to all comers at all levels. This network of centers could be and is used as a supplement to daytime education or as a substitute for it. It could merge work and study in the *Arbeitsschule* tradition.

(3) Primary and Postsecondary Education— the Danish Folk High Schools

From the nineteenth-century Danish educational tradition comes the prototype of cultural education designed to skip the secondary level. The folk high schools of Denmark and Scandinavia provide training for youngsters who have terminated their formal education at fourteen and have had work experience until the age of eighteen. Folk high schools offer general academic and cultural training for young adults in courses lasting from several weeks to several months. Their companions, the agricultural cooperative colleges, provide matching vocational education. The folk high schools are residential and are centers of training in morality and citizenship as well as in intellectual subjects. Observers unanimously report that they have contributed to an unprecedented social and cultural upgrading of the Danish farming population. These schools are now being criticized for lack of adaptability to urban industrial conditions, suitable adaption to which is certainly imperative.

The notion of return to school after interruptions is strong in Turkish military training courses, the Emergency Training scheme for teachers in England, and several forms of remedial education. They provide an informal way to recoup the educational losses occasioned by nonattendance and dropping out.

(4) Schools by Radio and Television—Escuelas Radiofónicas of Colombia and Others[5]

Schools of the new communications media have made a hesitant appearance in the last ten years in areas where distance and scarcity of resources make formal teaching impractical. Several types of networks for such education are available as models capable of great expansion. The Escuelas Radiofónicas of Colombia, the most modest of these schemes, consists of a one-

5. A more detailed discussion of the use of television can be found below in the essay on "The New Educational Technology" by Wilbur Schramm, p. 133 ff.

way network of broadcasts in religion, literacy, and vocational skills beamed from a center in Sutantenza into individual homes in the Andean hills. At each radio receiver is a specially trained local monitor, who acts as tutor and teacher to all members of a household regardless of age and advancement. An examination system administered from a center in Bogotá tests proficiency in each course.

The radio bush schools in Australia are a variation on this system. Regular school work is done by children in remote areas over a two-way radio system. Australian Schools of the Air operate from several small broadcasting studios and are a complementary service to the Royal Australian Flying Doctor Service whose network they use. Youngsters equipped with radio monitors can question the teachers and can participate in discussions with other pupils.

Teaching by radio is clearly capable of being extended to teaching by television. At present several school systems use educational television. The Italian *Telescuola* is one example. American Samoa is noteworthy as another model of total teaching through this medium with the aid of teacher monitors. Here the instruction takes place not at home but in schools. Courses are beamed from a special television center.

Teaching by communications media has great potential for totally overcoming the world's educational shortages. The available models demonstrate that the lack of teachers and insufficient school buildings are no great handicap to sound instruction. Here again discontinuous education could be provided to all in order to satisfy their interests and to complete their educational requirements outside established channels.

(5) *Vocational Non-Schools—United States*

A series of studies by Harold Clark and Harold Sloan describe the so-called non-schools of the United States.[6] In factories, in

6. Listed by Philip H. Coombs in *The World Educational Crisis—A Systems Analysis* (New York: Oxford University Press, 1968). p. 140.

stores, in military units, and in camps a vast amount of vocational education is satisfying the multiple needs of American organizations and industries. One such vocational system, that of the Raytheon Company in Boston, is currently reported to be seeking a charter as a four-year college. Equally significant is the recent work by Clark and Sloan on the so-called invisible classrooms.[7] There are several thousand schools in the United States whose existence can be discovered only by consulting the yellow pages of the telephone book. They range from jet-airline pilot training centers to fine arts colonies, from beautician schools to schools of egg production. Dropouts from formal schools are, as Clark puts it, dropins to this invisible network. It provides an excellent example of an ad hoc range of educational provisions which the necessities of life itself have brought into being.

(6) Out-of-School Institutions—Outward Bound Movement and Others

Youth activities from the Boy Scout movement to Soviet Pioneer camps extend the range of education. They are designed to school young people to appreciate, and to be able to cope in, uninhabited areas. The most dramatic example of this model is the Outward Bound School Movement conceived by Kurt Hahn in Austria. Transplanted to Scotland, the programs have now spread to several countries; in the United States there are five such centers. The training consists of short courses administered to adolescents and young adults. It combines school study with assault courses, training in seamanship and mountaineering, and training for survival in the wilderness. This rugged training is enhanced by involving the pupils in sea and mountain rescue operations. The aim is to provide moral training, but it would be neither difficult nor farfetched to extend it to intellectual training. The Outward Bound School pattern has been copied recently not for rural but for urban survival in an experiment in Trenton,

7. Harold Clark and Harold Sloan, *Classrooms on Main Street* (New York: Teachers College Press, 1966).

New Jersey. Here are models of direct training "for life" with the potential not only for teaching practical skills but for motivating better academic school study. No one major book describes the available provisions of this type of program throughout the world: from work camps in Holland to Peace Corps centers in Thailand there is a network, of low-cost spontaneous training, which could reclaim pupils affected by national shortcomings.

These examples of non-schools listed merely suggest the variety of educational provisions of different length, level, and intensity that could emerge to cope with the educational neglects of our time. They could appear piecemeal, ad hoc, in response to need, to answer the problem of illiteracy or the need for vocational skills, and above all to foster inner concentration and the willingness to seek self-perfection, the supreme gift of a school of any kind.

There is only one fundamental objection to a nonarticulated school system. It does not solve the problem of appraising the level of qualifications acquired. It gives no clue to the equivalence and interchangeability of different preparations. It does not satisfy the secondary but powerful source of motivation behind people's urge for education—namely their quest for social status. It provides no machinery of evaluation for employers to use as a criterion for placement.

This problem could be solved if nonarticulated educational tracks were marked out by national systems of certification. A ladder of schools could be replaced by a ladder of certifications, as is the case in French and German secondary schools and in English and American bar and medical board examinations. Many sound objections have been justly voiced against examinations. They tend to strangle school curricula from above. They are narrow in concept and enforce stultifying drills of preparation. They are only good tests of performance under duress. They reflect antiquated interests of once intellectually brilliant but now aging examiners.

To answer these charges, first of all, certifications are not necessarily examinations. Series of interviews, such as those employed by the British Civil Service; short periods of observation in residence, as required at the end of Soviet correspondence courses; evaluation of dossiers made up of teacher references, as practiced in American scholarship competitions; or aptitude and attainment tests are well-known devices to circumvent examinations. If as much ingenuity and effort went into improving examinations as are spent in criticizing and avoiding them, they could be made into perfectly equitable and noncontroversial means of evaluation.

We have on comparative record at least one examination system that has operated without major tensions and has permitted a multiple and flexible satisfaction of the many demands made upon it. The British General Certificate of Education is granted at the end of secondary school studies. The Ordinary Level Certificate is awarded at the age of sixteen, with credits available in any school subject and with no requirements as to the number and grouping of subjects offered. The Advanced Level Certificate is offered at eighteen and reflects levels taught in the sixth form. To qualify at all for admission to a university, the candidate must be successful in at least five subjects, and two at an A-level, scattered over the sciences and humanities. Apart from this stipulation, insisted upon by the universities rather than by the examiners, any one can offer most of the areas he has studied at a standard he feels prepared to attain. The British examination is not free from criticism. Framers of examination questions are senior teachers and Ministry of Education officials whose hardened arteries sometimes show up in examination papers. Questions are used and revised over the years, and collections of past examination questions are available in print, making possible a successfully specialized, but educationally not very fruitful, narrow professional preparation. Institutions admitting or employing successful candidates tend to make a fetish of the number and type of credits accumulated. But these charges simply mean that supreme care should be taken to select the examiners so as to ensure broad, humane, and fair appraisal of the capacities to be tested.

A system of examinations and/or certifications would remove the major objection from the proposal to build nonarticulated schools. It would provide the milestones to stake out the semblance of a structure that would otherwise be permitted to be a free-flowing quest for knowledge. The ramifications of a flexible, diversified, non-continuous school world would frighten those who seek neat structures. But to seek orderly education is one thing; to seek education with enough stretch to accommodate large numbers at a moment's notice is another, completely different matter. To ensure schooling for vast numbers of students, a laissez-faire educational scene buttressed by an orderly certification system seems the only solution.

Such an approach envisions the school to be like a skyscraper on fire, with people popping in and out through different windows and on different floors. It would permit pursuit of education wherever and however its accumulation is desired. It would once and for all challenge the right of any human structure to deny any human being his right to know, however humbly. It would do little to maintain the highest standards: that is the task of the brilliant and the profoundly specialized who in their care for extreme excellence are willing to stand as models, uncompromising and alone. But a nonarticulated school would have the vitality of the bulk of ordinary people in search of something good. The history of countries with mass education has suggested that having such a forward thrust is the richest capital at mankind's command.

TEACHER EDUCATION
AND MODERNIZATION

R. FREEMAN BUTTS

To paraphrase Jean-Jacques Rousseau, man believes that education has the power to set him free, but everywhere he is in chains for want of good teachers.

The purpose of this essay is to assess some of the basic reasons for this worldwide crisis and to produce a set of proposals for resolving it. How can the educators of different countries, possibly working together, improve the effectiveness of teachers already in the educational system and attract to the teaching profession a larger number of able young people, prepare them with higher qualifications, allocate them to the educational institutions where they are most needed, and hold them in the profession with high morale and steadily improving competence? And how can all this be done at a cost we can afford?

The world crisis in education, as it manifests itself in the preparation and supply of teachers, is composed of two powerful sets of ingredients which somehow must come to terms: these can be called the "drive for modernization" and the "tradition of educational disjunctivitis."

THE DRIVE FOR MODERNIZATION

The fact with which we start is the deep-seated aspiration of the leaders of the new nations to overcome the gap between their own predominantly traditional societies and the more modern nations of the technologically developed world. For ten to twenty years they have emphasized the needs both to industrialize as the prime means of improving the economic well-being of people, and to achieve the political status of a self-determining, independent sovereignty among the other sovereign nations of the world. Underlying these potent aspirations is the less obvious but possibly even more important psychological drive to be recognized as socially and intellectually equal to all other nations and thus deserving the respect and dignity due to free men.

Some national leaders have had their eyes so firmly fixed upon the race to catch up with the already modern nations that they have either overlooked or ignored tremendous gaps within their own borders between the vast majority of traditional men and the relatively small modern elite of which they themselves are a part. Although they have the benefit of a "modern" Western education, they have given little attention to analyzing what in a Western education helped to create the modernizing elites, what it is that now should be accepted, what adapted, and what discarded.

In any case, most nations have eagerly adopted universal primary education as a prime target of national independence and have set about to expand secondary and higher education as well. Sometimes without too much thought about the suitability of the inherited education to the process of modernization, they only say that education should pay more attention than it did under colonial rule to local life, culture, and values. Too seldom have political leaders, economic planners, and educational leaders seriously raised the question of what kind of education would enable traditional societies to become modern. Too often the planners have attended exclusively to producing the potential members of the modern elite, the ones who usually make up "high-level manpower." Too often leaders and planners have overlooked the dilemma of modernization as it must be faced by the "traditional" man and woman in Asia or Africa or Latin America or Europe or the United States.

The outside world is beginning to impinge upon the traditional man's circumscribed circle of behavior and is forcing him to change in many obvious or subtle ways his inherited loyalties to family and local rulers, his beliefs and outlooks handed down from ancestors or from the local guardians of religious faith. He must somehow broaden his traditional loyalties to his particular family, locality, or ethnic group and embrace a more general loyalty to his nation, which may now include social, ethnic, and religious groups once his ancient enemies. He may find that his inherited social class or occupation, which carried with it a recognizable status, whether high or low, may now be changed for the better if he works harder to achieve that change—or for the worse through no fault of his own if he merely continues doing what he has always done. His mother tongue is no longer sufficient to enable him to be a fully functioning member of his new nation or of the modern world. He must learn to read and write what he formerly knew only orally; formal education is therefore required, where informal learning had earlier sufficed. Indeed, he has often had to learn the written language of his ancient enemies or of his former colonial rulers. Strange sounds in words and music come over the radio, and many of these are fascinating yet disturbing indeed.

As his rural subsistence way of life is confronted by people who have adopted an urban way of life, he faces the prospect of radical change whether he stays at home or whether he himself is attracted by the magnetic pull of the city. Either alternative is deeply unsettling. His whole set of beliefs about what is good and proper begins to be challenged by new gods or new idols. His geographic isolation, his social position, his psychological security may all be disrupted by speeding motor buses, blaring radios, gaudy magazines, strange tinned foods, styles of dress that outrage the dictates of custom or morality, the crumbling of the familiar ties of family, an unfamiliar job in the city, and all the other trappings of modernization that those in highly industrialized societies have more or less learned to live with. But the effort to adopt a modern style of life and to find a reassuring sense of personal identity amid such disturbing change is traumatic indeed. It is hard enough for those born and brought up within a modernizing society, as the heart of any large city or rural slum in any country of the world can testify; but it is worse for those caught suddenly in the maelstrom of change. Fortunately many such people are turning to education as a fundamental means of surviving the transition without violence, blind despair, or chaos. But unfortunately the teachers they seek are not there or are not prepared to offer much help.

Why have teachers been lacking or poorly prepared to play a significant role in the modernization of traditional sectors in many nations?

THE TRADITIONS OF EDUCATIONAL DISJUNCTIVITIS

The answers to this question stem in part from what we can call "disjunctivitis": the disease results from dividing or disjoining an educational enterprise into separate, often mutually exclusive, parts. Such educational disjunctions tend to produce a number of professional dead ends which discourage able people from becoming teachers, and to perpetuate group divisions in the larger society which result in duplicated institutions and put further strain on an already short supply of teachers. The following are some examples of educational disjunctivitis that have curtailed the supply of teachers and interfered with their appropriate preparation and effective utilization. Traditionally the educational institutions of nineteenth-century Europe possessed several characteristic disjunctions, which have been exported to much of the rest of the world during the past one hundred years.

One, for example, is the wide gap between primary schooling, on the one hand, and secondary schooling leading to the university, on the other. In almost every respect primary schools and primary school teachers have been inferior to secondary schools and to secondary school teachers. Primary school teachers have less education; they have lower salaries; they have less status and prestige in the community; and their academic qualifications and professional training are inferior. This disparity has been still more marked in certain countries of Africa where primary school teachers were mainly indigenous and secondary school teachers mostly expatriate. Primary school teaching is widely looked upon as a professional dead end. Anyone able to do better does so.

A second gap is between secondary schools and teacher-training colleges (or normal schools). Just as primary schools are inferior to secondary schools in buildings, equipment, prestige, and status, so primary-teacher-training colleges are inferior to secondary schools. Most important, the students and the instruction in teacher-training colleges are inferior in quality to those in secondary schools; the students are lower in ability, academic achievement, social status, and cultural opportunity than the students in secondary schools. This means that there is little opportunity at a later time for the prospective primary school teacher to improve himself academically or professionally, because his only formal training has been at a primary school and at a teacher-training college that is often regarded as a second-rate secondary school. Not only does he often lack a secondary education, but he cannot acquire one, and therefore, of course, he can never attend a university. The fact that he attends a teacher-training college usually means that he was not academically qualified or was judged not to have the ability to attend a secondary school. This tends to instill a feeling of inferiority and a "dropout" mentality. Teaching in a training college is viewed as a professional dead end, except for a very few who can move into administrative positions.

Another of the principal signs or symbols of the difference

between primary and secondary school teachers is that secondary school teachers are expected to be university graduates, whereas primary school teachers are almost never university graduates, and training-college teachers or tutors are seldom university graduates. This is a third gap in the tradition of educational disjunctivitis—namely the social and academic distance between graduate teachers and nongraduate teachers. This gap has been widest in countries where most nongraduates have been African and most graduates have been European. It perpetuates a system in which primary school children receive an inferior education from teachers who themselves received an inferior education in training colleges whose teachers also received an inferior education in the same training colleges.

Here is a situation where those who finish a teacher-training college cannot go on to acquire an academic degree in a university, because they have not attended a secondary school and therefore cannot pass the external examination. On the other hand, most students who have the ability and the opportunity to pass the examinations of the secondary school and complete the university course and acquire a degree, do not want to teach, especially in a dead end institution. The opportunities for advancement in government or professional service have been so great that a university graduate with professional qualifications often prefers to do almost anything but teach in the secondary schools. There are only two worse situations: to teach in a training college and to teach in a primary school. The problem is highlighted by the fact that despite spectacular increases in attendance at primary and secondary schools in East Africa between 1953 and 1961, the attendance at teacher-training colleges did not keep pace; it even *declined* in two out of three countries.

Disjunctions occur not only between different levels of education, but also within the levels. The separateness of academic schools from technical or vocational schools is familiar, but training colleges for primary school teachers are also separated from training colleges for secondary school teachers. In the former the heavy emphasis is upon teaching method with relatively little academic work; in the latter the heavy emphasis is upon academic study with little attention to pedagogy. Training colleges for secondary school teachers of general subjects are often separated from specialized training colleges for health and physical education, music, commercial subjects, technical subjects, and agriculture; in all of these specalized institutions the general education is likely to be minimal.

At the university level the disjunctions continue, since "Education" is universally held in low regard. Some universities do not give special attention to "Education" at all. Those that do, concentrate on preparing secondary school teachers of academic subjects; and students in "Education" are often rejects from more prestigious academic or professional fields. Few universities give special attention to preparing teachers for the teacher-training colleges; this lack helps to perpetuate the disjunction between the universities, on the one hand, and primary and intermediate institutions, on the other.

The widespread disjunction between the arts or humanities and the sciences is too well known to describe here, but it has an influence on the highly specialized university degree programs, which in turn tend to reproduce specialization in the upper secondary schools; and thus prospective teachers absorb the specialist disease which is a subvariety of academic disjunctivitis. The all but universal disjunction between the university ideal of knowledge for the sake of pure scholarship and the professional or technical ideal of knowledge for practical application has persisted through centuries.

Still another kind of disjunctivitis in education concerns the difference between the relation of governments to the training colleges as compared with their relation to the universities. The governments feel that the training of teachers, especially of primary school teachers, is their province, and that therefore ministries of education should exert direct control over teacher-training colleges; while the universities feel that the training of

secondary school teachers is their province and that the ministries of education should keep hands off. But governments have
not been deterred; many have established separate and advanced
training colleges for secondary school teachers, when they have
become convinced that universities could not or would not provide appropriate training. And so disjunctivitis becomes still
more widespread.

Finally, many countries are torn by two drives: one, to use
education as a means of building unity among diverse racial,
ethnic, religious, and linguistic groups; the other, the drive of
different groups to demand separate schools to cultivate their
own language, religion, ethnic customs, or regional outlook.
Division among groups leads to demands for separate schools;
and the separate schools tend in turn to perpetuate the divisions,
perhaps to delay unification of the nation and even independence
itself. This disjunction is exacerbated by the fact that primary
schools are widely taught in a variety of languages or mother
tongues, which are different from the international language
which is often required of those who would continue in secondary and university education. Where the mother tongues are
also different from the official national language, disjunctivitis
may become especially virulent.

Many countries are thus faced with a formidable question.
What kind of educational system will enable them to overcome
group divisions and separatist tendencies and to build a unified
nation where people can live under laws and institutions devoted
to justice, while at the same time it encourages the diversity and
the flexibility that will allow individuals to develop themselves
and to live in security, dignity, and freedom?

PRESCRIPTIONS FOR HEALTHY TEACHER EDUCATION

If the drive for modernization is the most fundamental fact
of life in most nations of the world, and if the malaise of dis-

junction afflicts the educational systems of most nations of the world, what then are the prescriptions for a healthy increase in the supply and quality of teachers? The reply is that the whole educational system at all levels must be deliberately and thoroughly oriented to the task of modernization, and all the parts must become more congruent and integral within the total system. Teacher education at all levels must bend its efforts to these tasks and find its proper place in the over-all educational system.

The *supply* of teachers will be increased as the flow of prospective teachers upward from primary to secondary to higher education increases, but only if that flow can be directed into a variety of educational channels each of which is connected at several points with the institutions that train teachers, and if the teacher-training institutions are operated as integral connecting links between higher education and the total system. The goal is to provide diversity of opportunity without fastening a restrictive inferiority upon "lower" education simply because it comes earlier than "higher" education.

The *quality* of teachers will be improved as the educational system in general and as the teacher education system in particular develop curriculum programs and instructional materials calculated to aid the traditional sector of a nation to become modern as well as to produce high-level manpower for the modernizing sector. The educational system should be a bridge between the traditional and the modern sectors, assisting their integration rather than becoming a wall of separation that widens the gap between them.

Three levels of effort should be undertaken to attract, train, and hold able people in the teaching profession.

Teacher Education at the Intermediate Level

For those countries that maintain separate teacher-training

colleges at the postprimary and subuniversity level, the principle of greater educational congruence would involve one or more of the following steps:

1. The number of small, weak, isolated, and inbred training institutions should be reduced in favor of fewer, larger, stronger, and more diversified teachers' colleges. Many training institutions in many countries of the world impress one as depressing and inferior, with staffs who are scarcely superior to the students and are so cut off from the main currents of intellectual and educational thought that they do not even realize how deprived they are.

A high priority on any country's agenda should be upgrading present teachers college staffs and raising the academic and professional qualifications of new staff members. This may be a more important first step than raising admission requirements or lengthening the course of study for students. Afghanistan's emergency teacher-training program has demonstrated what can be done even at seventh- to tenth-grade levels when the staff has been specially trained to prepare the students to become primary school teachers. Systematic and prolonged in-service training programs to raise underqualified teachers to the level of those who have already had a complete pre-service training would constitute the other extreme approach to upgrading teachers now in service.

2. No general prescription can apply to all countries, but the goal should surely be university preparation and eventually degree status for teachers college staff members. Such preparation should include sound academic background in a scholarly field of study, thorough grounding in pedagogical methods, and—what is so scarce throughout the world today—a basic understanding of the political, economic, social, psychological, and cultural role of education in the modernization process as it manifests itself

in one's own country and in other parts of the world. This is a tremendous order, but nothing less will do if the most portentous crisis facing the world's educators is to be attacked seriously. If the goal of university preparation for teachers college teachers cannot be achieved at once, progress must be made toward it as rapidly as possible.

3. As staff members are upgraded in quality, the curriculum of the teachers colleges can be improved, the courses of study diversified, the academic quality raised, and the relevance of the curriculum to the modernization process heightened. Serious consideration might even be given to organizing teachers colleges into instructional departments according to the chief problems of education in the modernization, process rather than according to the usual academic disciplines: for example, departments of rural development and of urban development as well as departments of education and the usual academic subjects. Whatever the decision about such matters, the social sciences definitely should play a larger part in the new teachers college programs than ever before.

Teachers need to be "generalists" in the modernization process as well as specialists in their field of academic teaching. They must therefore be "literate" in more than their own specialty. They need to have a realizing sense of their country's past, its traditional society, its aspirations for modernity, the behavior patterns and attitudes of its people, the problems facing it, and its role in the world of nations. This calls for a general education of the highest order; and it calls especially for the application of the social sciences and humanities to the study and practice of education.

4. As the quality of staff rises, the length of the course for students can be increased, eventually arriving at university-level study and a degree. Meanwhile the academic program of teachers colleges should allow students eventually to go on to

university work and thus be able to raise their academic and professional competence after a period of years teaching in a school. Serious plans are being made in East Africa, Sierra Leone, Nigeria, and elsewhere for variable entrance schemes whereby experienced nongraduate teachers can obtain university degrees. Such plans could be a strategic breakthrough in one of the most pervasive disjunctions in education.

5. Another cure for disjunctivitis would be to diversify the teacher-training colleges themselves so that they could train more efficiently and more economically both primary and secondary school teachers in the same institutions. Much of the academic, professional, and social science study of modernization could be undertaken jointly by the two groups, and many of the common professional and national development problems could be worked on together. To some educators this would seem outrageously impractical; to others it would be a cure worse than the disease. But it is the direction in which the logic of the argument ultimately drives us. If those who run the primary and secondary schools could live together as students, perhaps they could bring their institutions closer together into an integrated total system when they become career teachers.

6. What can be done immediately in many countries is to remove the isolation of teachers colleges by bringing them more closely in touch with universities and with each other, as recommended, for example, in the Indian Education Commission Report of 1966. Regular contact through organized committees, conferences, workshops, in-service courses, syllabus committees, cooperative research plans, and publications would do much to remove the isolation and fragmentation of teacher training colleges.

On the other hand, the universities must be ready, able, willing, and qualified to take on the task of working closely with the training colleges. Admittedly, too few universities of the world have shown such interest or competence. Many have ignored their nation's educational problems and tasks. They have declined to engage wholeheartedly in the training of primary school teachers. When they have undertaken teacher training, they have often been interested only in the highly selected future students for university entrance; they have nearly always relegated "Education" to a low position in the academic hierarchy.

Ministries of education throughout the world have resented and resisted such attitudes on the part of universities. They have therefore almost universally set up their own training colleges to guarantee that their lower schools are manned by teachers who have been prepared to their liking—that is, prepared in professional practice and method and not solely in academic or theoretical scholarship. The proposition that training colleges should be more closely related to universities will not elicit widespread enthusiasm from many ministry of education officials. But affiliation with universities would be desirable, provided the universities were willing to accept the training colleges as genuine partners and would not stifle them.

Teacher Education at the University Level

In a modern society the education of teachers, and of members of all other major professions, must become a university-level enterprise. Unless they have acquired the requisite scholarly knowledge at the university level, a group cannot properly be termed professional; and, conversely, unless their knowledge is applied to the improvement of the human condition, their education may advance scholarship but does not fulfill the purpose of a profession. Thus, most training colleges do not produce true professionals, because although they emphasize practice, they do not require university-level achievement of their students; and many universities in the world, wrapped in a mantle of pure scholarship, do not produce true professionals, because they do not prepare their students to apply their advanced knowledge to the service of the public as expert practitioners.

The goal therefore is to work out ways whereby a nation's teacher-training colleges and its universities can help each other to improve the quality of teachers. The cooperative and mutual character of the relation has been purposely emphasized because each has something to offer the other in the modernizing process. Too often the university, if it deigns to deal with the training colleges at all, is likely to believe that the relation should be one way (a little like "technical assistance"): the superior institution improves the inferior institution by raising its standards of admission, by supervising the construction of its syllabuses, and by monitoring its examination process. It is not necessarily true that the goal of such a relation should be simply to change the training college into a scholarly university writ small. The university may need to take on some of the practical coloration of the best of the training colleges. There are several directions for a university to take:

1. A university can be an extraordinarily useful agent for modernizing teacher education if it can reorient its own narrowly conceived role as a transmitter of traditional knowledge and determines to serve the developmental needs of its society. This does not mean that it must simply do whatever the government in power requires, for a university must have reasonable freedom of action and dissent; but it does mean that it should embrace an expanded range of studies and an increased variety of programs in order to train effective leaders to do those things that a developing nation most needs for its modernization. High on the list of priorities is the obligation of preparing teachers for the tasks that face the nation. Somehow a university must serve the modernization and nation-building process but still be free to criticize it. Somehow academic and governmental authorities and the relevant public interests must work out methods of con-

sultation, policy-making, and university control that bring together the dual claims of national service and intellectual freedom.

2. A university that would improve the quality of teachers in its nation's schools, must improve the quality of its own instruction and reorient its own curriculum. This is more easily said than done, for universities are peculiarly tough and persistent specimens of human organization. There is need for more active student participation in the learning process, beyond the simple taking of notes in lectures which mark the confines of the set examinations. There is need for university teachers to give more attention to the quality of their own teaching either by formal study of the teaching process or by informal induction and acquaintance with a variety of pedagogical styles. There is almost universal need for university teachers who are dedicated—as they now rarely are—to sensitive and continuing inquiry into their own pedagogical techniques, with a view to professional improvement. There is need for more attention by prospective teachers to the general education they can acquire by ranging across the social sciences, humanities, and sciences as well as by delving deeply into their own specialties. The universities need to build up the scholarly and empirical study of the social sciences, which are relatively neglected in most parts of the world in comparison with the humanities on one side and the sciences on the other, and particularly those aspects of political science, economics, sociology, anthropology, social psychology, and history focusing upon the worldwide process of modernization.

3. Universities that want to improve the quality of teaching in their nation's schools must drastically upgrade the level of their own programs and courses in professional education. At the same time high-level work in education could be introduced into first-degree programs, thus accelerating the flow of trained

teachers into the schools. The colleges of the University of East Africa and the universities of Zambia and Nigeria, as well as the university colleges of Njala and Cape Coast, have launched first-degree programs in education.

This upgrading requires first-rate faculty members as highly trained at the postgraduate level as those in any other faculty, well versed in relevant academic disciplines as well as in pedagogy and the foundations of education, and excellent exemplars of the best possibilities of the teaching process. The curriculum in professional education should be thoroughly reformed so that the foundation studies focus upon the process by which all nations, young or old, learn to become modern. It is relatively easy to show how education in the physical and natural sciences contributes to the modern sector of a transitional society. It is desperately difficult to know how to deal with the problems created for social organization, personal attitude, moral behavior, and religious belief when the traditional sector is confronted by the revolutionary social changes of modernity. These are the basic problems of modernization with which a teacher must deal; these are the basic problems with which the teacher's professional preparation must somehow prepare him to deal; these are the problems that should infuse the courses in principles of education, history of education, comparative education, educational psychology, educational sociology, and the like. Teaching a child to be literate or to use a better plow is easy compared to the task of assisting the child to use new concepts or to adopt new beliefs that are not consonant with the life he has known.

Some of the educational disjunctions mentioned earlier can be remedied if the range and scope of trainees admitted to a university program of teacher education can be expanded to include primary as well as secondary school teachers—educational leaders and special officers (such as headmasters, supervisors, administrators) as well as teachers. Above all, it would be important for universities to take on the task of preparing teachers for the training colleges. This will be especially difficult in places where disjunctivitis is especially virulent, for many training-college tutors have not had the kind of secondary education usually required for university entrance. As stated before, a first step would be to admit experienced primary school teachers or training-college tutors to university study on the basis of their quality and experience rather than of external examination.

4. In the long run, one of the most strategic ways in which a university can improve teacher education is by mounting an effective and coordinated research enterprise as well as by extension and in-service programs whereby basic scholarly knowledge and disciplined methods of inquiry are brought to bear upon the role of education in the modernization process. The resulting knowledge should then inform and illuminate the instructional program in professional education, and it should serve as a basis for the development of instructional materials appropriate for use in the teaching process at all levels—from the most advanced graduate work to the earliest preschool level, in nonformal as well as in formal education.

Many universities of the world have already made significant contributions to the modern sector in the modernization process by their research in the sciences and social sciences. This approach should by all means be encouraged and applied to teacher education. But too few of the world's universities have concentrated on the processes by which rural transformation can be brought about effectively and democratically. Such research would be most appropriate for the improvement of teacher education in general and especially for the training colleges that prepare teachers who deal principally with the children of the traditional rural areas in every country in the world.

There is no better beginning agenda for the research that would benefit teacher education than the challenge to study what children are like, how they learn and develop as they come to school from their traditional cultures and are confronted with the modernizing influences of the school. And this is precisely the point where the training colleges and the universities need most to work together. The training colleges have access to the children; the universities have, or should have, the research techniques. They need to work together to forge the programs of research, pre-service education, and in-service training that will produce better teachers who, in turn, will be able to produce better-educated children and adults. As it is, a large proportion of all teaching is wasted on children who do not learn enough before they leave school to do them any good. The appalling figures of wastage and stagnation are all too familiar. The briefest way to sum up many school systems in the world is: high input, high wastage, low output. This is the debilitating result of chronic disjunctivitis.

One important key to the desired cooperation among universities, training colleges, and the governments that support and control training colleges is the development of institutes of education, especially as they have appeared in certain parts of Africa and Asia. The essence of an institute of education is that it brings together in a continuing and intimate dialogue the people who man the several principal agencies necessary for the improvement of the education of teachers. The better institutes do this with a maximum concern for the practical problems faced by governments and teachers in the day-to-day management of the schools. They can thus overcome the all-too-common gap between research and operation, because they have direct access to the top decision-making levels of government; but with freedom from the day-to-day operating pressures that necessarily mark any governmental or institutional bureaucracy, they have genuine opportunities to experiment with new ideas and practices. A variety of arrangements is appearing in many countries as different as Afghanistan, Britain, East Africa, West Africa, and India. In any event, the institute idea is peculiarly well adapted to international cooperation.

Teacher Education at the International Level

All nations would profit from large-scale, deliberately planned, long-range international cooperation in education. Cultural and educational borrowing and emulation have been an integral part of the modernization process wherever it has occurred. There are several areas in which further investigation would be worth while:

1. We might wish to engage in a critical assessment of twenty years of international technical assistance in teacher education. This would involve making judgments about the successes and the failures, the advantages and the disadvantages of the major types of educational assistance in teacher education that have been undertaken since World War II. Candid appraisals by "donors" and by "recipients" alike should be offered as openly and as objectively as possible with respect to:

a. bilateral versus multilateral arrangements,
b. governmental versus voluntary efforts,
c. the "exchange" approach versus the "institution-building" approach,
d. the supply of "doers" versus the supply of money versus the supply of "advisers,"
e. the relative contribution of trained professionals versus untrained volunteers,
f. the relative value of educational "innovation" versus the need to "keep the schools open" and to fit into the ongoing system,
g. how the foreign policy interests of the donor have been reconciled with the domestic policy interests of the recipient, or have not been reconciled.

2. We might wish to try to chart the course of preferred paths for international collaboration that would benefit teacher education in the future. The basic assumption undoubtedly will be that the next step beyond technical assistance is genuine educational collaboration across national lines. Guidelines regarding the desirability and priority of various ways to organize international collaboration in teacher education might be stated as follows:

a. Activities in teacher education should be supported not only bilaterally between governments but also by international organizations and by regional organizations of governments.

b. Long-term bilateral cooperative arrangements should be made between universities, teachers colleges, school systems, scholarly organizations, and professional societies.

c. Long-term multilateral networks of associated universities or other educational institutions should be established to enable them to learn to work together in training personnel, developing educational materials and conducting cooperative research.

d. International collaboration in the strategic and sensitive fields of teacher education is needed to promote: curriculum development for the schools of the world's nations (in the humanities and social studies as well as in the sciences and mathematics); instructional materials for the world's institutions of teacher education; improvement of the functioning of institutions of professional education; and improvement of testing and evaluation in teacher education.

e. International collaboration is needed in training career officers for active work in teacher education wherever it is demanded in the world.

f. International collaboration is needed in training

career scholars for conducting the research most
needed for the development and modernization of
teacher education throughout the world.

g. There is no international collaboration in educational
research across national boundaries in such a way as
to meet national needs for modernization and yet
possess the necessary autonomy and freedom to serve
the canons of international scholarship.

A special bias has been expressed in this chapter in favor of
teacher education as a strategic factor in assisting the fundamental changes by which traditional societies become modern
societies. The modernization process is essentially an educational
process, if it is to take place with a maximum of freedom and
a minimum of coercion. We need therefore to look again at what
we mean by a qualified teacher. The supreme qualification for
a professional teacher in any country of the world today is the
ability to lead the way to a modern style of life for his people,
in order to enable them to enlarge their perspectives on themselves and the world, to achieve a sense of identity in a world of
change, and to acquire the habits of rational and objective
thought as the only secure foundation for self-government.[1]

1. The following titles are relevant to the problems of teachers and
modernization:

Gabriel A. Almond and G. Bingham Powell, Jr., *Comparative Politics:
A Developmental Approach*. (Boston: Little, Brown and Co., 1966).

C. Arnold Anderson and Mary Jean Bowman (eds.), *Education and Economic Development*. (Chicago: Aldine Publishing Co., 1965).

George Z. F. Bereday and Joseph A. Lauwerys (eds.), *The Education and
Training of Teachers; the Year Book of Education*. (New York: Harcourt, Brace & World, 1963; London: Evans Brothers, 1963).

Cyril E. Black, *The Dynamics of Modernization; a Study in Comparative
History*. (New York: Harper and Row, 1966).

R. Freeman Butts, *American Education in International Development*.
(New York: Harper and Row, 1963).

James S. Coleman (ed.), *Education and Poiltical Development*. (Boston:
Little, Brown and Co., 1966).

Adam Curle, *Educational Strategy for Developing Societies: A Study of
Educational and Social Factors in Relation to Economic Growth*.
(London: Tavistock, 1963).

John Hanson and Cole E. Brembeck (eds.), *Education and the Development of Nations*. (New York: Holt, Rinehart and Winston, 1966).

Frederick Harbison and Charles Myers, *Education, Manpower and Economic Growth: Strategies of Human Resource Development*. (New York: McGraw-Hill, 1964).

Marion Levy, Jr., *Modernization and the Structure of Societies*. (Princeton, N.J.: Princeton University Press, 1966).

Dankwart R. Rustow, *A World of Nations: The Dynamics of Modern Politics*. (Washington, D.C.: The Brookings Institution, 1967).

Myron Weiner (ed.), *Modernization: The Dynamics of Growth*. (New York: Basic Books, 1966).

THE NEW EDUCATIONAL TECHNOLOGY

WILBUR SCHRAMM

When we speak of the "new educational technology" or "the new educational media," we refer to instructional television, radio, films, programmed learning, and language laboratories. The essence of all these educational devices is that they make it possible to share good teaching very widely. The usefulness of a skillful teacher or a well-planned demonstration can be extended as far as a film or a tape can be carried or a radio or television signal can reach. The new technology therefore makes it possible for schools and school systems to redistribute teaching resources and to extend learning opportunities.

We sometimes hear about these technological developments that "teaching is being turned over to machines," or that we are "replacing teachers." This is not the way things have worked out. Essentially the new media are merely pipes which carry teaching. In the classroom a television receiver is a diverting piece of technology for a little while, but the novelty soon wears off, and it has to stand or fall on the kinds of learning experience it brings to the classroom. School systems find that once they have mastered the technical problems of delivering broadcasts or films or tapes, the considerations are exactly the same as they always have been: to what kinds of teachers and teaching are classes being exposed? Furthermore, almost nowhere in the world are the new media being used *alone* to carry any heavy educational responsibility. In the case of television and radio, a *studio teacher* and a *classroom teacher* are working as a *teaching team*. Films are being used typically as a supplement and teaching aid *on call by classroom teachers*. Language laboratories and programmed instruction are used for individual practice *in connection with classes*.

Therefore, far from abrogating teaching responsibilities or replacing teachers, the new educational technology actually seems to be focusing *more* attention on teaching. The teaching that is televised has to be prepared with care because it is so much more public than teaching in a single classroom. The teaching that constitutes programmed instruction is prepared and tested more carefully than any ordinary textbook or lesson plan. The fact that a classroom teacher and a studio teacher share duties has caused more attention to be paid to the efficient use of teacher and classroom time.

Of course, the various technologies differ in the kind of teaching they can carry. Radio is excellent at carrying a teacher's voice and demonstrating such things as language and music, but it is hard to point at something on radio. On films or television it is possible to see the teacher, charts, demonstrations, or other visual aids—but these media are more expensive than radio. Films have an advantage over television in that a teacher can show a film whenever the time seems ripe for it, and can stop the film at any point and talk about it or repeat it. Television is limited by a schedule—at least until low-priced videotape recorders become common in schools. On the other hand, it is not always easy to provide a film for a classroom exactly when it is needed. Television can be distributed much more easily and quickly than films; and if the same films are going to be seen by a large number of students at approximately the same time, it is cheaper to distribute them by television. Programs can be altered and updated easily on television, and it is not necessary to go through the process of developing and editing. On the other hand, because of this slower process, films are often of higher quality than corresponding television programs. These characteristics help to explain why television tends to be used for direct teaching of courses and films to supplement or enrich or for specific short tasks.

Programmed instruction is different from either television, radio, or films, because it permits a dialogue between a pupil and a surrogate teacher—a computer, a teaching machine, or a printed program—in which the pupil responds to questions or problems and finds out at once whether his answers are correct. This same method can be used, and has been used, on broadcasts and films, but it is in some ways less convenient that way, and programmed instruction is turning more and more to the computer, which offers flexibility to fit the abilities of the user. Unfortunately the number of computer programs is not large, and computers themselves are not widely available in schools.

Language laboratories are essentially tape recorders providing an opportunity for pupils to practice a language by imitating the sounds of an expert speaker or to listen to the language, try to understand it, and answer questions in it. Language tapes can be put in the form of programmed instruction, and doubtless more of them, in the future, will be.

How widely are these technologies used? Instructional films are used in most countries, but in many they exist in very small numbers, and few projectors are available for them. Strip films or slides are somewhat more readily at hand. Instructional television is used in about fifty countries. In the United States between seven and ten million school children receive part of their teaching by television; and it is used extensively also in most of the countries of Europe, the Soviet Union, and Japan. Some of the most impressive uses of instructional television, however, are in developing countries; and we shall mention some of those. Instructional radio is used widely and has proved an effective partner of correspondence study, but has yielded center stage to the glamour of television. Programmed instruction is used mostly in the industrialized countries and is coming into use more slowly than had been anticipated, chiefly because of lack of adequate materials. Language laboratories are fairly common now in the industrialized countries and are appearing in the developing regions, but in small numbers. In general the new educational technology is still carrying only a tiny part of the world's educational responsibility, and the question has been raised many times recently whether it could not usefully be carrying more.

THE NEW TECHNOLOGY AND EDUCATIONAL PROBLEMS

The evidence says that the new technology used well can solve important educational problems. The amount and kind of evidence differs with the different media. There has been very little research, for example, on language laboratories. An experiment at Antioch College found that use of a language laboratory could save about twelve hours a week of the time of regular instructors in a foreign language course; and at the end of the year there were no significant differences in the performances of students taught largely with the aid of the language laboratory and of those taught conventionally in classrooms. There are a few other experiments with corresponding results. The chief evidence on language laboratories comes, however, not from experiments, but rather from a series of teacher reports on the use of these laboratories in many countries and in many situations. These reports have been almost universally favorable. However, there is nothing magic about the laboratories or about any of the other technology. For example, Lorge in 1962 published a large sample of secondary school students in New York City taken over a three-year period and found that practice with language laboratories did not significantly increase their listening comprehension of a foreign language over the level attained without use of laboratories, but it did contribute to their competence in speaking a foreign language.[1] On the other hand, numerous nonquantitative reports of experience with the laboratories have specified improved comprehension as their principal effect. Thus, the conditions of use will override any general rule for the effectiveness of educational technology.

Research studies of instructional radio have trailed off since the coming of television. Radio is still used in many countries for supplementary materials in subjects like music and drama, and it is used extensively for direct teaching in a few countries. In Thailand, for example, more than 800,000 pupils study parts of their language, music, and social studies from radio; and the research on these courses is encouraging. For a number of years Australia and New Zealand have combined radio with correspondence study to teach children who live in isolated places remote from schools. Many tens of thousands of children in those two countries have gone with no difficulty from elementary schooling by radio and correspondence into a residential secondary school, and some have gone also through secondary school that way. Recently the two top scholars of the second and third medical classes at the University of Western Australia were young men who had received all their training up to the university level by correspondence and radio.[2]

There has been a great flurry of interest in programmed learning since the published work of Skinner in the middle 1950's,[3] although some experiments on the method were done as early as the 1920's. Since the late 1950's, however there have been several hundred research studies, and programs have been made

1. Sarah W. Lorge, *Report of Study on Foreign-Language Laboratories in Secondary Schools* (New York State Research Project EP 120, Bureau of Audio-Visual Instruction, New York: New York City Board of Education, 1962).

2. For detailed accounts of the Thailand and Australia experiences, see International Institute for Educational Planning, *The New Media in Action* (3 vols.; Paris: UNESCO and the Institute, 1967).

3. B. F. Skinner, *Science and Human Behavior* (New York: Macmillan 1953), and "The Science of Learning and the Art of Teaching," *Harvard Educational Review*, 24 (1954), pp. 86–97.

and used at all school levels from preschool to higher education, all ability levels from retarded children to gifted children, and in business, industry, and military service as well as in formal education. Mathematics and language have been the favorite subjects for programs, but programs have been made and used for a vast variety of purposes from improving driver training to stimulating creativity. Specialists in programmed learning feel that any subject where the desired end-product can be specified in behavorial terms is potentially able to be programmed. Skinner points out that the characteristics of good program are also those of a good tutor.

The fairly frequent reports of student boredom with programs is a reflection of the scarcity of really good programs. The trend of research findings, however, is favorable: no significant differences where the comparison is tightly controlled; often a comparative advantage for programs in cases where the program is well made, and the classroom alternative is not a truly expert teacher; and numerous cases in which time or effort has been saved by the use of programs.[4] Reports of successful use for individual study and classroom practice have come from both developing and industrialized countries—from India, Zambia, and Rhodesia, among others.

Film research blended into television research in the 1950's, and there is now a great deal of evidence on the use of these two media in education.[5] Literally hundreds of experiments demonstrate that users learn effectively from either medium. There is typically no significant difference in learning when teach-

4. For summaries of this research, see R. Glaser, *Training Research and Education* (Pittsburgh: University of Pittsburgh, 1962); R. Glaser, ed., *Data and Directions*, Vol. II (Washington, D.C.: National Education Association, 1966); and Wilbur Schramm, *Four Case Studies of Programmed Instruction* (New York: Fund for the Advancement of Education, 1964).

5. For summaries of the research, see C. F. Hoban and E. B. Van Ormer, *Instructional Film Research 1918–1950* (New York: U.S. Naval Special Devices Training Center, 1950); J. C. Reid and D. W. MacLennan, *Research in Instructional Television and Film* (Washington, D.C.: U.S. Government Printing Office, 1967).

er's lesson and the program or media are the same; the differences arise from the way the media may be used. A film or television lesson can be prepared more carefully and with more teaching aids than are typically available in most classrooms; and the best, rather than the average, teachers can be assigned to television programs or films. In almost every part of the world, films have now been used successfully for enriching the content of classroom teaching; they have been used in many places for teaching the skills required, for example, by industry and military service; and in a few cases—for example, a filmed physics course in Turkey—they have been used for direct teaching. It is television, however—perhaps because it came into use when so many new countries were trying to speed their educational development, and when more attention was being paid to field evaluation —for which we have the most evidence concerning the variety of educational problems that the new technology can help solve.

A number of recent case studies of the use of television in education can be cited as examples of using television for a number of purposes:[6]

To Speed the Pace of Educational Development

For example, in American Samoa six open-circuit television channels are carrying the core of primary and secondary school classes to every public school on the islands, in an effort to leap from traditional rote learning to modern inquiring education in a few years rather than the century it has usually taken. The first research studies indicate that change is taking place very fast, and that the children are greatly improving their performance on standardized tests.

To Improve Educational Opportunities

The schools of Washington County, Maryland, centered in

6. These examples are taken from *The New Media in Action, op. cit.*

Hagerstown, wanted to offer science throughout the twelve grades, to begin foreign language instruction early in primary school, to have experts teaching art and music in every school, and to offer college-level courses to talented secondary school students. To do this without hiring a large number of additional teachers, they are using six channels of closed-circuit television, reaching every school in the county. In the first few years of television some of the improvements on standardized tests were spectacular; some classes rose thirty percentile ranks on national tests.

In Colombia more than 400,000 primary school children are now being taught in part by television in an effort to equalize opportunities. The research in Colombia, too, is encouraging; and the teachers favor continuing the program.

To Make Up for Shortage of Teachers

In Niger fewer than one hundred teachers have even completed secondary school, and there is no likelihood of increasing the supply very soon, because of the country's other needs for educated persons. At the same time it has become important to bring more children into school; only about 10 per cent of children of school age now have an opportunity for an education. Therefore some of the best teachers have been assigned to television teaching, and monitors are being used in the classrooms. In the first year of this experiment the classes taught by television and monitors did better than those taught by conventional classroom methods.

To Make Up for Lack of Schools

In Italy, as in numerous other countries, secondary schools are not available in certain areas. The Italian *Telescuola* was created to offer high-quality teaching to these young people, who gathered in study groups under a supervisor. No formal studies were made, but a high proportion of the students passed their examinations.

To Teach Pupils out of School

In parts of Peru, as in many other countries, there are not enough places in school for all children who would like to attend. Even among those who do get in, the dropout rate is high. Therefore television offers a variety of home-study and group-study courses to these children. In Japan, where educational television is well developed and serves practically the entire country, a combination of television—or in some cases radio—and correspondence is used very effectively to give further education to young people who have gone to work rather than to secondary school. The Japan Broadcasting Corporation (NHK) has created an NHK Broadcast Correspondence High School to experiment with these techniques; and about fifteen thousand students throughout the nation are now enrolled in it. Unlike most correspondence programs, the Japanese correspondence work requires students to follow a schedule parallel to that of residence schools and to take examinations at the end of the year like classroom students. One of the uses of television is to maintain this schedule.

In Chicago an entire junior college (thirteenth and fourteenth year) program is offered by television, and the students consistently do as well on examinations as do classroom students.

To Offer In-Service Training to Teachers

From almost every country where instructional television has been used, reports have come back about its contribution to in-service teacher training. The experience of seeing a skillfully prepared and illustrated lesson on one's own subject benefits many classroom teachers. In addition to this incidental effect, most countries that have instructional television use it formally for teacher training. Samoa, for example, has a kind of teachers' meeting by television at the end of every school day. Colombia used television to prepare its teachers for the "new math," and research showed that the course was highly effective.

To Support the Teaching of Literacy

Few people would claim that television can teach literacy effectively by itself, but the evidence is mounting that it can effectively *support* the teaching of literacy in study groups, even in some cases where the supervisors of those groups are not specially trained for literacy teaching. This happened, for example, in the Ivory Coast where it became desirable to prepare a large number of Ivorians to assume supervisory jobs in industry, for which they had to be able to read, write, and do elementary arithmetic. There were few skilled literacy teachers available, but the industries themselves made available meeting rooms and literate monitors, and expert teachers went on television to give the core of the course. These supervisors are now moving into their new responsibilities. Somewhat the same thing happened in Italy, where the large and effective *Telescuola* program of literacy teaching provided motivation, visual aids, and general leadership for study groups throughout the country.

To Provide Adult Education

Perhaps no use of televison for widespread education is quite so well developed as the radio rural forum in India, but teleclubs have been used successfully in France, Japan, and numerous other countries. Closed-circuit television has been employed in many places for technical training, and there seems little doubt that it is entirely within the province of this new technology to carry good teaching and demonstrations to adults as well as to children.

In contrast to these cases where the new technology has been used successfully, we might cite others where it has been used with less success: where students are bored, where teachers are dissatisfied, even where it has been tried and abandoned. But we can now hardly doubt, on the basis of a great deal of evidence, that the new media, used well, can contribute to solving some important educational problems. It is a wonder that these new developments have not come into use more swiftly, and that we do not really know about the difference between their effective and ineffective use.

SLOW SPREAD OF THE NEW TECHNOLOGY

The educational system is by nature conservative. Its basic task is to pass on the existing culture to new members of the culture. It is not receptive to innovations in the way that industry, military service, and commerce tend to be. And in most countries it is constantly scrutinized by parents, critics, and political groups who are suspicious of changes and are mostly interested in duplicating the experiences *they* had in school rather than in encouraging challenges to the status quo.

This characteristic of the educational system, of course, affects any innovation. In the case of the new media it is worth noting also that many technologies threaten, or seem to threaten, the teacher as well as the privacy of the individual classroom. The teacher is asked to share his classroom with a new and attractive teacher on television or to have his demonstrations compared with a fancy demonstration on film. He is asked to give up exclusive control over schedule and content, so that television or films or programs can fit in. He is asked to learn a new role, especially if television and radio carry some of the direct teaching in his classroom; and the classroom role seems to many teachers less honorific. (It often proves a more satisfying role, if the teacher can bring himself to give up the task of "telling" his students, and can concentrate on guiding them; but "telling" has been the central function of many school systems where teaching materials are not plentiful.) Furthermore, the cost of new instructional media takes money that otherwise might possibly go into raising teacher salaries. Therefore it is not surprising that teachers often resist the new technology, or that innovations requiring less role change—for example, language laboratories that simply remove some of the drudgery for the teacher, or films that can be used for enrichment when and if the teacher wishes—are less threatening and less resisted than other media innovations. A number of attitude studies have shown that teachers become more favorable to instructional television as they have more experience with it; but often the relation is handled so badly or the experiment is ended so soon that there is no chance for this amelioration.

Furthermore, it is unfortunate that these innovations are expensive. Some schools and some countries have tried the new technology expecting to save money. Almost invariably they have been disappointed if they have tried to save money over present program costs. The new media will sometimes save money when a school system undertakes expansion. For example, the cost for Australia of establishing conventional schools in the outback for the children who are now taught by correspondence and radio would be much greater than the cost of present technology. Samoa feels it is getting a good financial bargain by using television to buy time—that is, to speed change above the conventional pace. Hagerstown thinks it is saving money when it considers the cost of offering its improved and expanded courses by conventional means. But in each of these cases the new technology is being used to do something new and different and on a large scale. Most of the financial disappointments have come from using it gingerly and without a purpose adequate to it. And, needless to say, the initial costs have frightened away many users.

Many sad results have come from the inability or the unwillingness of school systems to meet the technical requirements of the new media: an adequate technical base and adequate maintenance for television, so that the signal is clear and reliable; an adequate delivery system and a sufficient number of duplicates for films; programmed materials of high quality; trained people; and, above all, the necessary planning and training to work the new technology into its classroom context.

There are two widely divergent opinions about the new technology: on the one hand, it is a miracle drug to cure the ills of ailing educational systems; on the other, it is a failure, if not a fraud. The first of these opinions is likely to come from enthusiasts who are more often broadcasters than educators; the second, from educators, who for the most part, have grown up before the newest of these technologies. The evidence supports neither position. It says that the new instructional media are neither miracle drugs nor frauds. They are sometimes failures and sometimes successes. Facing some problems, under some conditions, used in some ways, they are highly effective and helpful; under other conditions they are not. The central problem therefore is to define more closely and practically the conditions under which they will be successful and where they can be of help to educational systems that need them.

USING MEDIA EFFECTIVELY

We are far from knowing all we need to know about using media effectively, but a few touchstones emerge again and again from studies of the new media in action:

They Should Be Directed toward an Adequate and a Suitable Problem

If a school system or a nation begins with an educational problem, then there is a good chance of finding a technology or a combination of technologies to help solve it—or to decide, after having examined the alternatives, on a nontechnological solution. If a school system begins with a piece of technology, however ("we have television; now how can we use it?"), then it has already foreclosed most of the alternatives. The systems that really seem to be making a success of the new technology are

those that began with a problem sufficiently large and demanding to enlist the kind of support required: for example, Australia's children in the outback who could not feasibly be taught
in schools, Samoa's time schedule for development, Niger's
drastic shortage of well-prepared teachers, and the like. In the
United States it is an ironic fact that the schools most likely
to try television have been those with the least need of it—the
wealthy suburban school systems.

They Require Planning

An unbelievable number of details must be worked into a
system of new technology like television. Therefore planning is
a requirement for an orderly progression into one of these new
media. It is also an opportunity. A time of technological change
provides an unequaled chance to review the content, as well as
the form, of teaching against objectives and resources.

They Should Be on an Adequate Scale

Television, radio, and films, in particular, are mass media and
in most situations should be used as such. Economies of scale
can be most dramatic in educational technology. Thus, Colombia
can deliver instructional television to 400,000 pupils for less than
five cents per student per hour, which is not a cost that would
frighten most school systems. Thailand can deliver instructional
radio to 800,000 students for less than one cent per student per
hour. On the other hand, television used on a very small scale,
for enrichment, may cost as much as several dollars per student
per hour. And there are psychological as well as economic advantages in introducing these new methods in sufficient size to
attract respect and interest and to motivate general development.

The More These New Devices Are Used for Direct Instruction, the More They Require a Kind of Team Teaching

This is especially the case with television, where most effective projects have brought studio and classroom teachers together to plan and divide the work between them. The studio teacher cannot give individual attention to the pupils, regardless of the skill and effectiveness with which he can teach the main subject matter; the classroom teacher does not have access to all the opportunities of the studio to teach the core of the course, but he can build a context of preparation, practice, interpretation, and individual guidance around the television lesson. Thus each does what he is in the best position to do; and the more fully both can do this as a team, the better the product is likely to be, and the better the morale of the classroom teacher. This is, literally, a new and important form of team teaching, of which we are likely to see much more in years to come.

There Must Be a Great Deal of Attention to What Happens at the Receiving End

As we all know, learning is an active process. One of the most common mistakes is to think of television, radio and films, as media to teach passive students. This is not true of really successful uses of these media: classes are active both during the media presentation and afterward. There has been, during the last ten years, a considerable shift in attention from what happens at the transmitting end of the new media to what happens at the receiving end. High-quality content is necessary but not sufficient. It must stimulate learning among its receivers, and it must be received in a context where there is opportunity for practice, for discussion, and for other individual learning activities related to the broadcast.

They Must Have Support

Partly because of the resistance discussed above, but also because of the considerable financial outlays required, almost no large use of the new media has been successful without firm support, without financing for adequate material and personnel, and without involving the classroom teachers in partnership. Colombia made three starts at instructional television before it developed the support at the top and the financial base at the bottom to achieve success. American Samoa, it has generally been agreed, could never have introduced television into its schools in the dramatic way it did without the firm support of its Governor; without a generous financial contribution from the United States government for equipment, new schools, and operation; and without bringing classroom teachers into a summer-long work-shop, along with studio teachers, supervisors, and consultants, to plan the curriculum. Niger could not now have done what it has with television without the financial, technical, and advisory support of the French government.

Obviously the conditions of success for any given use of the new technology are likely to be more than six; but we are beginning to build up experience and research that make it possible to identify the key conditions. And in many parts of the world we have living examples of successes and failures for prospective users to examine.

THE APPLICATIONS OF THE NEW TECHNOLOGY

Many questions remain about the application of the new technology:

What Can We Do To Share Our Growing Fund of Information?

There are some useful documents on the subject in print. The twenty-three case studies of new media recently issued by the International Institute for Educational Planning are an especially helpful kind of information. And the United States Office of Education has just financed a new center (in the ERIC series—Educational Research Information Center) on research in the new educational media, which will try to collect such research from all over the world. But how can we cooperate to transmit this research to the new center? In what forms should it be disseminated and made available to governments, schools, and educational centers? Do we need more case studies? Especially, do we need to revisit some of the projects previously studied for a second look? How can we build research and evaluation into as many new projects as possible so that their experiences can be made useful to later innovators? Do we need a device such as a yearbook of new educational technology, describing projects and reporting results?

How Can We Train the Needed Personnel?

It is clear that certain new types of personnel will be required by the new technology. One such is the combined broadcaster-educator, now in short supply, who would be able to make an essential contribution to new projects. Even without these new types, however, there is still a shortage of trained personnel of all the traditional kinds who work with the new media. Would it be helpful and feasible to establish some regional schools to meet these needs? And how can we best use the more successful projects, particularly in the developing countries, as centers of training and internship?

What Can We Do To Increase the Supply of High Quality Materials?

The parochialism of school systems makes it difficult to prepare and introduce television programs, films, tapes, and programmed learning materials which are suitable for wide use. Yet the economy of the new media requires wide use to meet the expense of really high quality. If communications satellites come into use for educational purposes, broad sharing of the same materials will be necessary. Is there a solution to this problem? What mechanism and organizations do we need for exchanging material or for creating high-quality materials usable in more than one system?

Do We Need Demonstration Centers?

One of the most useful devices in agricultural innovation has proved to be demonstration-experimental farms. Would it be useful to have a few large demonstrations in which a variety of media could be tried on a variety of problems, with ongoing research to measure the results and opportunities for observation and perhaps training and internship? Are there existing projects that could be used for such purposes? Where should such centers be, if there are any?

How Can We Encourage and Assist Planning?

No one doubts that adequate and informed planning is necessary for the successful use of the new media. How can we encourage school systems and new nations to engage in this time-consuming activity? Are there sufficient opportunities for them to obtain expert counsel during their planning period? What kind of information do they need, and how can it be obtained? What kinds of travel or study opportunities would help them make informed decisions?

How Can Communication Satellites Contribute to the Advancement of Educational Technology?

We are only a few years away from having a usable distribution satellite—that is, a satellite able to feed rebroadcast stations directly—and could within three or four years, if we wished, launch a direct broadcasting satellite able to feed receivers not much more costly than present television sets in our homes. Political and economic barriers will probably delay direct broadcasting from satellites for a considerable time. However, either the distribution or the direct satellite could immensely expand the coverage of educational television or radio, could make teaching films available over an enormous area, and could broadcast printed material by facsimile. How could these capabilities best be used to advance education? What kinds of learning opportunities could gain by such a wide circulation, and what kinds of materials would have to be local in content? Could a number of countries cooperate in the use of satellites for educational purposes? And if so, by central programming, by sharing the task of programming, or by exchanging programs? What organizational patterns would be required for such cooperation—for instance, if a satellite were to be used cooperatively by the Latin American countries?

How Can We Speed the Acceptance of Innovation in Education?

This is a problem obviously wider than educational technology. A major push should be made to utilize the new educational technology in the developing regions. No one doubts that the new countries will have to make extensive use of new technology to share and distribute teaching resources if they are to come anywhere close to their educational goals and schedules. The problem is not so much whether to use the technologies, as how to use them and how to move into them. Caution is needed against a great crash program; we should move with all due speed consistent with deciding where the new media can be helpful and with making the necessary preparations for their effective use.

The new technology is but a single element in a teaching-learning system. It is the system, not merely the technology, that must be made to work. The new media have little educational magic in themselves, and they work magic only when they are put into a suitable educational context. For example, a great educational transmitter in the sky—a communications satellite—might seem like a magical gift to educational development on earth; but those of us who have studied the possibilities of satellites, know that the great bulk of the work required to make a satellite useful for education would have to be done on the ground, and very little of it would have anything to do with electronics.

There is no doubt that new educational technology can make a profound difference in the pace of educational development. A prepared and careful movement into extending its use—a program in which the related planning, building, training, and support go along with the technology—is needed. Over two years that would be less spectacular; over ten years, it would pay off richly.

FORMAL AND INFORMAL EDUCATION

BERTRAND SCHWARTZ

The universities have been offering courses for adults for a long time, but it is not pessimistic to say that the results are far from satisfactory. The number of adults who take such courses is low, and the intellectual level of the courses is comparatively high, which means that the mass of the people is practically never reached.

There are a number of reasons for this situation, which can be summarized as "inadequate facilities" provided by the universities. In the first place, most of the courses that adults can take are given in the evening; and obviously it is difficult, for both family and social reasons, to attend courses in the evening after the day's work. Few adults can attend courses on a part-time or a full-time basis and be paid just the same or can receive special allowances for that purpose. Moreover, and most important of all, the universities have made practically no effort to adapt their pedagogical methods and the content of their courses to adults.

In general the universities have not understood that adult education has characteristics of its own. Many think there is no difference between the education of children and that of adults. Moreover—and this is much more serious—many have not understood how the concept of instruction should greatly exceed the mere supplying of knowledge.

Hence some universities have rejected all the new methods

153

that nonformal educators have attempted to use; while others, willing to cooperate but unaware of their significance, have merely adopted a few of them. University professors, specialists to the core, feel their job is to provide knowledge in their respective specialties, and they see no difference between an audience of adolescents and one of adults.

Apart from institutions of "formal" education, various organizations and individuals have tried reforming and even revolutionary experiments. The first of these experimenters were responsible for "popular" education for adults. They followed or worked out for themselves absolutely new methods, which made them appear to be opponents of the formal educational tradition. The dissociation between the two forms of education became increasingly marked. As a matter of fact, the nonformal educators feared, and still fear, that they would be swallowed up by the many formal educators arrayed against them. That is why educators of adults, even when they believe that there should be no separation between education for minors and for adults—but a "lifelong education"—are very much afraid of being integrated. Paradoxically, it is they who want to maintain the separation.

Adult education in general has lacked funds and attention—essentially because the need for them has not been clearly evident. In order for any form of education to develop, it must be the object of strong social pressure: from the public who want to be educated, from government authorities, or from the educators themselves, who should be in the best position to appreciate the necessity for lifelong education. But so far adult education has not commanded such pressure.

Why does the public not pressure to be educated? Perhaps we should reverse this question and ask why the public would want to be educated? For vocational or professional reasons? Until recent times such reasons scarcely existed. Most trades and jobs required in the long run only vocational training in the strict sense of the term. Today that is undoubtedly no longer true. On the one hand, ever greater numbers of jobs require general knowledge, and on the other hand, many manual jobs are eliminated every year and replaced by work requiring higher qualifications.

Inasmuch as the conversion is affecting increasing numbers of persons and may affect an entire population within ten or fifteen years, it is becoming more necessary that everyone be capable of profiting by these changes instead of being their victim. That need is quite recent, however, and even now it is well understood only by few responsible authorities.

The public may want purely cultural education. The need exists, to be sure in latent form at least, among almost the entire French people, for instance; but generally for the majority, culture remains the privilege of an elite, and the bulk of the people feel that it is not for them. Moreover, it is undoubtedly a basic fact (proved by statistics) that the higher one's initial level of culture, the more strongly one feels the need for still higher levels. What can culture mean to a manual laborer whose only desire after a day of exhausting physical work is to earn a bit of extra money or merely to rest?

The authorities could—and should—be much more sensitive to the need for lifelong education. So far educators have not considered adult education as their problem, as they feel they have enough to do teaching children and adolescents.

Most political authorities have also not seen the value of such education. One wonders to what extent the Mandarin attitude has, consciously or unconsciously, entered the picture (the elite have always defended their privileges), or to what extent these same elites have tried to avoid educating too many people because they feared the growth of a new-found ability to challenge and to debate. Lastly, the political powers saw that lifelong education did not pay on a short-term basis, and that the results of large efforts along that line were not measurable and demonstrable.

One of the reasons adult education has not been greatly developed is that the first experiments did not "look very successful." In particular, the differing views—not to say the open hostility—between formal and nonformal educators appeared to noneducators to be a battle between specialists—a situation that led many to feel that adult education serves no purpose.

A compromise between formal and nonformal education would consist of a transformation of the formal methods based on consideration of what adults actually are and a transformation of informal education based on considerations of the objectives of lifelong education.

In this connection, we shall examine successively the two forms of education: the first is instruction in educational institutions (evening courses in particular), which is in the nature of formal education. Then, after having shown how this form is inadequate, we shall examine types of informal education.

INSTITUTIONAL OR FORMAL EDUCATION: AN INSTRUCTION OF ISOLATED INDIVIDUALS

Instruction of isolated individuals means instructing persons who come separately to attend courses, each of them from a different environment, each working in a different enterprise, and each having his own center of interest. Nothing exists in this form of education but the individual attending the course, the institution, and the teacher; and no thought is given to the adult society in which both the teacher and the student live. The problem is to change the traditional form of so-called formal education in order to take into account the specific nature of adults. In order to determine the right methods of instruction, the teacher and the institution must consider the adult himself, his motivations, and his characteristics, on the one hand, and their own objectives, on the other.

It must be noted that many adults have several motivations, which are not easy for the teacher to take into account. One of the most common—at least outside of the category of adults who are taking a sociocultural type of instruction—is the desire to change one's social status. Such adults aim not only at a salary increase but, to at least as great an extent, at a change in the type of work in order to have a better opportunity to assert their personalties. Along with that motivation has recently developed the desire not to become a victim of a downgrading changeover, but to be able to take it in stride. These motivations cannot be present, at least not in the same form, in children or in adolescents, as people who have been out of school for five years are quite different from them. It is not difficult to perceive the major differences:

1. Mental Image of Education

Some adults think of education as "culture," as "goods purchased"; in other words, they consider that once the schooling, or rather the "program," is finished, they have completed their education. Moreover they often tend to confuse schooling and knowledge, knowledge and memorizing, without being able to see that the essential thing is the formation of attitudes. To know is in some way to be able to "recite." To learn is for many a physical effort. There are even people for whom getting an education consists only of attending a course.

2. Difficulty in Learning

Adults, especially those who stopped their schooling very early —that is, those with the greatest need to go back to school— often find it very difficult to study again. They cannot easily read the documents assigned to them or take notes. They do not know how to listen or make use of the means available to them. Moreover, in evening courses, most adults encounter considerable material difficulties: lack of time, physical and nervous fatigue, lack of relaxation and of leisure.

3. Mental Image of the Outside World

On this point adults differ decidedly from the child or adolescent. While his occupational, family, and social experiences often give an adult better knowledge of certain phenomena, usually he also suffers from a decline in book learning and retains partial and hazy mental images of the life around him; an adult's observations are almost always based on the effect, not on the cause or the essence, of things.

The same applies, of course, to children; but many children do not try to form a mental image of their experience. Children admit, for example, that they do not know what is meant by atmospheric pressure or how and why an airplane flies, while it is probably rare for adults not to have ideas and mental concepts of such things.

Research has shown that certain mental images are so firmly established in the minds of adults attending courses that it is very difficult for them to absorb new knowledge. They cling to these images, even to those that contradict reality. For example, chemical workers define an acid as "that stuff that stings," while foundry workers describe a tempering bath as "what makes the metal shine."

THE INSTRUCTIONAL TARGETS OF ADULT EDUCATION INSTITUTIONS

An institution providing adult education should establish targets which should be, at least in part, those of the adult students themselves. These targets have a most important bearing on the teaching methods; for example, training technicians to do a special job is very different from training self-sufficient persons who are not dependent on others but are capable of making a place for themselves and of directing their own lives. The goal of adult education must be the determination to consider people as agents of change, as persons who not only receive from their environment but at the same time contribute to it—unlike children who go to school to receive but do not contribute anything to anyone else.

Such a target can be approached by observing a few principles.

First Principle: Starting with the Felt Needs

It is increasingly important to base the content of the instruction on needs defined by the adults to be taught and not on those defined by the teaching staff. The latter is basic pedagogical strategy, and it presupposes the right of the educational institution to adapt its programs in accordance with its analysis of its students' needs.

However, even where the instruction programs are not laid down in advance and where adult educators have full liberty the problem is still not solved. Actually in order to eliminate stereotyped instruction and to help adults discover what they really need to learn, it is necessary to put them in the position of learning. The best instruction always results from converting unfelt needs into needs that are really felt. For example, an electrician will consider instruction in electricity a step forward only when he discovers that he must know and understand certain laws. He starts with examples and goes beyond them in order to grasp the theory; then he needs to learn some mathematics and, in doing so, discovers problems of expression; thus one need leads to another. This is the generating force that puts the adult in a position of really learning and on the pathway to a truly lifelong education.

This is a difficult problem for the teacher who often instructs children or adolescents during the day by traditional methods. He must make an imaginative effort and at the same time be constantly sensitive to the progress of his adult pupils. In other words, he must struggle against his own tendency to plan that progress in advance.

Second Principle: Self-evaluation

In order to combat the common tendency of adults to reduce the concept of education to mere acquisition of information, the methods should facilitate thoughtful evaluation. In fact, the use of examinations should be open to question, for several reasons.

First, one of the justifications for examinations is that they constitute a stimulant for school pupils and students—but that is no longer necessary for adults. Second, the prospect of taking an examination will accentuate the adult's feeling of dependency, just when we are trying to make him self-sufficient. Finally, examinations strengthen the scholastic attitude, while the adult, in order to learn, needs constantly to link knowledge and experience.

If examinations are eliminated, it will of course be necessary to install in their place a constant and systematic control of the absorption of knowledge and also of attitudes. This critical problem is the object of much research. One site of such research is the Centre Universitaire de Coopération Économique et Sociale at Nancy, France, of which this writer is director. The conclusions and consequences of this research have led the Nancy staff to install so-called self-evaluation. After each session of a course or of practical exercises, all the adult pupils are given a written interrogation concerning a simple question. When they have finished, the teacher gives the correct answer and explains it. They are then asked to correct their own papers, not by grading or assigning a rating, which would be absurd, but by trying to analyze their mistakes, the causes of these mistakes, and their nature. The teacher collects the papers, which are anonymous—because the purpose is not to judge each adult pupil but to help each correct himself. He comments on the interrogations and the self-evaluation and then returns the paper. In this way each adult has the opportunity not only of knowing the answer but also of checking his own errors and of finding out what the teacher himself would have replied.

This self-evaluation does not, however, eliminate all evaluation of the pupils' results by the teacher. That is accomplished in small groups, so that there is a constant comparison between the teacher's evaluation and that of the adult pupil himself.

Considering the adult as an agent of change, the self-evaluation constitutes an essential element in his training, with a view to enabling him to judge himself and to reach a point of self-sufficiency in regard to his field of knowledge.

Third Principle: Teaching by Concepts and Mental Images

The obligation not to base the instruction on courses and not to use traditional textbooks has led the center at Nancy to a complete reappraisal of the methods of instruction.

The principle of instruction by the forming of concepts was the first to be established. When a teacher speaks, he normally uses terms that are strictly correct but generally mean nothing to an adult pupil. Take, for example, the definition of proportional quantities: "Two quantities are said to be proportional when the quotient of any value of the one divided by the corresponding value of the other is constant." That definition is not difficult to understand, or, to put it more exactly, it is easy to grasp if every word or term represents a perfectly familiar concept to the person who hears it; but it is, on the contrary, incomprehensible to anyone who does not yet possess those concepts and specifically to all those who are trying to learn them for the first time.

How can that lack of concept be remedied? The method consists in getting a group of adults to "discover" the concepts to be defined. In the case of proportional quantities, the teacher gives them one or two examples (an airplane flies 1,000 kilometers in one hour, 2,000 kilometers in two hours, etc.). Then the group must find other examples until finally either the teacher or a member of the group suggests one that does not fit (for example, a cyclist pedals 30 kilometers in one hour and perhaps 60 kilometers in two hours, but will not pedal 300 kilometers in ten hours because fatigue will prevent it). The group should then try to deduce what the examples have in common and how they differ. That is where the forming of a mental concept comes into the picture: the adults themselves formulate the difference. Only in this way, and after an hour or two, will the adults have grasped the concept of proportional quantity.

They will formulate it in their own terms, which will probably not be those of the teacher and probably not the official ones; but the important thing is that in the first phase they have absorbed that mental concept. A second phase will provide an opportunity to work out the terms to be used for the definition.

While this pedagogical method has proved very effective for subjects that are relatively new to the persons being instructed, it is not when mental images are already firmly anchored in their minds. The method then consists in getting them to discuss their different concepts or mental images, to realize the inaccuracy or incompleteness of their respective concepts, and then to reconstruct the concept by the entire group when all its members have realized that each of their individual concepts was only partially true.

COLLECTIVE EDUCATION

In spite of all attempts to improve it pedagogically the efficiency of the individual system of education is limited. It is generally difficult for an adult to make his new knowledge count —that is, by connecting what he has learned to everyday life— or to detect his own further needs and thus to be in a position to continue his training.

Probably this difficulty explains the small number of persons who take adult education. That is why it is necessary to introduce an essential factor, the context of the society as a whole. In individualistic education an adult who is receiving instruction such as we have described is "isolated." It is of course true that he is included in a group of persons, but they usually have nothing in common except the "institution," the teacher, and the instruction program. This environment is external to the majority of adults, and they profit very little from the instruction. In fact instruction is in many cases simply a surface coating and does not take root in their everyday subjective life. As a general rule each adult is the sole beneficiary in his own respective environment of the knowledge he has received, without any possibility of using it—and therefore really benefiting by it—or of communicating it to others.

From the intellectual point of view the teacher chooses concrete examples to clarify his instruction. But the fact is that what is concrete for one is not necessarily concrete for the others. Hence the example is not always meaningful for the entire group, but it creates in itself an additional difficulty of comprehension.

Still from the intellectual point of view it is almost impossible for the adult being instructed to understand and assimilate—in other words, to connect—what he learns with his previous culture, unless he can illustrate his new knowledge with examples that have been or are living ones to him. Since the teacher knows nothing of the experience of the adult he is teaching, he can scarcely help him find examples. In other words, in order for the adult to assimilate new knowledge, this knowledge must be connected with his own experience—in the general sense of the word and not exclusively occupational experience; and he must be taught to find his own examples and to process them. This is actually feasible only if the teacher comes from the same environment as the adult receiving the instruction, and has the same problems. The application of this principle has the additional advantage of allowing the instruction to be diffused and the number of persons instructed to be greatly increased.

There is, moreover, a sociological reason which leads to experiments with collective training. Not only is it very difficult for an isolated adult, sole beneficiary of the training, to communicate it to others, but he may find himself an object of hostility on the part of his fellows when he tries to put his knowledge to practical use. Witness those workmen who have been trained in good expression and in the preparation of reports, but who, on returning to their work, quickly drop back into the old system because they are ridiculed. Witness also those engineers given statistical training who give up using it because their superiors ask them to stop using "alleged sciences," of which they are themselves ignorant. Examples of that kind are numerous.

The instruction, therefore, is not fully fruitful unless it is linked with daily life, unless the adult is deeply imbued with it, and unless a sufficiently large number of adults in the same collectivity are training simultaneously. These conditions have led to the development of new forms of education directed no longer toward isolated individuals but toward groups, bringing together persons of the same collectivity and expressing similar needs and motivations. That type of instruction applies to all; it includes vocational, general, and cultural education; and it facilitates mutual understanding and the appreciation of sociovocational and cultural contacts. It constitutes in this way a real factor of personal development for all.

An Example of Collective Instruction

On the suggestion of a trade union representative, the center at Nancy examined the feasibility of providing a program of general instruction to raise the level of knowledge of the local iron miners. A rapid analysis of the economic and social context of the area—where, owing to declining sales of iron ore, men were laid off from work—showed that it would not be sufficient to install a standard program of evening courses. The idea was to undertake instruction that would be open to all and adapted to a population that had had little schooling; and it was, therefore, proposed that a general nonvocational program of instruction be based on the needs of the adults themselves and progressively adaptable to new needs as they appeared. This program had a chance to succeed and develop only if the community itself took the responsibility for it. It was essential that all institutions participating in the life of the area should act as agents of control and development for it, because the situation it was seeking to alleviate concerned the entire collectivity.

A committee composed of representatives of the various labor organizations, of representatives of the employers, and of representatives of the public authorities was therefore suggested. A survey was made of about one hundred persons of the area in order to ascertain their attitudes toward problems of instruction and to find out what needs were expressed, the major obstacles, and the motivations for obtaining more education.

The action then developed in three phases: The first phase consisted of an analysis of the sociovocational and cultural environment. The second phase enabled the committee to plan the action to be taken on the basis of the environment analysis report and to pool their efforts to overcome the initial problems. The third phase was the implementation of an experiment selected by the committee among four projects based on the environment analysis. This experiment consisted in organizing instruction cycles (twenty sessions of two and one-half hours each) for groups of twelve to fifteen adults on subjects of interest discovered in the original survey. The teachers belonged to the same fields of work as the adults to be instructed.

The response of the community to our publicity can be said to have been massive: 1,000 miners enrolled out of a total of 8,000. This response was cumulative. The instruction program was a subject of discussion on the job. A few problems were solved, but an increasingly greater number of other problems were suggested. One of the features of collective instruction is, precisely, the dissemination of knowledge, its transfer, and its utilization. It was also possible to analyze certain other pedagogical characteristics in the course of this instructional activity. First, the adults receiving the instruction belonged to the same vocation; they had mental images and points of interest in common. And, second, the instruction was adapted to the measure of the individual. Each one chose his initial cycle and then his general plan of instruction in accordance with the needs he felt and analyzed. The effort was also adapted to the over-all level, since the committee compiled opinions from outside of its membership, in particular from representatives of those enrolled, and adapted their action to the whole community.

Adult education is only beginning and is oscillating between the university rehashed type and the so-called cultural type of education. It must pass that stage and create an over-all system which will no longer dissociate—and, most of all, will not pit one against the other—vocational education, general and methodological education, cultural education, and the different types of training associated in a "culture" taken in the sense of "development." Development should be accomplished simultaneously on the basis of technical, scientific, and cultural content. And collective instruction, as we have seen, favors that development. Then, finally, adult education and the education of children and youth should join to become a lifelong education.

For these ideas to be converted into reality, it will probably be necessary to arrive at a system based upon institutions that could become regional university centers of an entirely new type, and that could be expected to: synthesize all the educational efforts of the region; conduct active and systematic research on educational activities of the institution itself or in association with other organizations, originating and culminating in educational realism; and train teachers for individual and collective work.

A system of this kind seems both feasible and capable of developing lifelong education. The university would be also associated in the adult educational effort at a level at which it alone is qualified (research and teacher training), but without being entrusted with the direct instruction which it is definitely not prepared, except in rare cases, to provide.[1]

1.   Sources of interest on this subject are:
Robert Peers, *Adult Education: A Comparative Study* (New York: Humanities Press, 1958).
Colin J. Titmus, *Adult Education in France*, (New York: Pergamon Press, 1967).
Mary Ewen Ulich, *Patterns of Adult Education: A Comparative Study* (New York: Pageant Press, [1965]).

THE FIELD OF EDUCATIONAL RESEARCH[1]

RALPH W. TYLER

Educational research is the disciplined examination of educational institutions and the processes of education. The adjective "disciplined" excludes investigations that lack methods for validating statements and findings and includes those that use disciplines of any field relevant to the problem and its phenomena. The terms "processes of education" and "educational institutions" are meant to include, respectively, educational objectives, learning, curricula, and evaluation, and schools, colleges, and other educational institutions. This broad field of educational research includes a variety of disciplines and problems, and it has been growing in both directions over the past forty years.

The United States affords excellent illustrations of the characteristic development of educational research. The American school has commonly been the means of social mobility and the agency to train personnel for new occupations arising from the changing structure of the economy. These functions require changes in various parts of the educational system which in turn create a demand for knowledge about education to provide an intelligent basis for action. Hence concern with educational research has been relatively intense in the United States. A brief

1. Revised version of Chapter 1 of *The Training and Nurture of Educational Researchers* (Bloomington, Ind.: Phi Delta Kappa, 1965).

review of its development there will serve as an example of similar developments in other parts of the world.

The early efforts in educational research were carried on by psychologists, historians, and philosophers. William James, Edward Thorndike, Charles Judd are the names that easily come to mind in recalling the early studies of school learning. James, in *Talks to Teachers on Psychology*, drew heavily upon the then current psychological concepts. Thorndike, in *Psychology of Thinking in the Case of Reading* and *Psychology of Arithmetic*, utilized his psychological research to disprove the theory of formal discipline and to formulate his own association theory. Judd, in *Psychology of High-School Subjects*, based his theory of generalization upon psychological research. These men carried on activities analogous to work abroad by such well-known men as Spearman and Vernon in England, Piaget in Switzerland, and Husén in Sweden.

John Dewey as a philosopher evolved the theoretical foundations for his school in Chicago, and his numerous writings provided an intellectual base for a kind of education going beyond classroom learning to include the range of transactions involving the learners and their school, home, and community environment. Paul Monroe and Frank P. Graves produced histories of education that provided rationales for the role of the American public school. John Dewey is in the class of Pestalozzi and Froebel and has had a wide hearing in many countries.

Today the disciplines of psychology, philosophy, and history are still used in educational research, but they have been joined by many other disciplines. Psychologists make up the largest group in the American Educational Research Association, and most of the presidents of this organization employ psychological methods and concepts in their research. But in addition to those who call themselves educational psychologists, psychologists from other divisions of the discipline are active in educational research; for example, Getzels, Bruner, Neil Miller, George Miller, and Daniel Miller. Philosophers today are not founding experimental schools or devising a comprehensive theory of education as John Dewey did, but they are studying educational aims and the logic of educational inquiry, and they are contributing to the clarification of terms and ideas. Although the history of education was in decline for several decades, currently historians both in and out of schools of education are examining the developments of educational ideas and institutions and of other major facets of modern life to which education makes an important contribution. The works of Baylin, Cremin, Edwards, Handlin, and Storrs are good illustrations of this sector of the field. Comparable work has been done in other countries. In England names such as Curtis or Tropp come to mind.

To the disciplines long involved in educational research are now added anthropology, economics, political science, sociology, and some of the biological fields. Spindler, Kimball, Henry, Alpenfels, and Lee are anthropologists who have been using the concepts and methods of this field to study educational problems. Schultz, Becker, Harbison, Myers, and Benson are economists who have analyzed the economic results of education. Ostrum, Easton, Snyder, and Agger are among the political scientists whose investigations have helped to develop new ideas on such questions as the relation of schools to politics, the political roles of school administrators, and the extent to which children acquire understanding of political matters. Warner, Hughes, Gross, Brim, Sewell, Rossi, Trow, Janowitz, Lazarsfeld, Barton, and Hollingshead are among the many sociologists whose works have dealt with a wide range of questions concerning education. Comparative studies are represented by Bereday and Kazamias. In communications research the studies of Schramm, Osgood, Carter, and Tannenbaum are further instances of the involvement of the social science disciplines in educational research; while the biological sciences are represented by the work of

Pribram on the neural physiology and anatomy of problem-solving, by the Social Science Research Council's Committee on Behavioral Genetics, by the studies of imprinting by Hess, Lorens, and Tinbergen, and by the sensory deprivation studies of Hebb and his colleagues. One cannot venture to list comparable names in other countries, but in economics Vaizey in England and Edding in Germany may be cited as examples.

In the current large-scale curriculum studies there are many with sound research value. These studies have involved investigations of learning objectives in the major academic disciplines and of the achievement of studies in working with new instructional materials. Even ten years ago one could not have imagined an internationally recognized physicist planning research studies in learning or equally renowned linguists investigating children's reading. Now these and other similar projects are under way. Educational research now includes persons from most of the academic disciplines. This trend is likely to continue for at least a decade, because of the discovery that there are important educational questions to which these disciplines can contribute and because the research on educational questions sometimes throws new light on the central theoretical questions of the disciplines themselves, as Dewey's work in education contributed to his philosophic theory.

INCREASING COMPLEXITY OF THE EDUCATIONAL MAP

Not only is educational research expanding to include a larger number of disciplines, but the conceptual map of the processes and enterprises of education is becoming increasingly complex. The prevailing notion forty years ago of the major areas to be investigated by students of the educational process was a simple one. There were subjects such as reading, arithmetic, handwriting, spelling. A different learning activity was inherent in each subject. There were learners of varying intelligence. There were methods of teaching each subject, characterized by terms such as "deductive," "inductive," "manipulative," and "incidental." Finally there were teachers who could be characterized as superior, average, or poor in their use of these methods. These four—subjects, learners, methods of teaching, and teachers— were the major features of the conceptual map of the twenties, and each of these was believed to have only one or two major dimensions that were important for their influence on the educational process. Educational research was focused on comparing methods of teaching a given subject, using matched groups of learners.

The conceptual map of the major features of educational institutions was equally simple. There were schools, differing in size of enrollment and in grade organization. There were administrators, varying in amount of training and experience. Finally there were administrative policies, which were commonly the area for study. They included pupil promotion policies, teacher salary schedules, teacher tenure policies, and the like. Two kinds of investigations were commonly conducted: one evaluated administrative policies and arrangements by the performance of pupils on achievement tests; and in the other, arrangement or policy among school systems were treated as a point of departure. The second kind of investigation was predominant, partly because pupil-testing was expensive, but particularly because most studies of the first kind showed little or no relation between pupil scores on achievement tests and administrative policies and practices.

Today the conceptual map has more features. The older ideas are still there but are now conceived with greater complexity. Every school subject is now viewed in terms of several possible objectives and of one or more structures which serve to organize its content either for use or for learning or for both. Each learner is now conceived as having many relevant characteristics in addition to his standing on a particular intelligence test. His cognitive development is important and includes such variables as his mode of approaching or withdrawing from new phenomena, his view of the world, his role concept, and his problem-solving abilities. His affective development is also considered relevant to many educational questions, and this development includes such variables as his interests and motives, his attitude toward education, his attitude toward work, his achievement needs, his self-confidence, the degree to which he identifies with others, and the characteristics of these others. His habits of work and study are often significant. And increasing recognition is given to physical development in certain kinds of educational problems. This includes rate and stage of development and the amount and variety of stimulation provided as sense organs and physical systems emerge and mature. This view of the relevant characteristics of a learner is not only complex; it also involves concepts from various disciplines.

The conception of teaching methods has undergone some elaboration also, though not as great as for the learner. This may be partly because many students of education consider teaching methods less important than learning processes and learning conditions. If the teacher's role is to determine the kind of learning required to achieve the educational objectives and then to help establish the conditions required for the students to carry on this kind of learning, the methods of teaching can more appropriately be viewed as functions of the learning conditions than as independent variables. However, the recently published *Handbook on Research in Teaching* provides a more complete discussion of teaching procedures and styles.[2]

The conception of the teacher has also been expanding. The amount of his schooling and years of experience are considered less relevant than such variables as his ideas about the objectives as a teacher, his concept of the learning task, his understanding of his materials, his attitude toward himself and his pupils, and the like.

2. N. L. Gage, *Handbook on Research in Teaching* (Chicago: Rand McNally & Co., 1963).

In addition, several new major features have emerged in this conceptual map of the research terrain. The school is no longer thought of as simply a place where teachers and children assemble for classes; the work of sociologists, anthropologists, and social psychologists has given the school meaning as a social institution in which traditions develop, aspirations are encouraged or dampened, communication is facilitated or distorted, activities are given direction and differential rewards, and students sense expectations that may greatly influence their own educational efforts. Hence the school as a social institution has become a relevant part of the map of education, and the variables involved are seen as potential factors influencing learning and teaching.

The home as the past and present environment of the learner is also being analyzed as a major feature of the educational process and the work of the school. Bloom and his students have developed indices of the quality of the home environment in encouraging and supporting learning. Bernstein in England has demonstrated the influence on later education of linguistic patterns used in the home. A number of studies like those of Sears and Maccoby relate the child-training practices of the home to cognitive and affective development of the child. Schramm and others have provided data on television-viewing in the home.

The environment created by the peer groups to which the learner belongs is now being characterized by several variables and is shown to mediate the influence of school, teacher, and home as well as to produce its own values, accepted practices, and "world view," all of which may result in differential learning among the pupils of the school. Investigations by Newcomb and other social psychologists indicate the importance of these peer group variables on college learning, while Hughes and Becker report peer group variables to be major regulators of effort put forth by medical students.

The larger community environment is recognized now as a feature of the conceptual map for educational researchers, but this idea has not been greatly elaborated. Edward Thorndike developed indices for the general cultural quality of a community; since that time some aspects have been identified, such as the availability of books, art and science museums, "quality" newspapers, and musical performances. But the significant variables have not been clearly established, so that current educational research generally divides the community environment into such rough categories as the suburbs, central city, slum sections, small town, and rural areas.

Another way of perceiving the larger environment—community, city, state, or nation—is in the attitudes of the people toward education. Surveys by the National Opinion Research Center and the Michigan Survey Research Center indicate the variety of attitudes among different sectors of the population such as parents of children in school, business leaders, labor leaders, farmers, professional people. Schramm and Carter have related attitudes of groups to the success of the schools in passing local bond issues. It has been suggested that community attitudes toward education are significant variables in attracting teachers and administrators and in influencing the educational aspirations of children and youth. This area is one under active study by researchers concerned with educational questions.

The foregoing brief review is sufficient to illustrate the great elaboration that has been taking place in the conceptual map of the terrain of educational research. The typical map of the educational process forty years ago included only four features; now there are at least eight major features. Forty years ago each feature was conceived in simple terms involving only a few variables; now each of these eight features has been developed into a complex involving a number of variables. Educational research is no longer guided by simple models but rather by a complex map where particular phenomena may be found, and where the variables involved are likely to be differential—that is, important under certain conditions, for certain objectives, for certain learners, and not universally significant. The field of educational research today requires much more sophisticated inquiry than was deemed necessary in earlier years.

THE FUNCTIONS OF EDUCATIONAL RESEARCH

In the earlier period, when education was not conceived as such a complex phenomenon, a common belief of educational researchers was that they could and would find definitive answers to questions about what and how to teach and, correspondingly, how to organize and administer schools. As research findings accumulated, however, it became obvious that clear-cut conclusions could not be drawn, and that the factors involved were more complex than the research designs had assumed. No longer do researchers expect to obtain direct answers to questions about what should be done in education and how it should be done.

A second function of educational research is now well established. It is to assess programs, procedures, and materials so as to indicate what educational results are being attained; what they will cost in time, effort, and materials; and under what conditions these results are being attained. Thus the new course-content improvement programs supported by the National Science Foundation commonly include evaluative projects in which students are given aptitude and achievement tests, and the conditions under which the course is used are studied. This procedure has given such results that students in the upper quarter of scholastic aptitude make substantial scores on the achievement tests, but students in the lower quarter show little achievement. This finding has led to the decision by the Biological Sciences Study Committee to devise and construct a special course for the so-called slow learner. Or, as another example, studies of a certain programmed text in high school English found that those who completed the course showed marked improvement in the mechanics of writing; but also many students did not complete the course because they said "they lost interest in it." Such an assessment suggests the need for more interesting or better-motivated learning experiences. This assessment of educational programs, practices, and materials is probably now the most common function of educational research.

A third function is to build up a body of information about the educational enterprise which is useful in charting policies and making decisions. The availability of information about our economic system represented by such indices as the gross national product and the unemployment rate is helpful to business, industry, and government in developing policies and plans for increased productivity. Correspondingly, information about the mortality rate of various diseases provides a basis for charting action in the field of public health. In like manner, educational research is beginning to produce basic data on matters of importance in planning educational activities, such as differential costs by geographic region, urban and rural; socio-economic level of the school; salaries of teachers in various categories; education of teachers; and numbers of school rooms meeting certain construction standards. We are in much need of continuing data on educational achievement by socio-economic categories by region—by rural area, town, central city, slum section, or suburban area. The National Bureau of Economic Research in the United States devotes a good part of its resources to identifying important factors in economic decision-making and to developing indices to assess these factors. This function will be of increasing concern to educational research.

A fourth function of educational research is to provide the outlook, the stimulation, and the fruitful guidance to educational innovation. Education today is the central task of each nation. Society, employment, citizenship, and productive family and group life now require a level of education far higher than ever needed before. For the individual's self-realization, he needs knowledge, skills in using a wide range of cultural resources, broad interests, and the habit of continued learning. These higher educational requirements come at the same time that knowledge is doubling every twelve to fifteen years. The goals of education cannot be realized by a little tinkering with our present schools and colleges. Widespread and fundamental educational innovations are required. Judging from experience in educational experiments and from analogous situations in agriculture, medicine, and industry, innovations are effectively developed and conducted in a research atmosphere. Increasingly, educational research will be expected to provide the dynamic core for essential and continuing innovation.

Finally a significant function of educational research is the development of a more adequate and valid theory about educational processes and the operations of educational enterprises. Educational theory deals with what is basic to the structure and function of education. Those facets that are open to casual observation do not include such important matters as the thoughts, the attitudes, the feelings, and the perceptions of the people involved; and they provide no basis for distinguishing the relevant from the irrelevant, the important from the unimportant. Questions of relevance and importance require the study of consequences. Hence a sound theory is one whose elements are shown to be significantly related to consequences of concern to education.

The choice, of course, is not between having a theory or not having one. All educators have a conception of what they are doing and of what is relevant and important, but most have theories that have not been carefully examined and tested. Thus some teachers talk of covering topics in their courses. The idea that to have students come in contact with a topic is equivalent to getting desirable learning, has clearly not been thought through or stood an empirical test.

We need sounder and more comprehensive theories of learning, of teaching, of testing, of guidance, and of administration. A sound theory provides a much more usable guide to action and to further inquiry than does a series of specific answers to questions about education. The growing complexity of the conceptual map of educational research is a beginning in the development of more adequate educational theory. This is a function of educational research that needs much attention.

RESEARCH SUPPORT

Forty years ago, when many bureaus of educational research were established, they were provided with little support, either for personnel or for other expenses. At that time Charles Fordyce, a professor at the University of Nebraska, was relieved of one course in his teaching assignment to direct the research bureau. His research was on testing and diagnosing learning difficulties. He either administered the tests himself or was aided by unpaid graduate students. He had a part-time secretary and $500 for supplies and other expenses. Many better bureaus were as meagerly supported; those at Illinois, Minnesota, and Ohio State were much more adequately financed. The budget request for 1929 for the Ohio State University Bureau of Educational Research was for $100,000, a large sum in those days; and the increased appropriation enabled the director, W. W. Charters, to bring to the bureau that year W. H. Cowley, Edgar Dale, and this author. Two years later the Depression brought a sharp cutback in the support of education generally.

Even as late as 1950 the support of educational research in the United States was nominal indeed. Except for the special studies financed by large private foundations, the vast majority of the research was done by professors of education during time squeezed from a full teaching schedule and by graduate students preparing dissertations. Then came the Cooperative Research Program of the United States Office of Education, which began operating on July 1, 1956, with an appropriation of $1,000,000 for the first year. This amount has steadily grown, reaching more than $75,000,000 during the fiscal year 1966–1967. At the same time the Office of Education has provided financial support for research on educational media under the National Defense Education Act. Also the Office of Education is directed to spend on research 10 per cent of the funds appropriated under the Vocational Education Act of 1963.

Other American agencies, particularly the National Institute of Health, the National Science Foundation, and the Department of Defense, are now supporting educational research projects, so that the federal government is by far the chief source of project funds for educational researchers. Corresponding efforts are made by many other governments. The Soviet Academy of Pedagogical Sciences and the Japanese National Institute for Educational Research are only two examples. It is estimated that more than $100,000,000 was spent from federal sources in the United States in 1966–1967, and that the more than 600 research projects conducted involved about 1,200 principal investigators and nearly 2,200 graduate students. With the authorization for funds for research on vocational education and for support of research on manpower retraining by the Department of Labor, the money available for educational research in the future is likely to be greatly increased in the United States. This may be less true in several other countries and in research funds at the disposal of international organizations. But even for the world as a whole the bottleneck we face now is not likely to be a shortage of research funds, but inadequacies in the number and the quality of educational researchers. This is already a matter of serious concern and will continue to be as time goes on, unless the present recruitment, training, placement, and utilization of potential researchers is greatly improved.

EDUCATIONAL AIMS AND
CONTENT OF INSTRUCTION

C. EDWARD BEEBY

Within the limits of this chapter one could do little more than list all the problems posed by curricula throughout the world, many of which are already well documented. For that reason this discussion ignores such hardy curriculum perennials as the balance between science and the humanities or between general education and technical instruction, and it bypasses with a word more recent topics such as the relation of educational aims to the socio-economic aims of the country. A single problem that has been grievously neglected by research workers and finds scant notice in most books on the curriculum will be discussed here. It is the diffusion of new aims, new curricula, and the teaching practices essential to them, throughout a whole school system.

Brave words, new ideas, and pilot projects in selected suburbs are of no less interest to the good administrator than to any other educator, but his deepest interests are aroused only when he sees how they can be applied in his average schools by the great mass of his average teachers. It is at this moment, when the real difficulties begin, that he finds himself most alone, left to handle what appear to the specialists to be mere administrative problems. The aims and content of an educational system must be based on the aims of society as a whole—though in a democratic country, society can be a hydra-headed master speaking with many tongues. But although in theory the aims of school systems should be diverse, there is, for practical purposes, a fair measure of agreement throughout a wide range of countries on a common core of skills, habits, and attitudes that *should* be taught in a primary school at least. (This does not necessarily correspond to what *is* taught.) At the secondary level there is more diversity, but even here there is a roughly common understanding that general education will include languages, the humanities, mathematics, the natural sciences, and the social sciences, with perhaps a gesture toward physical education and the arts. The ways in which they are taught, the groups to whom they are taught, their relation to vocational training, and the relative weights given to the subjects admittedly vary so much as to make agreement on abstract aims less significant than might at first appear; and plenty of room remains for debate.

Although they give different weights to the factors, writers generally agree that the curriculum should be based on three things: the nature of society, the nature of the child, and the nature of the subject. To these one would add the nature of the teachers. The choice of the aims and content of a school system must depend on, among other things, the capacity of the teaching service to carry them out. It is amazing how frequently this factor is overlooked in writings on the curriculum.

THE PROBLEM: TWO "EXPLOSIONS"

The fact that the term "explosion" applied to education is already faintly hackneyed is proof that the conditions to which it refers are now fairly well known. The two explosions having the greatest effect on the curriculum have been well reviewed and need little elaboration. First, knowledge, we are told, is being accumulated much more rapidly than it can be imparted by the schools with the conventional means at their disposal, particularly in the sciences. Many of the "facts" and "laws" now being taught are already out of date. Secondly, an explosion of the school population is occurring in countries of all types. In developed countries it shows up as a rapid increase in the percentage of each age group demanding secondary education. In developing countries it usually begins with a clamor for universal primary education, which soon extends to the next higher level. In both cases it is exacerbated by the natural growth of population.

The effect of these two explosions on the teaching profession, and on what it should and can teach, is to drive a school system in opposite directions.

The explosion of knowledge has made the teachers' job harder and more complex than ever before. They must be better educated, must keep their own knowledge up to date and must, in the words of an Organization for Economic Cooperation and Development committee, "think of educational changes not in terms of periodic revisions but as a continuous process, a 'rolling' adjustment of courses and textbooks."[1] At least at the primary and secondary levels, teachers as a whole have not been known for these particular qualities; and without vastly more help, encouragement, and resources than they have been given in most countries, it would be unfair to expect them to keep themselves and their courses abreast of the swift stream of modern research.

But minor adjustments to books and courses, even of the "rolling" variety, are not enough. Curricula in most developed countries were overcrowded twenty years ago, and the subtraction of one fact for every one added will not meet the situation. A new concept of the curriculum and a new view of the very purpose of education are called for.

The most hopeful attack on this problem has been made by groups of scholars from different disciplines who see the teacher's job not so much as the transmission of the "given" as the guiding of the pupil to discover the structure of the subject, the body of principles and methods that will enable him to extend

1. OECD, *Curriculum Improvement and Educational Development* (Paris: OECD, 1966), p. 31.

his knowledge as the content of the discipline changes. Jerome Bruner writes: "Every subject has a structure, a rightness, a beauty. It is this structure that provides the underlying simplicity of things, and it is by learning its nature that we come to appreciate the intrinsic meaning of a subject."[2] So education, while not spurning facts, becomes a process of learning to learn that in some measure frees teacher and pupil from the awful burden of accumulating facts.

While this subject-centered view does not ignore the nature of the child, it does involve a rejection of the child-centered philosophy of the "progressive," whose picture of the child would be regarded as romantic and idealized and his treatment of the subjects as sloppy. However that may be, it is certain that the "structuralist" concept (if one may lump together people who differ widely in many respects) of the curriculum and teaching methods makes far greater demands on the teacher's intelligence, scholarship, and ingenuity than do the more routine practices it seeks to replace. The "simplicity" of which Bruner speaks is a sophisticated form of simplicity that dawns on the individual as the result of a complex mental process. To teach in this way a teacher must have a deeper understanding of both the subject and the child than is necessary for drilling a class in the rote memorizing of a set of relatively disconnected facts. The administrator's natural response to Bruners much-quoted statement that "any subject can be taught effectively in some intellectually honest form to any child,"[3] is, "But can it be taught *by any teacher?*"

The explosion of population forces the schools to dilute their offerings. The rapid expansion of the demand for schooling has affected in three ways the aims and curricula of the schools. First, at the secondary level the nonacademic newcomers to a school

2. Jerome S. Bruner, "Structures in Learning," in Glen Hass and Kimball Wiles, eds., *Readings in Curriculum* (Boston: Allyn and Bacon, 1965), p. 286.

3. Jerome S. Bruner, *The Process of Education*, (Cambridge, Mass.: Harvard University Press, 1961), p. 33.

system devised for an elite usually suffer, for a time, from a curriculum that is irrelevant to their abilities and their interests. Some advanced countries are still struggling past this stage; developing ones are just entering it. Second, developing countries, in their haste to extend their schools according to what seem to be the best world models, frequently borrow from developed countries aims and curricula that are largely irrelevant to their immediate needs.

Finally, the most serious effect of the school population explosion has been on the quality of the teachers. In developing countries the demand for more teachers coincided with the opening of new opportunities for boys and girls, and in many places the standard of the teaching profession has dropped over the past decade. In developed countries the shortage of secondary teachers has meant that classes in mathematics and science are taught by teachers with little grounding in the subjects. Even when there has been no actual decline in the educational level of the profession, few countries, if any, have been able to bring their teachers to the level demanded by the sudden expansion of knowledge. Thus, the reforms demanded by one explosion are made extraordinarily difficult by the other. Nowhere is this as obvious as in underdeveloped countries.

TEACHING AND THE CURRICULUM

Throughout great areas of the world—and in some schools in even the most advanced countries—classroom practice is almost the opposite of that demanded by the change in the nature of knowledge. In the majority of classrooms in most developing countries, teaching is dull and routine, and education consists of mastering simple skills and memorizing a fixed collection of facts and laws, the acquisition of which is later tested by examinations. The measure of truth in this dreary picture varies with the level of development of the country and its school system, but reports coming in from all over the world leave little doubt that rote memorizing, rather than "problem-solving" and "understanding of structure," is the dominant characteristic in underdeveloped areas and is not unknown in developed countries. One of the main causes of the dependence on rote memorizing is the low level of general education of the teachers (particularly in the primary schools), and there is, therefore, a limit to the improvements that can be made by exhortation or by training in new pedagogical techniques.[4] The teacher who has only a thin and routine knowledge of his subject and is compelled or cajoled into using a technique he does not understand or does not really believe in, is possessed of a strange inverted alchemy which can turn the brightest idea into lead. The syllabus may change, but he goes on doing the same old thing under another name.

An educational reformer who wants to adapt the aims and content of a school system to the demands of the modern world must begin in any country with some classrooms where teaching is of this routine type; in many countries it will be the commonest pattern, with, happily, a few striking exceptions everywhere. The reformer, like the golfer, must play the ball from where it lies. It is not some abstract education that is to prepare our children for a brave, new world, where understanding will be deeper, minds more sensitive to change, and the rules of the game radically revised—*it is the teachers*. And teachers in mid-career who tend to dominate the work of the profession are the product of the very schools they are to reform, and are deeply embedded in the society they are to change. Many books on the aims and content of education would be shorter and more down-to-earth if they substituted "teachers" for "education" in most of the sentences, especially when the reference is to developing countries where a fair percentage of the primary school teachers have themselves no more than seven or eight

4. For a discussion of this idea, see C. E. Beeby, *The Quality of Education in Developing Countries* (Cambridge, Mass.: Harvard University Press, 1966).

years of inferior general education, with perhaps a year or two of teacher training. Anyone who expects the average teacher in such a country to adopt, without major amendment, sophisticated methods based closely on problem-solving and the analysis of structure is guilty of the very romanticism and sentimentalism for which child-centered education has been criticized.

The concept of the average teacher is itself deceptive, and no strategy for the general reform of a big school system can succeed unless it takes into account the range of ability and of capacity to change in the teaching profession. (This is another topic that plays a minor part, if any at all, in most books on the curriculum.) It is not the average teacher who initiates reforms in school practice, but the exceptional individual. If he is to be able to experiment with new content and methods, he must have a considerable measure of freedom from rigid outside controls, such as a fixed syllabus, compulsory textbooks, authoritarian inspection, and narrow examinations. But, especially in developing countries with ill-educated teachers, the below-average teacher may need just this kind of rigid structure to give him guidance and intellectual security in the strange world of book learning. Perhaps the most difficult problem in educational administration is to devise a system of control that gives freedom to those who can take advantage of it, and a supporting framework just firm enough for those who cannot get on without it.

It would be easy to assume from this gloomy sketch of the limitations of the average teacher that, without waiting for a new generation of teachers, there is little point in attempting curriculum reform. This would be an unfortunate conclusion to draw. But any new curriculum must be as carefully adapted to the powers of the man who is to teach by it as to the children who are to learn by it. It is not a question of evolving a teacher-centered curriculum, but of remembering, whether the starting point is the child or the subject, that the main link between the two is a member of a semiprofession which includes Nobel prizewinners as well as teachers who are barely a page ahead of their pupils in knowledge and far behind the best of them in sheer intelligence. At least in developing countries, the limitations of the great bulk of average teachers create a greater barrier to curriculum reform than do the abilities of most of the children they teach.

TOWARD A STRATEGY FOR THE REFORM OF EDUCATION

The most hopeful point at which to begin the search for a strategy of reform is the work of subject specialists who have devised new courses on the basis of the structuralist view of learning. Perhaps the best known of these are the Physical Science Study Committee Physics Course and the New Mathematics in one or another of its forms. These courses are based on an authoritative analysis of the subject to be taught; progression in the textbook follows this structure; the teachers' guides go far beyond pious generalizations to detailed suggestions on method; and pupils are encouraged to discover for themselves rather than accept and memorize the given.

The strength of most of these courses lies in the fact that they have been worked out by top-level subject specialists in the universities in collaboration with groups of particularly able teachers from the schools. For certain purposes this could also be one of their weaknesses, unless special precautions were taken. Some of them have proved remarkably successful in the hands of the able teachers who were the first to adopt them, but they may have to be modified with the average and below-average teacher. (For the sake of simplicity the other problem of the average and below-average pupil is being ignored.)

The problem is intensified when a course, devised in prosperous American suburbs, is transferred to a country whose poorly educated teachers have achieved their position by rote learning and have little conception of any other form of education. The question is not whether the aim of making children think for themselves is desirable (though in traditional societies some would challenge even this); the task, rather, is to make a systematic study of the conditions under which the newer methods will work—the level of education and training they demand of the teacher, the maximum size of class and the minimum amount of equipment, the books and materials essential for success, and the kinds of resistance that must be overcome in the minds of teachers, inspectors, administrators, and parents. In a narrower sense it is a matter of deciding the "dosage" of the new method that can be taken in each case. How much rote memorization must be retained to give pupils and teachers the feeling that this is still education? Where and how far can problem-solving be introduced? If the children are encouraged to ask questions (and modern education cannot exist if they do not), at what point will the average teacher begin to panic and clamp down because he does not know the answers and cannot afford to lose face? In short, just how far along the selected road can teachers of any given level of general education be taken by new teaching materials and ad hoc training?

The same argument applies to the new educational technology, which is so often advocated (but not usually by classroom teachers) as the answer to the explosion of school populations and the shortage of trained teachers. There is no evidence as yet that television, films, radio, and programmed instruction will ever bypass the teacher or be made "teacher proof"; but they could be used to improve the work of all but the most hopeless teachers, if we only knew better how, where, for what purposes, and at what cost they can be employed. In general, the content of the newer instruments and techniques devised in developed countries has been based on the most modern concepts of education, which may represent for the average teacher in developing countries too great a leap from his present practice of teaching by rote. With few exceptions, we have still to explore the possibilities of such techniques for helping the ill-educated and poorly trained teachers take a few steps toward modernity under physical and financial conditions that would appall the best teachers in the most advanced countries.

What action does all this call for? In each country there is obviously room for widespread reforms in education; but if these reforms are to be fully effective, especially in developing countries, there is need for some such programs as the following on a world scale.

SURVEYS OF PAST AND PRESENT PRACTICE

Surely no other "industry" throws away its experience as recklessly as does education. In highly developed countries some well-publicized innovations now spread relatively rapidly, and even a humbler experiment in classroom practice has a chance of percolating through to other members of the profession; but all sorts of promising practices spring up, flower, and die in out-of-the-way parts of the world and are never heard of beyond a radius of a few miles.

There is a need for a series of surveys (comparable to those made by Wilbur Schramm and his associates on the new media)[5] of hopeful experiments in curriculum, school organization, and classroom practices in countries at various stages of development with as full an analysis as possible of the practices they superceded, the reasons for their success or failure, and their feasibility in other countries. Such surveys would give us much more than tips and suggestions for specific practices. They would provide the first systematic and authoritative picture of what is actually going on in the classrooms of the world, and would give a new basis for the theory we so much need of the development of school systems. Useful surveys have been made, by the United Nations Educational, Scientific, and Cultural Organization and other agencies, of administrative problems and practices in edu-

5. Wilbur Schramm, Philip H. Coombs, Friedrich Kahnert, and Jack Lyle, *The New Media: Memo to Educational Planners* (Paris: UNESCO, International Institute for Educational Planning, 1967).

cation; but when it comes to the real business of teaching and learning in developing countries, each educator has to rely on his own limited experience and on passing references in the literature.

There is, secondly, a need for a series of simple, straight-forward accounts of long-range experiments in improving the quality of education, written if possible by people closely involved in them over a period of years, giving an account not only of the final results but also of the daily failings and frustrations. If there were twenty statements from different countries like the account by V. L. Griffiths of his twenty-year experience in training teachers in the Sudan, we could begin to reexamine some of our theories.[6]

We must have a carefully planned series of experiments, where new teaching techniques and materials are tried out with groups of teachers of varying levels of education and training, to see to what degree and under what conditions teachers at each level are capable of adopting aims, curricula, and methods that break with their traditional practice.

There seem to be three distinguishable but closely related approaches to this task. First, we must focus on the preparation and adaptation of teaching materials. There is already a fair amount of evidence that the average teacher finds it difficult to apply abstract educational theories in practice, and that the best method of inducing him to change is to provide him with detailed courses embodying the theories in practical suggestions that can be used directly in the classroom. There is little doubt that this is especially true of most teachers in developing countries and that the poorer their general education, the more detailed and specific must be the texts and the teachers' guides. Therefore, the preparation of new materials and the adaptation of existing materials to meet varying conditions must be at the

6. V. L. Griffiths, *An Experiment in Education* (London: Longmans, Green, 1953). This book is out of print, but a booklet based on it is soon to be published by UNESCO, International Institute for Educational Planning.

basis of all these practical experiments. This is true about books, which will probably continue for a long time to be the basic tools of the teacher, but the same principle applies to television programs, films, programmed courses, and the like. In every case the final adaptation should be made as close as possible to the place where it is to be used, and in collaboration with the teachers who are to use it.

Second, we need field experiments. There are already a few field experiments in the transplantation of sophisticated materials and techniques to developing countries: for example, the attempt by the Educational Development Center, in conjunction with national authorities, to establish the teaching of the new mathematics in East Africa; the similar experiment on a smaller scale by the Department of Education in Papua and New Guinea; the work in India of the team from Teachers College, Columbia University; and the team teaching project in Barbados being conducted by the Ministry of Education, Harvard University, and the University of the West Indies. There is need, however, for a far wider range of practical experiments of this type. To be of the greatest value to theory as well as to practice, they should be especially devised to show the types of methods and materials that are most suited to teachers with different amounts of general education and training. They should be more than pilot projects; for the administrator it is of less interest to know what miracles occur when the educational prophet lays his hands on a few disciples than to see the results when the disciples themselves talk to the multitude. These experiments should have a built-in systematic method of evaluating the results. The experience of Wilbur Schramm in the survey mentioned earlier bears this out.

Finally, experiments in administration are needed. In addition to knowing what the individual teacher can do with new curricula and methods in his classroom, we need to know a great deal more about the best kinds of administrative structure and policy to start the process and to keep it growing. The only two ways to find out are to observe what has already been done in progressive areas and to persuade other authorities to experiment with new forms of administration. In many developing countries, the best points of leverage for the reform of classroom practice (assuming interest and enthusiasm in the central ministry of education) are the training colleges, the inspectors, and the textbooks and teaching aids. A method of administration that brings these three together at a focal point has a fair chance of succeeding. A training college in Poona, India, where the faculty, the local inspectors, and the teachers have got together to produce new textbooks, teachers' guides, and teaching aids, may be pointed to as an example. This training college, moreover, does not confine its training to its present students but takes responsibility for training in the use of the new materials the experienced teachers who can make or mar any widespread classroom experiment in the schools they dominate. The college is, in effect, a corporate workshop for the area. It would take relatively little money, but no small amount of skill and persuasion, to have administrative experiments of this kind established in a number of countries. The institutions that were successful would provide admirable training grounds for the teachers of teachers, who, all too often in developing countries, merely confirm their students in the stale old practices, because these are the ones they use in their own teaching.

One side effect of these field experiments, whether in administration or in the classroom, is that we should be able to see more concretely the significance of the "systems analysis" that is mentioned frequently—but vaguely—in the modern literature on educational planning, and that we should, in consequence, forever kill the false hope that reforms in education can be brought about merely by altering curricula. If you make a major change in the curriculum, you find yourself inevitably committed to changes in the education and training of teachers, inspection and promotion policies, publications, examinations, specialist field staff, school buildings and equipment, public relations, administrative structure, and, as likely as not, the relations between central and local educational authorities.

RESEARCH AND THEORY

There is need for much more research on the diffusion of educational practices. The monumental work of Paul Mort was for the most part not directly concerned with teaching methods and was, moreover, done before the recent developments in educational technology and before the new interest in education in developing countries vastly expanded the field for research.[7]

There is a need also for research on the capacity of teachers to absorb and use new techniques which is as thorough and systematic as the corresponding research by modern psychologists into the capacity of children to learn. Many aspects of the psychology of teachers have been neglected by the experts, not the least of them being the effect of individual differences of teachers on their ability and willingness to change standard practices.

There is need to study theory. However much each knows about the history of education in his own country, educators are grievously ignorant of the natural life history of an educational system as such. Not only is there no general theory to explain or predict its growth, but they are not even sure that there is any consistent pattern in it. If there *are* recognizable stages as a school system proceeds from simple beginnings to sophistication, developing countries should be able to make rough predictions of the problems they will meet over the next decade and take steps to handle them. If there is no such pattern, they may have more freedom of choice, but they will certainly have less reliable guidance, and planning will become very risky. Administrators in

7. Synopses of this body of work are to found in an article by Paul Mort appearing as Chapter 13 of Matthew B. Miles, ed., *Innovation in Education* (New York: Bureau of Publications, Teachers College, Columbia University, 1964); and in Donald H. Ross, *Administration for Adaptability* (New York: Metropolitan Study Council, 1958).

developing countries have every right to expect help from theoreticians of education on this basic issue; if they cannot be given what they need, it is not for lack of raw material for study.

Nor have educators in developed countries had time or inclination as yet to rethink their own educational theories in the light of the mass of new experience that has just become available in developing countries. The theories on aims, curricula, methods, and administration are all based on countries at one end of the spectrum of development. They may be tolerably valid in the bright light of the reds and the yellows; how will they look when viewed through the gloomier indigos and violets?

Educators have never been noted for their capacity to relate their theories to their practice, but in the present educational crisis one of the most practical contributions that any individual or group could make to schools throughout the world would be to work afresh on educational theory.

Any of these suggested programs would involve massive work at the national level where the control of school systems lies, but this clearly would be more effective if some attempt were made, if not to coordinate the work, at least to report on it systematically. There is an urgent need for a world clearing house on activities and experiments bearing on the curriculum and on teaching methods and materials. As a profession, education can no longer afford to discard experience with such abandon.

FROM GOALS TO RESULTS
IN EDUCATION

WILLIAM W. TURNBULL

"When a man does not know what harbor he is making for, no wind is the right wind," wrote Seneca. This chapter is concerned mainly with one thing: relating educational attainments to educational purposes. This modest aspiration is far from easy to realize. But unless it can be realized with some degree of success, the educational ship of state will of necessity have neither rudder nor compass.

Relating results to goals is one crucial element—in many ways *the* crucial element—in the "systems approach" to education. This term is used here to indicate a deliberate effort to set forth what one wants to accomplish, to examine all the possible means that might be used to meet the desired ends, to make a reasoned choice among the means on the basis of their anticipated effectiveness, to monitor their degree of success or failure, and to adjust the system continually in response to the findings.

This definition has many parts, and the procedure it defines is complicated. Nobody has followed it satisfactorily in the field of education to date, partly because educators have not had the analytical tools of operations research or systems analysis, but mainly because explicit attempts at educational planning are a phenomenon of only the last ten years. Now in a great many

195

countries there is some form of educational-planning service.[1]
Perhaps for the first time educators are in a position to look
broadly at available strategies for improving education on a
national basis and to apply the most powerful analytical tools
to help in the process.

To some people this approach has a formidable ring—cold and
mechanistic, with no room left for human values and certainly
none for frivolities or indulgences. Systems analysis can be used
just that way, but it can also be a commonsense approach to
achieving a balance among esthetic, economic, and scientific
values in order to achieve a more satisfying life. Or it may mean
simply proceeding with one's eyes wide open—like a man who
knows all about calories, but decides on a second dessert anyway.
It may also reassure some to note that the completely successful
application of the systems approach in education is not so much
dangerous as unlikely. But it is worth a try.

The press of growing aspirations against a hard ceiling of
available assets is a worldwide phenomenon. So, too, is a human
reluctance to abandon hopes and desires in the face of scarce
resources. As Alfred North Whitehead said: "The vigor of civilized societies is preserved by the widespread sense that high
aims are worthwhile. Vigorous societies harbor a certain extravagance of objectives. . . ."[2] The answer to the "extravagance
of objectives" has to be a choice, if not of which goals to
abandon, then at least of which goals to defer. Any approach
that can help defer as few aspirations as possible, and can point
the way to realizing the greatest number in the shortest time,
deserves a hearing. Educators need not abandon their vision
of beauty and goodness in striving to lend architecture to their
purposes.

1. See Maximo Halty Carrere, "Some Aspects of Educational Planning
in Latin America," in Raymond F. Lyons, ed., *Problems and Strategies of
Educational Planning* (Paris: UNESCO, International Institute for Educational Planning, 1965), pp. 53–63.
2. *Adventures of Ideas* (New York: Macmillan, 1933), p. 375.

NATIONAL OBJECTIVES AND EDUCATIONAL GOALS

In applying a systems concept to an enterprise such as education, the logical starting point seems to be to state directly and exactly what one wants to accomplish—what the result is to be. In practice it usually turns out that this is not the place to begin.

Take the case of setting goals for education, for example. It is axiomatic that the educational goals of any country are derived from a broader set of long-term, national objectives—economic development, public health, national defense, and so on. But education must compete with such other purposes for its share of scarce resources. The urgencies of each country's present circumstances inevitably set the priorities among the entire array of needs. A country afflicted by drought imports grain and invests in irrigation plans; one swept by disease seeks doctors and medicine; one at war drains its treasury for arms. Education's needs are determined against such competing demands. Only when these over-all priorities among national objectives have been decided for each period ahead, in the light of present urgencies, and when the resources have been allocated accordingly, is it realistic to begin the job of setting the broad objectives of the educational system. And, of course, the objectives in all areas of public policy interact. The need for health services places demands on the educational systems; the availability of skilled manpower helps to determine realistic aims for technological development. The pattern of objectives at any moment in time is interconnected at all points and is subject to change through a constant, dynamic interplay.

Assume, however, that the broad objectives for education at all levels, primary through postgraduate, have been established. They may include such general and disparate aims as increasing the literacy rate, developing a greater appreciation of the cultural heritage, inculcating a positive attitude toward school and learning, developing self-understanding, building a corps of technicians below the professional level, and so on. Establishing these broad objectives involves choices among educational levels, between engineering and the arts, between concern for the individual and concern for the society, between institutional and on-the-job training. The priorities are likely to be influenced by transient circumstances, by slow-changing conditions making up the nation's stage of development, and by the policy-makers' view of the essential functions of education: whether to train manpower, to provide an enlightened citizenry, or to help individuals to personal fulfillment. The choices are entirely open. The process of making the objectives explicit in no way constrains the philosophical or practical bases on which they may be set.

The foregoing describes in words what may be thought of as the first loop in an educational systems analysis, as illustrated below (Figure 1).

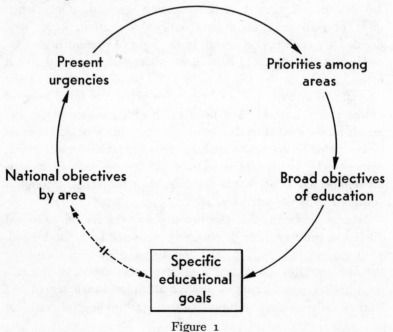

Figure 1

It is probably true that the hardest step in the entire sequence —other than finding more money—is the one we have yet to deal with: translating the general objectives into specific goals. The aim should be to express the goals in terms exact enough to allow planners to say, in three years or five years, whether they have met the goals or how far off they are. For example, the general objective of increasing the literacy rate needs to be translated at least into such subgoals as "in five years 90 per cent of all twelve-year-olds and 75 per cent of all adults should be able to read a minimum of 500 words." Such a goal as tripling the output of teachers in ten years, while specific in numbers and time, has shortcomings. In the first place, it is primarily a means to an end, not a goal for its own sake. For a phase immediately ahead, however, it may be defined as a necessary, though intermediate, goal   —an end for the first period and a means for the next. Even so, it is much cruder than it should be. What should the teachers be able to teach? Mathematics? Geography? To whom? And, specifically, what standard of knowledge and skill in teaching their subjects should they possess? A critical part of the job of setting out specific educational goals is making just such matters explicit in terms that can be measured.

EDUCATIONAL GOALS AND EDUCATIONAL RESULTS

The reasons for seeking such tangible definitions of goals will become clearer in the description of the second loop that completes the systems approach, the "feedback loop."

Starting with the goals specifically stated, the planners next must decide the broad strategies for attaining them. Specifying the target to be hit in precise, measurable terms and the segments of the population to be involved is likely to be useful in suggesting possible strategies for reaching the goals. For example, a decision that the literacy rate of twelve-year-olds should be raised from 60 per cent to 90 per cent and that of adults from 50 per cent to 75 per cent may suggest the strategy of concentrating on basic education in primary school and employment centers, while the goal of tripling the output of teachers may lead to proposals for investing in facilities at a higher level. Alternatively, however, the greater number of teachers might be attained by means of subsidies for study in other countries, importing teachers, incentives for qualified women to return to teaching, or a combination of several approaches.

This suggests another essential element of the systems approach. *The statement of the goal should not stipulate how the goal is to be attained.* Rather, it should lead to formulation of a number of possible alternative means toward the end—as far as possible, all of the preconditions that are capable of leading to the goal. The requirements implied by each such precondition can then be explored, and so on. The planner thus traces backward from the goal through each alternative and its chain of logical antecedents, comparing these chains to see which one or which combination leads to the goal in the most satisfactory manner. "Most satisfactory," of course, in different situations may mean different things—fastest, cheapest, most politically acceptable.

The selection of the broad strategy, then, can be accomplished only after a careful comparison and selection of the detailed tactics to be employed: the number and dispersion of new schools, the study materials needed, the number of new university lecturers required. And obviously where goals are multiple, as they always are, a particular tactical move may be optimum for one goal and at the same time help or hinder progress toward another. The selection of the best strategy may involve the analysis of a rather intricate network of interrelated chains or sequences. Computers and simulation techniques may help in this process, but here we are concerned with the logical flow rather than with the computational or mathematical techniques used.

Finally, the time comes when the plans must be executed. This activity results in two kinds of reports. The first kind consists of action or process reports (the schools have been built, the books bought, the television system set up), which say that the intended means have been employed. The second consists of reports of results (90 per cent of the twelve-year-olds can read at the level specified, the number of people qualified as mathematics teachers with the knowledge and skill specified has tripled), which say that the intended ends have been achieved (see Figure 2 for a diagram of a feedback loop).

Figure 2

The final step in closing the feedback loop is all important: comparing results with goals. Note that the arrow in the diagram goes both ways. The essential reason for stating the goals so explicitly in the first place is to make the comparison of results with goals sharp and informative. The goal has to be a statement of the desired results expressed in the terms in which the final measurement will be made (90 per cent of twelve-year-olds can read at least 500 words, and so on).

The systematic comparison of results with goals is the key to the responsive capability of the educational enterprise. It is the means by which those responsible for education can recognize successes and failures and can check the actual efficacy of a procedure against their initial expectation, thus learning from experience. It is the signal that adjustments are or are not needed, and therefore is basic to the self-regulatory capability of an educational system.

The two loops involved in the systems approach taken together make up "the figure-eight approach to educational planning" (see Figure 3).

DEFINING THE GOALS

Explicitly defined goals stand at the center of the Figure 3— at the core of the systems approach. The job of arriving at them, therefore, merits closer attention.

First, the importance of an educational goal is quite independent of the present ability to measure progress toward it. Indeed, it may well be that the more subtle, and in some ways the more crucial, the goal, the more difficult it will be to devise descriptions of observable behavior that give evidence of its attainment. It would be folly to abandon the attempt to achieve a highly desired end simply because only clumsy ways exist of expressing how near we have come to it.

At the same time, without any techniques to measure degrees of attainment of any given goal, there is no basis, other than blind faith, for believing that what is being done to try to reach it is making the slightest difference. Luckily conditions are seldom that bad. A persistent search will usually suggest "for instances": examples of how the more analytical, more appreciative, more tolerant, or more dexterous person can be distinguished from his peers who are not similarly endowed. The techniques

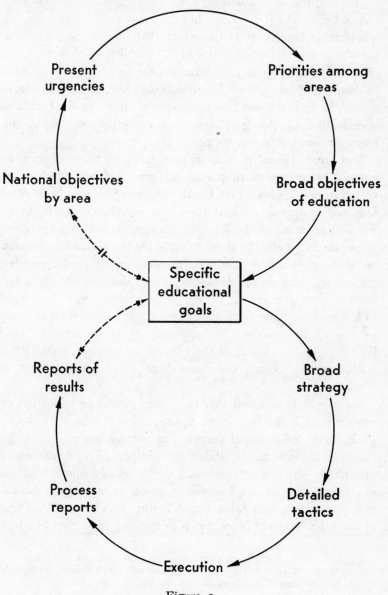

Figure 3

for making the distinctions may not have much in common with conventional school measures, but they may produce meaningful, quantifiable results. It is important that we not neglect these hard-to-measure characteristics in the initial goals, but that real effort is made to specify, in advance, the techniques to be used in determining degree of accomplishment and what that degree should be to make our efforts successful. It is the final, precise specification of the goal that makes possible the later, all-important comparison of results.

The usual statement of goals is couched in terms of means—amount of money or proportion of gross national product invested, number of teachers hired, number of schools built or of libraries equipped. At best these are short-range goals, to be justified in terms of the learning they are intended to produce in pupils. More closely allied to ends are the measures centered on students—number enrolled, number of dropouts, number graduating, and so on. However, these also are usually intermediate measures. Even though at present we may be forced to fall back on them for want of something better, they are only substitutes for more precise statements of what students should be like or do as a result of the educational process. These latter goals are the direct and immediate outcomes expected of education.[3]

Suppose it is assumed that the direct impact of education on the students is the best level, theoretically, at which to specify goals for an educational system. For some areas of knowledge or appreciation it may be fairly straightforward to devise measures of the students' attainment. Take the rather simple example of concern with accomplishment in music, as in a recent evaluation project in which Educational Testing Service is active. One of several component objectives is to discover the extent to which

---

3. At a more remote level, education's outcomes interact intimately with and feed into other objectives of the nation: full employment, decrease in crime, responsible voting behavior, and the like.

students can listen to music with understanding and enjoyment. This component has again been analyzed into four parts:

A. Recognize and identify instruments, musical forms, and particular works by sound.

B. Perceive the unity of musical selections and perceive gross and subtle changes in musical performance.

C. Discriminate between different related aspects of music by sound.

D. Attend to simple and complex pieces of music.

For each part (A, B, C, and D), a number of tasks have been prepared and a goal of student performance has been set. For example, one of the ten questions under Part A is:

1. Listen carefully to the instrument playing the music and decide how the sound you hear is produced. (A tape of a trumpet is played)

How was the sound of the instrument made?
(a) By blowing into the instrument.
(b) By plucking the strings of the instrument.
(c) By striking the instrument.
(d) By drawing a bow across the strings of the instrument.

We might say, depending on the importance we place on musical education, that 75 per cent of the nine-year-olds should be familiar enough with musical instruments to answer correctly. Or the goal might be 90 per cent. The important point is to express as many as possible of the goals of musical education in terms as specific as this, so that when the time comes to apply the yardstick, a meaningful comparison between the aspiration and the actual results can be made.

It is worth noting that the effort to assess the progress of a group of students toward a particular goal ordinarily will not require measuring each student's attainment. Since the concern is with group rather than individual accomplishment, a fairly small sample of representative students will be adequate to assess the level of attainment for all.

The example above admittedly does not establish the most elusive of goals with which to illustrate the process of measurement and comparison by way of the feedback loop. Considering that education should be more than the imparting of knowledge and skills, how can we state the full breadth of its goals in terms of desired student characteristics described specifically enough to permit later measurement of results and comparison with goals? At present the answer has to be that we are a long way from having any completed system of goal statements and available measures of progress for the full gamut of educational aspirations. But there have been promising beginnings which suggest the job can be done. An illustration may be of interest.

Three years ago the Educational Testing Service was asked to work with a committee of educational leaders in Pennsylvania to appraise the "adequacy and efficiency" of education in the state. Part of their report follows:

> After much deliberation, the Committee decided upon a broad interpretation of what was meant by the "adequacy and efficiency" of educational programs. It concluded that an educational program can be regarded as adequate only if it can be shown to contribute to the *total* development of students. Recognizing the central importance of the academic subjects in any educational program, the Committee also stressed its belief that the goals of education having to do with the growth of youngsters as individuals and as useful members of society are just as important as the goals of conventional academic achievement. . . .
>
> In attempting to state the goals of education in Pennsylvania, the Committee posed this question: "What should children be and do and know as a consequence of having gone to school?" The question stemmed from the Committee's belief that measures of quality in education should focus on the behavior of students. Committee members wanted a set of goals that would reflect the problems society faces

in the world of today. They also wanted the statement of goals to be short enough to be discussible in public meetings, yet definite enough to indicate clearly the kinds of behavior that students who had attained the goals would exhibit.

The definition of 10 goals was developed after an extensive review of the literature, much discussion, and close collaboration between the Committee and members of the Educational Testing Service project staff. The proposed goals, covering the personal, academic, social, and civic development of students, were formulated into 10 general statements:

I. Quality education should help every child acquire the greatest possible understanding of himself and an appreciation of his worthiness as a member of society.

II. Quality education should help every child acquire understanding and appreciation of persons belonging to social, cultural, and ethnic groups different from his own.

III. Quality education should help every child acquire to the fullest extent possible for him mastery of the basic skills in the use of words and numbers.

IV. Quality education should help every child acquire a positive attitude toward school and toward the learning process.

V. Quality education should help every child acquire the habits and attitudes associated with responsible citizenship.

VI. Quality education should help every child acquire good health habits and an understanding of the conditions necessary for the maintenance of physical and emotional well-being.

VII. Quality education should give every child opportunity and encouragement to be creative in one or more fields of endeavor.

VIII. Quality education should help every child understand the opportunities open to him for preparing himself for a productive life and should enable him to take full advantage of these opportunities.

IX. Quality education should help every child to understand and appreciate as much as he can of human achievement in the natural sciences, the social sciences, the humanities, and the arts.

X. Quality education should help every child to prepare for

a world of rapid change and unforeseeable demands in
which continuing education throughout his adult life
should be a normal expectation.[4]

Following each general statement was a paragraph or two of
elaboration, which made the brief goal statement more explicit.
The first general statement appears at first glance to be a restatement of a common and never-defined objective, but the para-
graphs of elaboration begin to help. The proposed goal reads in
full as follows:

I. Quality education should help every child acquire the greatest
possible understanding of himself and an appreciation of his worthiness as a member of society.

Self-understanding should increase as the child matures. That is,
he should become increasingly aware of his strengths and weaknesses,
his values and interests, and aspirations, so that the decisions he makes
about his educational and occupational future will be informed, reasonable, and rational. He should be helped to know the strengths in
himself that he should exploit and the weaknesses that he should try
to overcome or that he must learn to live with.

On the other hand, regardless of the level and pattern of his particular talents, the school experience should be such that it will
strengthen, not damage, his self-esteem. The school should be operated in such a way that children at all levels of talent can achieve a
growing awareness of their worth as persons in a society that claims
to have an equality of concern for all its members.

Although this statement does not fulfill the criteria of behavioral
specificity we are seeking, it suggests many clues about where
and how to look for the behavior, as a basis for setting up the
goals related to it. How closely should students be able to forecast their performance in different areas of accomplishment at
successive age levels? How clear and consistent should they be
in stating their educational objectives at age ten or fifteen?
Samples of explicit self-description would not be hard to obtain.

4. Educational Testing Service, *Annual Report 1964–1965* (Princeton,
N. J.: Educational Testing Service, 1966).

Similarly, one could proceed systematically through the paragraph and by specifying procedures for assessment relating to each of its elements, devise a method for describing in quantitative terms the extent to which students of various ages can meet an objective that on first reading seems entirely beyond measurement.[5]

We have concentrated in this chapter on one particular application of the systems approach in education: its use in planning the objectives of instruction and monitoring progress toward them. There are many examples of a different kind, in which systems analysis has been applied to important administrative problems in education and more broadly in problems of national resource allocation. Those who are not familiar with the work done in these areas will find excellent accounts in publications of the Organization for Economic Cooperation and Development. We have chosen here to concentrate on a systems approach to achieving specific behavioral goals in education, because this task, although extraordinarily complex and difficult, lies at the heart of the educational enterprise.

The systems approach is characterized by successive approximations at every point along the diagram in Figure 3. And the process is continuous, cycling and recycling through both loops of the figure. The whole point is the sensitive, continuous adjustment and calibration of the resources applied as the results are assessed. We may be forced to realign our expectations—our goals—as we see what results are attained, or we may be stimulated to vary the strategies by which we seek to achieve the goals. In either case the essence of the matter is to state the goals in testable form and to assess the results regularly and with perseverance and ingenuity.

5. Further examples of efforts to express educational goals in terms of measurable behavior may be found in: Nolan C. Kearney, *Elementary School Objectives* (New York: Russell Sage Foundation, 1953); Will French *et al., Behavioral Goals of General Education in High School* (New York: Russell Sage Foundation, 1957); Educational Testing Service, *A Plan for Evaluating the Quality of Educational Programs in Pennsylvania: Highlights* (Princeton, N. J.: Educational Testing Service, 1965).

INTERNATIONAL COOPERATION THROUGH UNIVERSITIES TO STRENGTHEN EDUCATION

HEIMAN G. QUIK

The topic of international cooperation in education, notably at the university level, has been discussed at a number of international conferences in recent years. From these discussions one learns that international cooperation can occur through an incidental and entirely voluntary decision by the collaborating parties. It can also be viewed as initiated by sense of a common responsibility. Educational systems are not bound up only with their own national society; they are also related to educational systems in other countries. The body of knowledge that is handed on in the educational process is not national property alone; it is universal property as well. Universities cannot operate in complete independence behind man-made national frontiers; they transcend those frontiers and are interdependent. International cooperation exists therefore whether or not it is openly recognized and declared.

The Ashby report on higher education in Nigeria sets forth the specific point that *education should be explicitly viewed as an international undertaking*.[1] As such, any strategy framed to promote it must extend from the educational establishments of the given nations to the international level.

1. Report of the Commission on Post-School Certificate and Higher Education in Nigeria, *Investment in Education* (Nigeria: Federal Ministry of Education, 1960).

THE RESPONSIBILITY AND TASKS OF THE UNIVERSITY
IN INTERNATIONAL COOPERATION

An important proposition follows from the preceding point: universities have a responsibility of their own to foster the kind of cooperation that can help bridge the great and growing gap in conditions of life among the rich and the poor countries and spur the development of the latter. One of the reasons for this special responsibility is the universal character of learning and the growing interdependence of institutions of learning in various parts of the world. Further, not only are the universities in the developing countries dependent on sister institutions in countries with a high level of economic development, but the dependence works in reverse as well. As universities in the developing countries increasingly adapt themselves to their own social and cultural environment—and hence display greater variety in their educational and research programs—all other members of the international academic community stand to gain by remaining in close contact with them.

Another reason underlying the special responsibility of universities here is the place held by the universities in the young countries of the Third World. In these countries the university, at one and the same time, stands at the forefront of the search for a national identity and as a symbol of that identity. It is of central importance to the socio-economic and cultural development process. It is responsible not only for higher education but is, or should be, responsible for building up the entire educational system. Unlike the case in Western countries, its role in scientific research in a nation is often exclusive, for there are not as a rule many other research bodies created by the government and business with whom the research task can be shared. If the universities are to fill that role to benefit the nation, they must keep abreast of and be able to draw on research work throughout the world of higher learning.

The relation between research and national development points to yet another reason that universities have a special responsibility to cooperate. It is often difficult to find a common meeting ground between the advanced countries and those of the Third World, especially in matters that touch on economic and political relations. But these difficulties can be materially reduced if universities provide the forum for contact. Here is where people have learned to work with critical judgment and with a sense of the relative nature of things. Here, too, despite other inequalities between the haves and the have-nots, there can be a dialogue at a level of equality and in a spirit of mutual respect —with consequent beneficial effects in the work of national development.

Until recent years Oriental and African studies were centered in universities like London, Paris, and Leyden. Of late, however, it has come to be recognized that the universities in the East and in Africa offer research possibilities unavailable in Europe or the United States. The range of subjects includes tropical agriculture and tropical medicine; certain fields of biology, anthropology, archaeology, meteorology, oceanology; languages, religion, and legal structures; and sciences dealing with developmental problems such as development economics and development sociology.

It is worth recalling that the general development of science was closely bound up with the social processes and the technological progress of Western society and was adjusted to the specific needs of Western society and culture. But the view is now gaining ground that a greater part of the scientific potential will have to entail the adaptation of science and technology to the highly varying needs of non-Western societies. Many scientific institutions of the West are increasingly trying to work according to this view. But the results of scientific research cannot be successfully transformed into action within the domain of the universities, let alone that of the Western universities. The task calls for close cooperation of universities and other scientific institutions in the rich countries with their sister institutions in the poor countries.

The division of labor among universities in various parts of the world will have to be accompanied by an expansion of research facilities at universities in the developed and the developing countries alike. In this effort, among others, reference must be made to the International Education Act of 1966, enacted by the Congress and signed by the President of the United States. One of the aims of this act is to use a system of grants to institutions of higher learning or combinations of such institutions to establish, strengthen, and operate graduate centers to provide national and international resources for research and training in international studies and the international aspects of professional and other studies. The framers of the act wisely realized that universities left to themselves are not automatically fit to join in international educational undertakings, but must be helped to reach a position where they can adapt and reinforce their resources for that purpose.

Aside from needs related to research facilities, virtually all universities in the developing countries have to contend with a shortage of staff. These universities have made considerable efforts to fill university posts as soon as possible with their own nationals, but it will be many years before expatriates are no longer required. Although reliable figures are not available, it is safe to assume that in the case of Africa, for example, the process of Africanization will not go as quickly as was expected in 1961 at the time of the Tananarive Conference. In the foreseeable future one of the most pressing problems for the young, rapidly expanding universities of Africa—and elsewhere in the developing world—will continue to be the need to engage an expatriate staff.

There are five principal obstacles in the way of staff migration:

1. Manpower needs at home. There are staff shortages everywhere, and only a few universities are adequately equipped to perform international tasks in education.

2. The lack of a real involvement of the home university in

such international tasks. As a result, work abroad often becomes a personal venture of the person concerned; he must himself bear the risks of an interruption in his career and reinstatement in the university system after the end of his stay abroad.

3. Inadequate financial inducements.

4. Unfamiliarity with foreign university systems, academic tradition, level, research facilities, etc.

5. The difficulty of adjusting educational facilities abroad on behalf of families with children.

Various countries have devised schemes to overcome these obstacles. While the schemes are addressed to specific local conditions, they deserve to be more widely known, and their possible application in other countries merits investigation.

One group of schemes is designed to overcome the shortage of staff for international work:[2]

The Home Base Scheme of the British universities is the first. These universities have created a number of additional posts in order to help in recruiting staff for overseas universities—by providing security for the supernumerary man and by facilitating the secondment of British staff to those universities. The scheme promises to work best in large departments, preferably those with an inherent interest in overseas development. It is hoped that it will enable staff to spend normal tours overseas, besides making possible short-term secondments which are of particular value where interdepartmental links exist.

Visiting Scientists Teaching Abroad (VISTA) is a scheme for seconding British university scientists to new universities in the developing countries. Its appeal is directed to junior- and middle-level scientists of established university status whose commitments and prospects make it difficult for them to contemplate a secondment of the normal length. There are two main advan-

2. Information on schemes in Great Britain comes from a circular published in London by the Ministry of Overseas Development, August 26, 1966.

tages to the scheme. For British scientists it means only one term overseas, which relieves them of the need to uproot their domestic arrangements and replant them in a foreign country. For the overseas universities it means a succession of experienced staff giving courses planned well beforehand and fully integrated with the university teaching program.

Study and Serve Overseas is the third scheme. Under it Great Britain's Ministry of Overseas Development provides the funds for selected British postgraduate students to spend a year at an overseas university studying for a higher degree on the condition that the student agrees to remain at least another year in approved employment in the overseas territory concerned. Experience has shown that the Study and Serve program yields best results when the student spends two years at an overseas university, dividing the time between study for the higher degree and tutoring or demonstrating in the host department.

Still, the creation of an acknowledged source of supply for staff migration does not mean that the universities themselves are necessarily an active party cooperating with overseas recruiting agents. Better results can be expected where it is possible to give the cooperation an institutional character by establishing a direct bond between two university partners who jointly determine the content and form of their collaboration. The advantages of institutional cooperation over incidental recruitment are:

1. The opportunity provided to the institutions to take the initiative and to choose men on the basis of their special interests, relations, capacities, and in accordance with staff policies.

2. The possibility of joint consulation and of short- or long-term planning depending on circumstances or opportunities.

3. The opportunity for relatively long-term selection and preparation of university teachers and other staff to be seconded and also for scientific "accompaniment" during their overseas tour and ready reinstatement upon their return.

4. The opportunity for an exchange with staff of the foreign

institution and for their effective placement within the home university.

5. The establishment of lasting institutional and personal relations.

6. The opportunity to do research that is impossible in one's own environment and thus to keep up and extend knowledge on developing countries and the process of development.

7. The integration of international tasks in the program of the university.

There are other advantages for universities in developing countries. First, the collaboration with sister institutions abroad is a normal phenomenon in international scientific intercourse, whereas receiving aid from foreign government stresses dependence and in the long run arouses ill-feeling. Secondly, the principle of freedom of learning, highly esteemed in university circles in many developing countries but difficult to realize, is better served by direct cooperation among universities than by governmental involvements. And again, the useful effect of the teachers and advisers seconded to them is considerably enhanced by the fact that these persons are assured of the lasting cooperation of the institution that made them available.

In some countries the system of direct university-to-university cooperation is well under way. In the United States it is an established practice in the Agency for International Development programs. In Great Britain interdepartmental links between British and overseas universities have rapidly increased in recent years. But in other countries many obstacles still have to be overcome. Their university circles often lack the necessary interest; the structure and organization of universities is not entirely equipped for collaboration; or their governments are not willing to give the universities the necessary scope for this collaboration.

An important aspect of international cooperation is student migration. Few of the developing countries possess an adequate training capacity in their own universities, so they must send sizable numbers of students to foreign countries for university training or part of it. But the system of study abroad has its disadvantages, the most important probably being alienation from the home country, its culture, and its socio-economic conditions. More and more young students, therefore, are being urged to take their first degree in their home country and to attend foreign universities for graduate specialization only. This arrangement is intended to support the new universities in the developing countries and to diminish the dangers of alienation. At the same time it is often a positive contribution to the work of the host university.

The phenomenon of study abroad is too often seen as a one-way street. The great possibilities the Third World can offer students from Western countries are still too often neglected. Why shouldn't one attend universities in Africa for African languages and culture? Where could one better study tropical agriculture and tropical medicine than in the research institutions of tropical areas?

In many European and American universities the student community shows a willingness, and even enthusiasm, to participate in this type of study abroad. It is not, of course, to be done at random, and students must be carefully selected and prepared. But it seems clear that here lies an untapped reservoir which could serve to intensify and enlarge international cooperation to the benefit of all parties involved.

THE ORGANIZATIONAL ASPECT AT THE UNIVERSITY LEVEL

In the wide sector of international *service*, the universities have an important task to perform in the years to come—a task that will sometimes also take them outside the traditional fields of education and research.

There will have to be adjustments to a further expansion of

international intercourse in the various functions of the university: teaching, research, and service. The fact that these functions are interrelated and cannot be detached from one another will have to be recognized. It will also have to be recognized that the issue here does not involve one-way traffic, or the provision of aid, but that cooperative efforts can be of mutual benefit if the parties concerned view their cooperation as a whole instead of fixing their thoughts on a single specific matter, such as the temporary loan of teaching staff. In other words, the international task of the university is not equal to the sum of unrelated activities. It consists of interrelated activities viewed as the international dimension of a university's role in society. Unfortunately, while this idea is gaining wider acceptance in the university world, it cannot be said that it has been followed through in the realm of practical action.

The problem is with the nature of the university. A university is not a business or a government service. Many universities do not have a strong central authority or a bureaucratic structure. University staff members are not the easiest men to organize. To make the idea of an international dimension a reality within the university does not mean the imposition of an operation from a central point. It means the search for equilibrium between centralization and decentralization suited to a situation. It is not so much issuing orders that have to be carried out, as bringing people, groups of people, and university institutions together to work in concert so that the various tasks reinforce and support one another. It is a matter of knowing which tasks can best be performed by particular university institutions.

Many universities are trying to make the international dimension of education pervade various university activities. Michigan State University, for example, has done this deliberately and persistently. President Hannah, of that institution, has said: "We have not, and we do not anticipate creating relatively isolated pockets of international studies on our campus. Instead, we are trying to create a general environment and an international dimension which will permeate all relevant segments of the university over the years ahead."[3]

Thus, a conscious effort is being made to familiarize the students in various fields with the international aspects of the tasks that will face them upon completion of their studies. This means an international dimension in education, but it also means further research into the international aspects of the branches of learning concerned. It entails overseas research, for which are used the international technical assistance contracts into which the university has entered. This aid thus provides a feedback on behalf of education and research at the university itself.

The international idea has been promoted at Michigan State University, for example, in the creation of a number of area study centers for Africa, Asia, and Latin America. Efforts have been made to reinforce the international atmosphere of the campus by attracting foreign students, while opportunities have been created for study abroad by American students. The coordination and administrative leadership of all these international programs have been centralized in the Office of International Programs, headed by the Dean of International Programs. The details cited indicate how a university can approach the problems of international cooperation in education.

Some of the recent developments in a number of Dutch universities illustrate such efforts. These universities have created special agencies to foster international cooperation. They are concerned primarily, but not exclusively, with collaborative efforts with developing countries. The assumption underlying these agencies is that the university has many-sided tasks to perform with respect to the problems of the developing countries—tasks that find expression in various sectors of university activity:

3. Education and World Affairs, *The University Looks Abroad: Approaches to World Affairs at Six American Universities* (New York: Walker, 1965).

teaching, research, and service. Like Michigan State University, these Dutch universities are convinced that these tasks are interrelated. Moreover, only in rare cases is such a task the sole responsibility of a given chair, faculty, or department. In most cases it is interdisciplinary or interfaculty, and its proper implementation requires the active participation of curators, senate, (faculty or subfaculty) scientific staff, university office, and students.

All this poses a communication problem within the university, and efforts are being made to solve it by creating a permanent committee for international cooperation. Within that committee the necessary consultation can take place among the individual university agencies and assorted groups who can contribute to international cooperation. This committee can combine the experience and expertise required to stimulate initiative and to direct the collaboration.

Within the Dutch university the committee doing this work resembles the centers of initiative that have been created within a number of British universities in order to stimulate university interest in international work. It is assumed that consultation among a committee of persons whose main function lies elsewhere does not in itself automatically lead to action. Executive machinery, therefore, has been created. It consists initially of only one official, who acts as secretary to the committee, collects material for documentation and information, structures tasks that can be performed within the university by faculties and institutes, and maintains contacts with the national and international institutions concerned with the performance of these tasks. As these university tasks grow, the executive agency will also have to become a center of expertise in international cooperation, capable of acting as a stimulator, source of information, organizer, and coordinator.

Only a few Dutch universities have such an organization, but a recent national conference organized by the University of Utrecht and attended by delegations from all universities recommended the creation of such agencies at all Dutch universities. As is the case at Michigan State University, the key question confronting Dutch universities is how a central administrative leadership can be combined with decentralized implementation. In both cases a solution has been found without straining the existing university structure.

ORGANIZATIONAL PROBLEMS AT NATIONAL AND
INTERNATIONAL LEVELS

A solution to some of the organizational problems is to combine the resources of various universities and to have programs carried out by a consortium of universities. A number of universities in the United States work in this way. In the Netherlands the institutes of technology of Delft and Eindhoven are working together on a project for the development of a faculty of engineering at the University of Nsukka in East Nigeria.

The organization of a university consortium creates a number of new problems. The task of establishing an equilibrium between central leadership and decentralized implementation is more difficult than when the activities are performed inside one institution. But through a consortium resources become available that otherwise would remain untapped. Moreover, within the consortium, tasks can be allocated according to the special qualities of the participating institutions, thus enhancing the level of the joint campaign. In implementing a given project, it is therefore far better to encourage one nation to combine and use the appropriate resources provided by a group of universities. Indeed, too little application has been made of the consortium idea.

In addition to collaboration in support of a special project, interuniversity contact on a broader basis is also developing in many countries; this contact is related to several aspects of the international task of the universities. Among the examples of such national forms of organization, the following may be mentioned:

United States   Education and World Affairs

                 Overseas Liaison Committee of the
                 American Council on Education

Great Britain   Inter-University Council for Higher
                 Education Overseas

                 Committee for University Secondment

Canada   International Programs Division of the
                 Association of Universities and Colleges
                 in Canada (AUCC)

Netherlands   Netherlands Universities Foundation for
                 International Co-operation

As the differences in tasks and forms of organization of these national bodies are closely bound up with local situations, it is impossible to draw a general picture that will be universally valid. It is possible, however, to indicate the kind of task such national organizations can successfully perform:

1. Founding and maintaining institutes and courses where teaching in a world language is given at the postgraduate level to an international community of students. Such institutes, of course, chiefly apply to countries where the language of instruction is not a world language.

2. Fostering and coordinating university programs of international scope and also providing administrative services for the realization of these initiatives.

3. Being a clearing house for other countries in the field of university education and research.

4. Setting up a documentation and information service on matters of international cooperation in university education and research, which acts for all universities in the country concerned.

5. Promoting the study of problems of international cooperation in university education and research, either by stimulating
and coordinating the tasks performed by the existing universities,
or by founding new research institutes to perform them.

Organized collaboration of universities at the national level
is only the first phase in creating an international network to
link the universities of the world. Organized collaboration at
the international level is more difficult than collaboration within
one nation. It is slow to grow and, as an extra handicap, must
often overcome the opposition of old or new nationalism.

Cooperation at a level higher than the national one takes place
initially in a regional context, as in the cases of the Association
of Southeast Asian Institutions of Higher Learning and the Association of African Universities. The majority of these organizations have a limited task: they provide a forum for consultation
on matters of common interest; they can play a useful part in
providing information and documentation; and they provide
clearing house facilities.

The International Association of Universities operates at a
world level. It organizes five yearly conferences and thus provides
university leaders around the world with a useful meeting
ground. At the same time it maintains in Paris a small but effective bureau whose main function is providing information.

There is great value in setting up and improving these regional
and worldwide university organizations. With the active aid of
these organizations, the idea of education as an international
undertaking must be translated into action. For this purpose they
must be more active in the operational field and reinforce their
executives.

A GLANCE INTO THE FUTURE

The world in which we live has changed fundamentally in
the last twenty-five years. Through greatly improved means of

communication, distances have shrunk to nothing; countries have become each other's neighbors; and a realization of interdependence has grown. We know that we are living in one world, and we know that our children will live in one world or none. We know, too, that social and economic development is above all a matter of science and technology and, thus, of education. Science pervades society, and society is exerting increasing influence on science.

As a result, the social function of the university has changed radically. The university has the job of educating people who will have to live in the world of tomorrow, and who will have to understand something of what it means to be a citizen of the world. The research that is performed by the universities can no longer be aimed at the country's own society but will have to direct itself with equal force toward other societies. To this end, the creation of cooperation with institutes in other parts of the world is essential.

The changed social function entails a change of the attitude in which university work is performed, a change of university tasks, a change of forms of organization for the university, and a national and international view of the meaning of university cooperation. These changes will take place gradually—too gradually in relation to the revolutionary development of science and technology and their potentialities. But this gradualism is a natural result of the stability or conservatism that inheres in a university.

II

AFRICA

ARTHUR T. PORTER

Notwithstanding individual and regional diversities and complexities, certain broad generalizations can be made about the pattern of education on the continent of Africa. Attention by way of an example will be focused in this chapter on the region broadly defined as "Middle Africa" and more particularly on the Anglophone areas of the region. The pattern of education in these areas originated from the former colonial power and still reflects this dominance.

HISTORICAL REVIEW

Until almost the time of the Second World War, education in the former British colonies was largely controlled and organized by the Christian missionary societies. The British government played some part in the provision of education after the start of the nineteenth century, but it was insignificant compared to the efforts of the missionaries; and such government activity as there was retained the same clerkly rote learning, in both method and content, characteristic of the Christian charity school education in nineteenth-century England.

This pattern was first reproduced in Sierra Leone with hardly any adjustments to meet the new situation and context, and it was extended to other parts of West Africa and later to East

Africa. There were schools in Sierra Leone almost from the colony's founding in 1807, and its citizens generally regarded education as an important avenue through which the advantages of civilization would reach all Africa.[1] Partly because of the variety of languages spoken by the people manumitted in Freetown, no attempt was made to adapt the education provided or to utilize any of the African languages. Laurie's report of 1867 to the Colonial Office supported this essentially English type of education, and in 1882 the system was extended to the other West African dependencies.

By the eve of the First World War some disquiet was already discernible about the "un-Africanness" of the system. Some modifications were made; teaching in the vernacular was introduced in the elementary schools; and some ill-equipped technical institutes were established. The system as a whole, however, especially in the secondary and tertiary levels, still reflected the dominant English model—a situation criticized by the Phelps-Stokes Report of 1922.[2]

The only institution of higher education in all middle Africa where African students could obtain university degrees from 1876 to the establishment of the "Asquith" colleges following the Second World War, was Fourah Bay College in Sierra Leone. Yet even there no attempt was made to broaden the curriculum or to adapt it to the existing African environment. It was firmly based on the arts and theology courses of the University of Durham, with which it was affiliated.

Thus, before the pre-independence period and the era of African nationalism, the pattern of education was narrowly English and circumscribed. The prime purpose of missionary education was to prepare souls for that other kingdom not made with hands; its institution of higher learning was intended

1. In commenting on the fourth quarterly examination of the scholars of the Colonial School, the Sierra Leone *Gazette* for January 3, 1818, records: "It is from the foundation of education that we must expect the stream of civilization to flow; it is that which enlarges the mind and thus renders it capable of every other development."

2. African Education Commission, *Education in Africa: A Study of West, South, and Equatorial Africa* (New York: Phelps-Stokes Fund, 1922).

primarily to prepare teachers and pastors who would be the door effectual through which it was hoped the blessings of industry and civilization would permeate the continent. In addition to being narrow in scope and content, the education was also narrowly based. By 1924 there were still only fifty-six elementary schools in Uganda and nine intermediate schools which took children from twelve to sixteen years of age but did not bring them to the level of the London matriculation university entrance examination. In 1935 there were still no full secondary schools for Africans in Kenya, Malawi, or Zambia.[3]

The Africans themselves had come to accept the education provided, despite its narrowness and elitism, as the source of the white man's magic. It was an important part of the road to success and to positions of status and prestige. Not surprisingly, therefore, there was an increasing demand in the years between the wars from Africans themselves and from voices in Britain that educational opportunities, particularly for higher education, in the then colonies should be increased.

These aspirations were partially realized after 1943 with the announcement of the Asquith and Elliot commissions and their reports, which led to the establishment of the university colleges in Ibadan, Accra, Khartoum, and Salisbury in special relationship with the University of London.

The emphasis in the late forties and fifties, both by donor agencies and colonial governments, was therefore on providing high-level manpower in the form of secondary and university graduates. In East Africa, as elsewhere, a large portion of Commonwealth Development and Welfare funds were devoted to university and other postsecondary education. In Kenya, for example, just about one-third of the £3,890,000 in educational grants between 1946 and 1965 went for these purposes.[4]

---

3. Eric Ashby, *Universities: British, Indian, African* (Cambridge, Mass.: Harvard University Press, 1966), p. 199.

4. F. X. Sutton, *Aid and the Problems of Education, Employment and Rural Development* (Paper prepared for the Conference in Education Employment and Rural Development organized by University College, Nairobi, at Kericho, Kenya, September 1966).

The new institutions still reflected the dominant philosophy of the earlier education. The new colleges were to produce, in the words of the Asquith Commission, "graduates who have the standards of public service and capacity for leadership." Though they failed to reflect their African backgrounds, they nevertheless served an important function by producing the leadership that independence required. It should also be remembered that in the colonial period Africans measured their worth in terms of the metropolitan country, and educated Africans were agitating to be regarded in all matters as equal to the imperial administrators whom they wished to replace. Admission to the "senior service" at that time required degrees, and no one wanted to qualify for a degree that could give rise to any suspicion of inferiority or of a double standard.

To the politicians at independence, education was not merely a matter of filling much-needed gaps in the leadership cadre. Education was considered to be a right of all citizens. Thus, at the eve of independence and in the first flush of national sovereignty, the emphasis was on mass education.

In the early 1960's there were two clearly discernible pressures on the structure of the education system in the tropical African countries: the pressure to provide high-level manpower and popular pressure to expand primary education and mass literacy. The conference of African ministers of education, finance, and economic affairs, which met at Addis Ababa in 1961 under the auspices of UNESCO, and the published plan of the conference for the accelerated development of education at all levels in Africa was a response to one of these pressures. The conference the following year, at Tananarive, on African higher education, also under UNESCO auspices, was a response to the other. Both dealt with the plan period 1961 to 1980.

Universal primary education was accepted as a desirable goal for this plan period, and target dates were set for its implementation. Universal primary education was in that period a popular and vote-catching slogan for party manifestos. Kenya's ruling party, Kenya African National Union (KANU), for example, promised in its manifesto that "every child in Kenya shall have a minimum of seven years free education," though it laid down no date for achieving this target.

The basic philosophy of the early 1960's was that an investment in education in a developing country would pay off; that it would generate much-needed employment. But within a few years it became increasingly clear that this assumption was not supported by results. The Western Region of Nigeria, which first implemented the proposals for universal primary education, was being faced with unemployed primary school leavers. When it responded by establishing secondary modern schools for the school leavers, the problem became unemployed modern school leavers.

Today the emphasis has shifted from both improving the tertiary level and providing mass education for its own sake. Many African governments are finding it difficult to support both the expansion of primary education, required by a policy of mass education, and the facilities of higher education, which seem necessary when political factors and other considerations such as Africanization demand a massive build-up of cadres. These are needed not merely for normal turnover but for a deliberate and conscious replacement of expatriate personnel in the shortest possible time. Today the assumptions of the early sixties are being questioned as African governments as well as donor agencies work to alleviate the present crisis in African education.

The priorities in African education have been different at various times in colonial history. They have ranged from an emphasis on the need to save souls, to the colonial preoccupation with providing a moderately educated minority to perform the subservient administrative roles, to an emphasis during the war years on providing colonies with leadership personnel, to the belief that education is the panacea for all problems, and, finally, to the current phase of disillusionment and crisis. African education has stumbled forward, influenced in turn by the passions and prejudices of its proconsuls on the spot.

An important first conclusion born out by this review is that the pattern of African education is the result of neither systematic nor long-range planning and does not reflect clearly defined objectives. The most effective ways to help Africa resolve its present crisis in education is to provide adequately for the training of Africans to wrestle with their own problems. Trained personnel are urgently required in sufficient numbers not merely to plan but to implement all sorts of development efforts on which solutions to problems depend. The dilemma facing most African countries is that while this need is known and accepted, limited manpower and finance may make it impossible to make that leap forward. There has to come a break with the European pattern without which the present crisis cannot be resolved.

INTO THE AGE OF PLANNING

Many African countries are now attempting to take stock of the present and to spell out the targets aimed at through their various development plans and manpower surveys. In Kenya, for example, with a population of nearly 10,000,000, as of 1965 about 1,000,000 pupils were enrolled in the seven-year course, and about 60,000 in the four-year secondary course (excluding the sixth-form work)—or 60 per cent and 7 per cent respectively of the appropriate age groups. About 80 per cent of the primary school teachers have had no secondary education other than their training; and in the secondary schools 90 per cent of the graduate teachers are expatriates or noncitizens. Only about 12 per cent of primary school leavers can gain places in government-maintained or -assisted schools. Since independence in 1963, however, a number of self-help, or *Harambee*, schools have been opened, which provide places for some primary school leavers who cannot enter the aided schools. Unfortunately because of severe shortages of equipment and trained teachers, the education provided in these schools is far from satisfactory.

It is difficult to give an exact picture of the cost of formal education to the government of Kenya, but it has been roughly estimated at £20,000,000 annually. This figure does not include expenditures on adult education, youth programs, apprenticeship schemes, training institutions, and other schemes outside the formal education system. Even with these omissions, the total expenditure is equivalent to 7 per cent of the national income, a very high figure in comparison with many other countries.[5]

The 1964 High Level Manpower Survey showed that Kenya had then about 70,000 jobs in the range from skilled manual to professional and top management. Of these, about 6,000 required a university education, and the total number of jobs in this category is expected to increase to about 10,000 by 1970. In the technical and semiprofessional category it estimated a requirement of about 13,000 in 1964 rising to 31,000 by 1970; and in the skilled office and skilled manual category it estimated requirements of 32,000 rising to 41,000 in 1970.

The government's 1966–1970 development plan has been influenced by these findings; and although the requirements of high-level manpower have been revised upward, the 1964 survey remains a determining factor in the government's plan for educational development. Yet there has been some criticism of

5. Cf. Friedrich Edding, "Expenditure on Education: Statistics and Comments," in *The Economics of Education*, E. A. G. Robinson and J. E. Vaizey, eds., (New York: Macmillan, 1966), p. 41. Edding's figures for around 1960 show educational expenditure at 7 per cent of national income in the Soviet Union, 6.19 per cent in the United States, 5.87 per cent in Canada, 5.85 per cent in the Netherlands, 4.41 per cent in the United Kingdom, 3.79 per cent in West Germany, 3.50 per cent in France, and 3.49 per cent in Australia. Edding observes that "in practice to spend even 6 per cent of the national product on public education will prove very difficult for the poorer countries," since so much of this is public sector expenditure, and the extent of the public sector is limited by a narrow tax base.

several important details of the plan. Manpower surveys are worthless unless they are reviewed each year by an expert manpower board.

A particularly pertinent criticism of the survey and of the development plan—and, indeed, of most of the planning so far attempted—is that the plan period is too short for long-term targets and covers the period of abnormality when the country is shifting from colonial to independent status, with all the problems involved in rapid staff turnover, Africanization, and so forth. Thus, one of the problems all African governments face as they review the educational structure they have inherited is the overriding need for long-term planning.

Further, in the early phase of manpower planning, opportunities for wage-earning employment and economic development were emphasized. But African governments are beginning to find that the situation is not that clear-cut. A government, whether in Britain or in Africa, cannot effectively fulfill its role unless it can keep the loyalty of its citizens. In certain situations the determination of choices cannot depend on what is most economically beneficial. Compromises may be required in the face of traditionalism or populist pressure.

This can be illustrated—with relevance to education—by the problem of rising unemployment in the towns and cities. Harbison has argued that modernization generates unemployment. He writes:

The forces of modernisation all work to swell the number of job seekers, as traditional agriculture has little holding power in a developing society. Once a farmer's son has completed five or six years of primary school, where the curriculum is almost exclusively oriented to the modern sector, he will not want to sentence himself to a life of digging yams on the family plot. He wants a position with the government, a job in industry, more education, or almost anything except traditional agriculture. . . .

As wages continue to rise in the modern sector, the greater is the aspiration of young people in the rural areas to seek employment in the cities. The progressive extension of primary education to the rural areas raises these aspirations even more. And the high wages in the modern sector enable those already employed to house and feed more relatives and friends from the rural areas. . . .[6]

It is estimated that in Nigeria the modern sector can absorb no more than one-third of those who aspire to find employment within it. Guy Hunter has estimated that in Tanzania, for each 250,000 of an age group entering the labor force, only about 25,000 jobs are available in modern sector employment, in addition to 6,000 places annually in secondary schools; and that in Kenya, where the annual output of primary school leavers is 150,000, there are only about 40,000 jobs and 15,000 places each year in the secondary schools.[7]

Hardly any other problem poses a greater threat to African stability than this one of rising unemployment and its control. Increasing employment is partly a consequence of modernization, but it is also a consequence of the increase in education and a reflection on the relevance of the education provided. Many countries in trying to tackle unemployment are also reappraising their school system.

As Harbison has pointed out, the only way unemployment can be kept under control is by improving the rural sector of the economy; and this can be achieved only through a dedicated commitment on the part of government, through massive investment of resources which the African governments unaided cannot sustain and through appropriately trained manpower and efficient organization. The latter directly concerns us in this chapter, for it means a reorientation of more than 50 per cent of the current educational practices.

6. Frederick Harbison, *The Generation of Employment in Newly Developing Countries* (Paper prepared for the Conference on Education, Employment and Rural Development organized by University College, Nairobi, at Kericho, Kenya, September 1966).

7. Guy Hunter, *Manpower and Education Needs in the Traditional Sector* (Paper prepared for the Symposium on Manpower Aspects of Educational Planning held by the International Institute of Educational Planning in Paris, May 1966).

African governments faced with the total problem of modernization are expanding their educational systems at all levels. Recently, for instance, the Kenya government negotiated a $1,500,000 loan with the World Bank for expansion of its secondary school system. Its development plan also envisages a more moderate expansion of primary school enrollment.

PROBLEMS IN LOWER-LEVEL EDUCATION

But the crucial problem, if balanced growth is to be achieved and unemployment controlled, is whether the expansion should involve merely growth of the existing system of formal education which is demonstrably inadequate for modernizing both the urban and the traditional sectors. The more than 50 per cent of the nation's young who must earn their living in the traditional sector need a different kind of education. The task of providing it cannot be left to the Ministry of Education alone. In Kenya part of the work of rural development education is performed by the Ministry of Agriculture through its Community Development Program and its Agriculture Training Colleges. Ministries of education are not adequately equipped to deal with these problems, which are not in the area of formal education. But dividing the educational task between two ministries is also hardly satisfactory. Some more cooperative endeavor between ministries seems necessary. Fresh ideas are called for from all who are concerned about the much-needed rural transformation. Educational planning is interdisciplinary; and an interdisciplinary approach seems mandatory.[8]

In spite of the widening gap between urban and rural and the increasing unemployment, which is already critical and destined

8. "The successful, effective educational planner must be fully conversant with the needs of industrial and agricultural development, know the problems of foreign exchange and those relating to the terms of trade, be able to integrate all these factors with human resource development." Frederick Harbison, *Educational Planning and Human Resource Development* (Papers in the Fundamentals of Educational Planning, Paris: UNESCO, 1967), p. 22.

to become worse, governments are increasing the facilities, and the costs, of formal education without any imaginative or bold expansion of the educational services required to achieve rural transformation.

Kenya's development plan, for example, as has been pointed out, provides for expanding both primary and secondary facilities, giving highest priority to the latter while recognizing the need to improve the quality of the former. Enrollments in primary schools are expected to rise from 60 to 62 per cent of the age group by 1970 at a recurrent cost of £11,000,000. The current output of the primary schools is already more than adequate for the secondary expansion contemplated.

Lower secondary enrollments are expected to rise from 31,700 to 60,700, and upper secondary (the sixth-form course) enrollment from 1,800 to 4,800. There is real danger that, because of political and other factors, the Kenya government may be compelled to increase enrollments beyond these figures. Even more critical, the government may have to take over administrative and financial responsibility for the *Harambee* school, because it feels that all planning will be meaningless if this self-help exercise is outside its control.

The problem of the primary school leaver is a familiar one throughout middle Africa. As has been pointed out, only 12 per cent of these leavers can gain entrance into the state-aided secondary schools; the rest, at the primary school leaving age of about 13+, are too young in modern terms to do a man's job even at a boy's pay. Their absorption, either in industry or in agriculture, poses one of the critical problems for Kenya, for Nigeria, and for every other newly developing country.

The Kenya government is currently preparing a white paper on its education policy, which will, no doubt, consider this and other pressing questions. A number of alternatives to the present structure have been suggested, including a later school-entry age. It has also been estimated that should the Kenya government take over the *Harambee* schools, it will, in effect, have to provide by 1970 for an enrollment of as many as 120,000 pupils. This is almost double the number needed by the economy according to the manpower survey.

Equally important, of course, is the content of the education provided. Attempts are being made to improve this, and the New Primary Approach and new mathematics and science teaching in many African countries have given encouraging results. Governments also realize that the most direct way to improve the primary schools is to improve their teachers and, as much as possible, to replace untrained with trained teachers. Small teacher-training colleges are being regrouped into larger, more effective units.

The secondary curriculum is also being broadened; in Kenya, with the help of a credit of £2,300,000 from the International Development Association and the World Bank, facilities are being provided for general training in manual skills and for optional courses in agriculture, technical subjects, commerce, and home economics. Entry to the teaching profession at the secondary level is also being encouraged by the use of the system of tied bursaries: 50 per cent of the university students in arts and 30 per cent of those in science who hold government bursaries, are requested to sign a bond agreeing to teach at least three years after graduation. The recently established Department of Education at University College, Nairobi, the Kenya Science Teachers College (a Swedish project), and Kenyatta College will considerably reduce the present heavy reliance on expatriate teachers by Kenya's secondary schools.

University College, Nairobi, recently received a grant from the United Nations Development Program for technical assistance to its Department of Education covering its postgraduate and undergraduate courses in education; a program of research on selection procedures, teaching methods, African psychology, and the economics and sociology of education; and a program for upgrading the education of secondary school teachers through in-service, vacation correspondence, and residential courses. Teacher education in Africa today needs the emphasis on the economics and sociology of education and on African psychology. African teacher education has been based too long on a Greek philosophy of education and on an historical and comparative view of education. This view has tended to underestimate the relevance of the African background and the imperatives of national development—a term that, as Harbison rightly put it, "encompasses economic, cultural, social and political development in the building of national identity and integrity."[9]

But more needs to be done. Systems analysis is still foreign to most African teacher-training colleges and institutes. There is an incipient danger that in order to increase the number of teachers, governments may establish separate teacher-education institutes divorced from the universities. These institutes, usually financed by external aid funds, compete for scarce competent academic personnel with the countries' universities; and because of their external funds, they are able to pay more attractive salaries, though they are not always able to attract the highest quality. These institutions, competing also with the universities for students, tend to attract the less qualified and thus to set up the vicious circle of poorer staff, poorer students, and consequently poorly trained teachers for the nations' schools.

A developing nation must guard against the dangers of unbalanced growth; it must also avoid a hiatus between citizens and decision-makers, between high-level and unskilled manpower. But this hiatus is being created in the absence of adequate middle-level personnel—an absence that is putting many development programs into constant jeopardy.

In Kenya technical education is provided in three types of school—junior trade, secondary trade, and secondary technical—and, at a higher level, at the Polytechnic, the Mombasa Technical Institute, and the Faculty of Engineering of the University College, Nairobi. One of the most serious shortages revealed by the Kenya manpower report was of technicians, and the plans are to

9. *Ibid.*, p. 25.

meet this shortage with students from the Polytechnic. Most of these students are on sandwich courses or are already sponsored by employers; there is consequently no problem of overtraining or unemployment.

Vocational training in Kenya is generally regarded as the responsibility of the employer; but, except in a few large industrial concerns and government departments, little training is actually given. To overcome deficiencies in pre-employment, institutions such as the Kenya Institute of Administration (which serves mainly the public sector), the Management Training and Advisory Centre (for the private sector), and the government Secretarial College have been established. Plans are being prepared for a National Industrial Vocational Training Centre.

But despite the undoubted usefulness of the existing institutions, the question has been raised whether the harassed and hard-pressed African governments should take on added responsibilities for vocational training. Pre-employment training facilities in secondary vocational schools have proved a poor investment. The Latin American experiment in which training related to industry is financed by a payroll tax on employers has been recommended as a pattern for developing African countries.

PROBLEMS IN UPPER-LEVEL EDUCATION

On-the-job training, continuing education, and in-service training are areas of opportunity that seem to be underutilized in many developing countries. The philosophy that the basic training in the three R's should be a once-and-for-all exercise has influenced also some of the patterns and content of higher education. The Bachelor of Arts degree has been regarded as evidence that the recipient can read and study for himself, that further training as such is no longer necessary. This is a familiar part of the dispute over whether the schools should strive for quantity or quality, whether research should be pure or applied, and, ultimately, whether higher education should train a professional elite or managers of all types or, perhaps, even everyone. There is a growing awareness that, to cope with the recent advances in knowledge, there must be a continuing, and not a terminal, evaluation. African countries must review their higher education systems to see whether their priorities are right.

The continuing popularity of the one-subject honors course at the African universities is part of the difficulty. Lord Eric Ashby has dealt exhaustively with this problem in his recent book *Universities: British, Indian, African.* He refers to a meeting of six principals from universities in developing countries (four from Africa) held in Jamaica in 1955, and writes:

Some of the principals plunged into heresy by asking whether post-secondary education in a developing country might not have something to learn from a "mass" university, on the American land grant model; and whether it might not be desirable to include in institutions of higher education a far higher proportion of the school product and a far broader range of studies than that to be found in British universities.[10]

By 1960 the Nigerian Commission, under the chairmanship of Lord Ashby, was able to come closer to the desires of some of these principals by recommending broader courses of studies in Nigeria's new universities. But Lord Ashby has acknowledged that "with the aid of hindsight it can be said that the Nigerian Commission did not emphasize the point forcefully enough."[11]

An ambivalence toward the special single-subject honors course still pervades official documents on higher education. To illustrate from the East African scene, the Committee on Needs and Priorities commented in 1962 as follows:

For the present, we are obliged to express our regret that the 3:1:1 first degree is envisaged as a possibility when the University of East Africa comes into being. We regard it as unfortunate that individual Departments have been permitted to opt, as between the 3:2:1 and

10. Ashby, *op. cit.*, p. 260.
11. *Ibid.*, p. 274.

the 3:1:1 pattern. Of these two alternatives, we prefer the former, on educational grounds.[12]

The Economy Commission of 1963 also commented as follows on the organization of study in the sciences:

> As with the Arts and Social Sciences, we would hold that such marked specialization (3:1:1) at the undergraduate level is unwise as well as uneconomical, especially with the small numbers now flowing into the Natural Sciences at each of the Colleges. Therefore it can only be justified where a clear need exists in East Africa for specialists in a particular field.[13]

Finally, the 1964 Report on Entrance Levels and Degree Structure conceded that single honors "degrees might be offered to only a small percentage of the most able students and that the majority should read a broader degree of at least two subjects."[14] Such statements amount to no more than lip service to adaptation and change, which can be also illustrated from other areas of university life.

Today most African countries are spending over 20 per cent of total government revenues on formal education, and the costs are rising both absolutely and relative to total income. Most of the presently advanced countries never had population growth rates of more than 2 per cent in their comparable period of development. In most developing countries population growth rates are higher, and the indications are that the rates are on the increase. What then are the prospects for the future? Whatever the eco-

12.   Report of Committee on Needs and Priorities (1962), p. 87. The 3:1:1 and 3:2:1 patterns refer to the number of subjects studied in a course leading to the bachelor of arts degree. Each course in either arts, science, or social science lasts three years and begins with three subjects. The choice is between having one subject in the second and third years or having two subjects in the second year and one in the third. In either case, subjects taken during the second year must be a continuation of those taken in the first year, and subjects taken in the third year must be a continuation of those taken in the two previous years.

13.   Economy Commission Report (1963), p. 22.

14.   Report on Entrance Levels and Degree Structure (1964), pp. 3–4.

nomic or financial argument, it cannot be denied that there are critical manpower gaps which must be filled in all the developing African countries. On the other hand, access to education results in all African countries in more graduates than the manpower requirements; this is the result of political promises of education. In Kenya, to continue the example, the number of entries for the Kenya Preliminary Examination is now about 150,000 per year, compared with only 30,000 six years ago. The possibility of a K.P.E. holder getting a place in an aided school has dropped from 14 per cent in 1964 to 8.7 per cent in 1966; it is estimated at 11.7 per cent by 1970.[15]

Because of shortages brought about by Africanization and independence, the primary stress in a number of developing countries is on providing for short-term requirements. But sometimes these are not consistent with the long-term requirements; and the result may be unbalanced development and awkward surpluses in some areas once the immediate gaps have been filled. The signs that this could happen in the absence of the most careful and continuous planning are already apparent. In Kenya, for example, about 70 per cent of those who sit for the Kenya Preliminary Examination gain the award; K.P.E. in itself is thus becoming of little value in the search for jobs. The experience in other countries warns that it is not impossible for the situation to worsen so that, first, higher school certificate leavers and, then, university graduates find difficulty in obtaining employment. Some developing countries already have a higher proportion of university students in their population than do the United Kingdom or the Federal Republic of Germany.

In a situation where, with the passage of time, the qualifications needed to obtain jobs are rising, there is ever increasing pressure for improved educational opportunities at the higher levels. African countries are bravely trying to meet this demand,

15. This information was supplied by the Ministry of Education for the Conference on Education, Employment, and Rural Development organized by University College, Nairobi, 1966.

but it seems clear that the gap between their needs and their possibilities will hardly be obliterated without outside assistance. The prospects for such massive external aid are not encouraging.

CONCLUSION

Today the gap between rich and poor nations continues to widen, as the former provide the latter with ever less capital and other assistance. This situation is leading an increasing number in the developing African countries to the conclusion that massive assistance from outside will not be forthcoming, and that their development must be based on their own efforts. Another deceptively attractive viewpoint, prompted by cynical disillusion, advises retreat into traditionalism from the uneven struggle or violence to awaken the conscience of the world.

There is in fact a crisis in education in the newly developing countries of Africa. The systems they inherited create expectations without providing corresponding fulfillment. Costs are rising far more steeply than the economic growth. A fundamental review of whole systems is urgently required if scarce resources are to be rationally utilized.

Much has been said about the "inner logic" of educational systems, about universities being like organisms because they evolve and adapt themselves by successive small mutations, large mutations commonly being fatal. This argument maintains that some inertia, or preservation of the status quo, is necessary in education to provide both stability and direction. But what defense can be made for a system whose only result seems to be taking children off the farms to towns where they cannot find employment?

The purpose of this chapter was not to attempt solutions but to delineate the background of the urgencies in African schools today. It is tempting to remark that, despite the advance in technology and the undoubted breakthroughs in educational methods by the armed forces during the war, no sustained attempt has been made by the affluent societies to combine the technological advances and the methodological innovations in the service of African education. It is also unfortunate that more emphasis is not placed on adequate and continuing research at all levels before even the smallest, allegedly nonfatal mutations are made. It is too much to expect that the necessary changes will emerge spontaneously from overworked and undersupported teachers and administrators in the African schools. The system must receive the necessary shocks and stimuli from outside. The costs of tackling today the problems posed by the crisis in education in Africa will be great; but the costs of tackling them tomorrow will be greater.

SYMPOSIUM ON ASIAN EDUCATION

CARLOS P. ROMULO

with notes by Prem N. Kirpal and Uday Shankar

THE DEEPENING CRISIS IN ASIAN EDUCATION[1]

In recent times the late and esteemed Adlai Stevenson, referred to the crisis of the "revolution of rising expectations." It is this crisis that we in Asia face today. Philippine President Ferdinand E. Marcos began his term of office with a stirring call to his countrymen to rally in the face of a widespread crisis affecting all facets of contemporary society and government in the Republic of the Philippines.

The form and substance of this crisis are not unique to that country. Parallel experience, histories, and cultural urges give the educational problems of Asia a distinct cast and urgency. Crisis feeds upon crisis, dilemma upon dilemma; there is not a single difficulty in the educational enterprise that does not stem from the dynamics of the system or from the imperatives of the larger society. We are also much aware that the triumphs and disasters of human institutions are ultimately to be attributed to the success or failure of education. The educator is in a fatal embrace with every program, every institution in his society. In Asia as in Africa and other underdeveloped regions, this is a dance unto development or death. The death of any man, John Donne said, diminishes everyone. Education is both cause and effect of any

1. This first, and major, section of the chapter was written by Carlos P. Romulo.

244

vibrancy, or stagnancy, evidenced by any other part of society. In the Philippines as in the rest of Asia, education is under extreme pressure to produce miracles. But, paradoxically, these are made difficult to produce by society itself.

Dimensions of Asia's Problems

The crisis of education in Asia has two major aspects: one involves the rest of the world, and one is peculiarly Asian. Both have been a part of Asian cultures since the beginning of this century, but only since the end of the Second World War have they become crucial factors in the mobilization of resources coincidental with grants of independence and the start of forced-draft programs of change and development throughout most of the region.

The first aspect is that major inputs into the educational systems of most Asian nations come from abroad, particularly from those countries that were once their colonial rulers. In itself this could be an advantage, especially if the model institution provided the answers to local problems or to the larger problems of development. In most cases, however, the educational institutions in the West were not designed for conditions in today's societies. In transplanting the forms and substances of Western educational institutions into Asian cultures, colonial regimes planted the seeds of present-day dysfunctions. In most Asian countries these negative effects are long-lasting.

A parallel input results from the other aspect of the crisis: that Asian societies face the universal problems of modernization, urbanization, and industrialization. Thus their educational systems share in a rapidly growing fund of knowledge accumulated by all countries on the road to development.

These two problems identify two major dimensions by which the crisis of Asia can be better understood. One is the set of influences sweeping through most countries of the world, which tend to have a leveling and a universalizing effect on all educational decisions. The other dimension is the forces, more or less indigenous, which constitute an inner dynamic of societies and cultures in Asia and inevitably affect their responses to external influences.

We shall now discuss specific dimensions of the educational crisis which falls under these two general categories. Asia is too complex a region to generalize about easily, so that much of the time we can only make statements about limited areas, but not about the whole. How else can we deal with a region that runs the gamut from highly organized industrial conditions, as in Japan, to nomadic food-gatherers?

The Educational Establishment in Asia

As the largest industry in any country of Asia, the educational enterprise poses problems of size and coverage approached by only one other establishment in Asia—the military. There is no comparison in terms of mission and complexity of tasks. In general, the Asian tendency—unlike that in the United States—to centralize the administration, funding, and supervision of education, lays on the central government a heavy burden, which perhaps could be better shared among local communities. Here of course the dilemma is between strong central direction—with the attendant benefits of uniform standards, articulation with national policy, and planning—and greater local participation and involvement in schools, with presumably better responsiveness of schools to local conditions and a greater sense of responsibility among the citizenry for maintenance and improvement of schools.

The largest industry threatens to run away with an even larger share of the country's public budget. In Asia the share of education hovers around 25 per cent; in the Philippines, where public commitment to education has been one of the highest since the beginning of this century, education claims one-third of the national budget. Continuing expansion as a result of population growth will bring Asia close to the point where an additional share of a country's income will threaten other national programs. At the same time, expansion raises the dilemma of quality versus quantity. Although the time has not yet come, one can foresee the day soon when a country like the Philippines will have to decide whether to continue expanding along familiar lines which perpetuate the heavy concentration in academic subjects and the popularity of certain courses such as law, literature, and medicine, or to initiate a deliberate attempt to deflect its youth into vocational streams and to effect a more discriminate selection at higher levels, in order to mitigate the wastage and the imbalance that are now the rule rather than the exception.

Education and National Goals in Asia

The last point raises a problem that is basic to countries whose nationhood is closely linked with a colonial past: the problem of creating the identity and unity needed for the tasks of concerted action, particularly toward development. The diversity and pluralism of most Asian societies are the bases, not yet for unity, but for divisiveness. Most are suffering from identity crises and uncertainty about their future, which makes it difficult to have any consensus about specific goals and means toward goals. Under these circumstances it is not easy to use education as a tool for the mobilization of resources that development requires.

Parallel to this problem is the lack of articulation of schools with the community and with the culture. One aspect of this problem is that the curricula of primary and secondary schools still reflect those of the colonial regimes. In general, however, many observers say that Asia's educational practices are "bookish, examination-ridden, and completely out of tune with the life and needs of a very large section of the population," or "the curriculum carried over from the past . . . is classical and highly academic in nature. . . ."[2]

2. D. F. E. Panagoda, "Ceylon, A Nation Seeking Unity in Diversity," *Phi Delta Kappan*, 39, no. 3, December 1957, p. 153; C. W. Wood, "Post

There is evidence of a growing relevance gap or meaning gap in the educational systems of Asia, which needs to be corrected by greater efforts at articulating curriculum with national goals and by innovations such as practicums, internships, and, in general, more intense confrontation with realities of factory, field, and shop.

The Language Dilemma in Asia

It is perhaps not an exaggeration to say that in many parts of Asia each school is a veritable Tower of Babel, with teachers and pupils speaking different languages. The language problem, perhaps more than any other, has been responsible for the confusion, the lack of direction, and, at times, the bitter conflict that characterize the school systems of Asia. Part of this problem is, in some Asian countries, the question of what to do with English: should it be taught as a second language? In many Asian countries, primary and secondary students spend an inordinate amount of time, which otherwise could be devoted to science or vocational subjects, trying to become familiar with alien tongues. In the Philippines, as in Malaysia and India, the quest is for a national language, which will be viable for all, to serve as a vehicle for unification. Meanwhile the schools are in quandary. Often the child begins with the vernacular, at the lowest levels—a process that under a different system normally flowers into a full-fledged acquaintance with the idioms and nuances of the language. But in Asia, after a few years, the student is told to abandon formal use of the vernacular and is required to learn a new language,

---

Liberation Problems in Korean Education," *Phi Delta Kappan*, 39, no. 3, December 1957, p. 116. See also other articles in this issue of the *Phi Delta Kappan*, especially Muhammad Shamsul Huq, "Pakistan Education— Plagued with Problems of Quantity and Quality," pp. 126, 127. The League of Nations' report noted much the same thing of pre-Communist China's educational system; cf. C. H. Becker *et al.*, *The Reorganization of Education in China* (Paris: League of Nations, Institute of Intellectual Cooperation, 1932), pp. 21–22.

English, or, in the Philippines, two new languages, Tagalog and English. At the upper reaches of the educational ladder he virtually abandons one and is asked to work in a language that is essentially alien to him, but that is a universal medium—English.

Asian realities must never exclude the overriding influences of, on the one hand, the colonial heritage and, on the other, twentieth-century nationalism and its antiforeign manifestations. The answers each offers to the language problem, in the context of the patent ambivalence of many Asians toward foreign influence in general, serve at the moment only to exacerbate the dilemma.

The Social Dynamic of Asian Education

The language problem ushers us into a source of many imponderables in the educational crisis—the real loci of both input and output of the educational system.

We are impressed by the study of the International Institute for Educational Planning on the interaction between education and the rest of the social system, making the search for solutions also a search for contributory causes. There are some reasons to believe, however, that the circle is not a closed one in Asian societies, and that it can be, and has been, breached at crucial points. Time and again this has been well demonstrated by the initiative, the energy, and the visionary zeal of men who may come from the ranks of followers or even dissenters. Systems analysis postulates some degree of dynamic consensus among forces that are essentially indigenous in origin. But this has not always been the case in Asia.

Where the input is not easily incorporated as a result of the "rubbing together" of differing social systems, education may be regarded as an alien intrusion; and unless it undergoes radical change, as apparently it has in Communist China, it remains dysfunctional in the social system, acting at variance, propelled by its own internal dynamic. In some countries of Asia educational systems have been more or less autonomous, as in the higher institutions of learning in Ceylon and India or the private educational systems in the Philippines. It is partly for this reason that until recently education has tended to be ivory-towerish in most of Asia and to produce graduates who are literally misfits and later to join the swelling ranks of the educated unemployed and unemployable. In effect, the schools are implementing the inputs of another society, and the fact that they have been allowed to do so for so long throws serious doubt on the workings of a system in which the elements are supposed to be mutually dependent.

The symptoms, the manifestations, of this lack of articulation are, for Asia, quite clear. There is, first of all, the childlike regard for education as a panacea for all the ills of society; this attitude finds a parallel in the unquestioning trust in educated persons, particularly those educated in certain professions like law, the priesthood, and medicine, as latterday shamans.

There are the differences in social status that result from the continuing impact—of certain Western values. For instance, possession of an education has merged with the ideal of the privileged status for the scholar-gentry. The result is the rise to dominance of a class of Westernized, white-collar elite, extending rather far down the economic ladder, to whom education has become important for the status it confers, and not because it is useful in serving the needs of the people or of the social system. By the same token, there is the phenomenal concentration in Asia in courses in law and literature, while courses in the sciences and the trades go begging. By contrast there is the situation in Communist China, where enrollment in engineering institutions has increased 300 per cent over a five-year span, while other areas of higher education increased by only twice as much, and in the case of nontechnological subjects, not at all.

In certain areas the schools have been only too successful in their mission. They have succeeded in meeting the demands of people, but not of the social systems; they have created a gap between society's ability to absorb the output of schools and the rate of production by the schools. The result is an "intellectual proletariat" who become prey to all sorts of desperate influences in order to requite unfulfilled aspirations. The "brain drain" is only one of these consequences.

There is reason to believe that in responding to the values of the West, Asian culture is following its own dynamic, selecting those values that reinforce earlier patterns. A derogatory attitude toward manual labor is only a sporadic rather than a universal feature of the rise of technology in the West. But school systems in Asia have succeeded too well in adjusting to Western patterns in this case, by selecting from the range of Western practices attitudes toward work which suit their own tradition. What is perhaps necessary is a more incisive analysis of the problems of confrontation of Eastern and Western cultures. It may even be desirable for Asian educators to adopt an exploitative approach, to see what in the arsenal of educational weaponry they can seize for the needs of their own system. Thus, for example, the avidity for status could be turned to advantage by giving importance to certain types of occupation—not just white collar ones—and alleviating chronic shortages that have resulted from mindless aping and complacency. For instance, all of Asia needs more medical doctors who are trained and motivated to work in the countryside; all of Asia needs middle-level technicians, especially in the fields of health, agriculture, science, and technology.

Mounting Pressures in Asia

It is increasingly obvious to those who are concerned for the future of Asian education, that if present trends continue, most Asian countries face anxious times ahead. The pressures are recurrent, as evidenced by the annual school crisis: the outcries for more schools, more classrooms, more teachers, textbooks, teaching aids, better salaries for teachers. The inventory of Asia's woes is familiar, and their recitation would serve no purpose other than to discourage further the pessimists among us.

These pressures will have to be met head on, not in order to be resisted, but in order to be solved, through unremitting struggle with the budget committees of national parliaments or congresses, through belt-tightening in less essential areas, and through a process that the British with characteristic humor call "muddling through." As the revolution of rising expectations engulfs the hitherto silent and unmoving masses of Asia, as the demographic revolution adds to already swollen populations which constitute more than half of the world's population, the educational leaders of Asia may soon realize that the tiger they now have by the tail is not going to be tame for long.

It is equally clear that should there be no determined effort to come to terms with the many facets of the crisis, the ultimate effects on society may not be pleasant to contemplate. Mr. Hla Myint, has warned about the possible effect of education on modernization: among other things, it may destroy indigenous initiatives for the mobilization of resources and even break down that social discipline that may have kept communities viable and vital. Humayun Kabir sounded much the same warning when he said that education must be reoriented to make sure that society does not "disintegrate."

Toward Solutions

The problems are many, and the shadows are deepening all around us. But if there is one characteristic that must strike every observer of Asian societies, it is resilience, a certain ability to yield to adverse circumstances but afterward to spring back undismayed. In this spirit all educational leaders in Asia believe that their countries can get by in spite of predictions to the contrary. The peoples of this region have enjoyed civilizations that have withstood many storms, and have emerged much the stronger for the experience of getting something new while giving much in return.

To begin, there will have to evolve a way for the national societies of Asia to make decisions by themselves about the directions and shape of national aspirations and the implications they have for the educational enterprise. This will require no less than a working development model of society with the essential pieces all in place, so that, for example, it will be immediately obvious how many people in particular occupations are needed by particular sectors of society. With this model it should be possible for educational planners to make projections that provide useful information not only for the youth knocking on the doors of schools but also for the schools themselves.

One cannot, of course, entertain any illusions about the ease with which any development model can be agreed upon in societies long marked with fragmentation. To get this model adopted at all, tremendous educational effort will be needed. Afterwards there will arise the problem of seeing that the decisions this model made possible filter down to the agencies and the institutions that will make them work. In the main, this type of solution could be accomplished by a better national integration than now exists for most of the countries of Asia. Disparities of perception, as exemplified by Manning Nash in the case of Burmese villagers versus Burma's educational planners, make the task difficult but not unattainable.[3]

The Basic Tasks of Educational Reform

There will be no quarrel with the two goals set forth by Philip Coombs as the "two towering challenges of our time," which are: "the thorough-going adaptation of educational systems to greatly altered social aims and conditions, and the creation of conditions

3. Manning Nash, *The Golden Road to Modernity, Village Life in Contemporary Burma* (New York: John Wiley & Sons, Inc., 1965).

of peace in a world wracked by dangerous tensions."[4] Without
these conditions all of us here can consider ourselves to be the
last historians of the human race.

Running through all discussion about Asian education is the
conflict apparently inherent in the polar extremes of the national
versus the international emphasis on education. However, the
ambivalence of Asian peoples, as well as the history of education
itself in countries we consider advanced, convince us that the
polarity is more apparent than real. Indeed, one may be rash
enough to suggest that the proper road to internationalism in the
modern era, as in past eras, is through national routes. Nowhere
is this better exemplified than in the history of the humanities or
of the social sciences or of law and philosophy. If, and only if,
national systems of education strengthen their relevance to the
local and extend their declarations of independence to their
educational systems, will they eventually find their way toward
a fruitful collaboration with other nations of the world in the
common task of facing up to the challenge of develoment.
Neither a school nor a university relishes the thought of meeting
as an unequal in any forum for international exchange.

The time, then, has come for truly international or regional
conferences to approach the problem of adequate school and
university programs by means of reinforcing the school's or the
university's ability to cope with its immediate environment. In
the case of international exchanges and programs of educational
assistance, this piece of insight can help overcome the narrow
view that any program that does not incorporate the latest fash-
ions in academic practice is somehow backward.

It should, then, be feasible, with local and national programs
well on the way to realizing potentials for full cooperation, to
provide a continuing international exchange of the experiences,

4.   Philip H. Coombs, *The World Educational Crisis—A Systems Analysis*
p. 197, in the International Institute for Educational Planning document.
The quotation has been rephrased in the Oxford University Press volume,
p. 161.

problems, and solutions of all educational systems. We in Asia have just begun to feel the need for regional cooperation in order to integrate our disparate national educational programs. We now have the Association of Southeast Asian Institutions of Higher Learning (ASAIHL). Ministers of many Asian countries have held conferences to discuss similar possibilities for all levels of the academic enterprise, and we have organized the Southeast Asian Ministers of Education Council (SEAMEC). There are at this moment a number of schemes—some on a bilateral basis, others making use of growing numbers of cultural, economic, and political groupings among Asian countries—which envision academic exchange over the next few years. A novel idea, the formation of a federal University of Southeast Asia, is proposed. All these are in line with the suggestion of Philip Coombs that assistance be extended to "develop research capabilities in developing regions—sometimes on a regional basis . . ." and that "the dialogue among universities within developing regions, and between them and universities in industrialized countries, should be strengthened so that knowledge, experience and ideas for educational improvement may circulate more fully and swiftly throughout the world. . . ."[5]

To help these ideas along, it will be necessary to establish formal—or informal—machinery, either separately or as part of an existing world body, to facilitate the exchanges across national boundaries. To this end, an international commission of education should be established as a clearing house and agency to proffer assistance in the form of survey teams, for example, wherever such aid is needed and solicited.

There is a deep sense of crisis, but there is also a profound certainty that educators in Asia—or, for that matter, educators everywhere—face nothing that cannot be transcended by human spirit, spurred by a mission in which we dare not fail for the safety and future happiness of the generations that follow us.

5. *Ibid.*, p. 160.

ASIA THROUGH THE PERSPECTIVE OF INDIA[6]

This is the age when Louis Cros and the editors of the *World Year Book of Education*[7] have popularized the concept of educational explosion. First, there is the explosion in numbers—increase in population, increase of enrollments, increase of targets—and these increases are like a flood no one can stop. This explosion of numbers is an accepted fact in most Asian countries. Asia has to live with it and to solve the problems caused by it.

Secondly, there is an explosion of expectations on the part of the common man. For the first time in the entire history of Asia, there has come into being a faith in education. This is something truly revolutionary. In Indian villages the image of the god or another deity is being replaced by a book kept on the mantelpiece, dusted every morning, and looked upon with reverence. A book is truly a precious treasure in the villages of India, because it symbolizes the explosion of expectations. The villager sees in education the means of solving all his problems, of escaping the wretchedness of poverty, of catching up with the change that is around him. Asians have accepted the Western concept of education as investment, but with some reservations. They have heard a great deal about the connection of education to economic productivity and have taken up the slogan. They justify, or try to, the increase in the national budget on that basis. But, in fact, most Asian countries believe not only in education as investment, not only in economic development, but in social transformation: not only in increasing material productivity, but also in bringing about a change in society that will increase public welfare.

Thirdly, we have around us an explosion of time. Time has come to matter in a world that until recently was not very con-

6. This section was written by Prem N. Kirpal.
7. Louis Cros, *L'explosion scolaire* (Paris: Comité universitaire d'information pédagogique, 1961); and George Z. F. Bereday and J. A. Lauwerys, eds., *The Education Explosion: The World Year Book of Education 1965* (New York: Harcourt, Brace & World, 1965).

scious of the movement of time. Asia is now exhorted to hasten to catch up with the advanced countries of the world and to make changes that other parts of the world took much longer to accomplish. This explosion of time means that Asian nations have to work in a hurry.

To deal with these three explosions, the objectives of education are being formulated in Asia in two ways. One is the objective of education and work. Education has to contribute to national development, and it has to help in creating work. It must train people for all kinds of jobs and generate work that will contribute to national development. This raises questions of the kind of general education needed, of its relation to specialized on-the-job training, of vocationalization, of the place of informal education. Most Asian countries are beginning to realize that the key to the achievement of harmonizing "work-oriented" education is to provide opportunities for on-the-job vocational education and to develop simultaneous formal education opportunities that assure literacy training. The connection between work and education is one of the great preoccupations of educational planners in Asia.

Secondly, Asians are conscious of the social objectives of education: social integration, the breakup of the old hierarchical structure, more equality, and the fusing of people and regions into nations. Asians expect education to achieve these new objectives. Here the Asian nations have special problems, because almost all of them have inherited traditional values, which are treasured and considered by many people to be of great merit. Thus, Asian educators have to be conscious of the crisis in culture: they must devise means for preserving or adapting traditional values to the process of modernization. Not only new values, but also new vision is sought as a result of good education. The crisis of education in the world is due mostly to the lack of vision in society and of the search for a new future, a new synthesis, a new transcendence on the part of the individual.

Four major problems are the main causes of Asia's crisis. First is the lack of resources, the tremendous financial poverty. Matching finance with needs is truly a depressing task. Secondly, there is a lack of trained manpower: of teachers, educational administrators, and other professionals needed to improve the quality of education. There is thirdly the problem of quality, which suffers from the explosion of numbers resulting from population and enrollment increases. Asian planners are very conscious of it as they confront the difficult choice between expansion of opportunities and improvement in quality. The fourth problem is caused by the pursuit of modernization. Asians have to build science and technological education to create specialists, especially the middle-level workers, the technicians. The problem of modernization, of converting knowledge into action, is not easily solved when dealing with old, resilient customs and traditions.

These are the elements of the Asian crisis, and its tremendous difficulties are offset only by hope. There is the tremendous resolve of the countries and their peoples to forge ahead and to put great faith in education. These national resolves have expressed themselves through hard work, through dedication, and through the fullest exploitation of the human capital. Secondly, Asians see hope in international cooperation. Increasingly, educators are meeting to reflect on international education problems. In India, for instance, it was decided to form a national commission to survey the whole field of education; this decision was followed by invitations to a number of educators from other parts of the world to participate as full members. The United Nations Educational, Scientific, and Cultural Organization supplied the specialists on that occasion, thus providing a further example of international cooperation in the planning of education. Cooperation, in the true sense of the word, is people working together and not merely some giving money to others in a relation of recipients and donors. The third saving grace for the future comes from the application of the scientific and technological revolution of our times. The new techniques of communication promise to add a great deal to the educational process in the Asian countries. Perhaps they are capable of reconciling the simultaneous need to improve quality and increase quantity in education.

Asians realize that the crisis of education must be solved by better planning and more research in the schools. They are becoming more and more conscious of the new potentialities of education, but their hopes are pitted against the constant threat of insufficiency. Spirit contends against matter. If Asia's ancient philosophers are any guide, there is no question which will prevail.

EDUCATIONAL CRISIS IN INDIA, ITS DIAGNOSIS AND REMEDIES[8]

India is a vast country with a population of about 512,000,000. At the present time there are 21,000,000 births and only 8,000,000 deaths every year. It is therefore estimated that in another twenty years the population will be nearly 750,000,000, and at the end of the century it may be 1,000,000,000. With this growing population, food and industrial production have increased by 62 per cent and 150 per cent, respectively; yet the national per capita income is only 350 rupees per month; ($1 equals 7½ rupees) the lower 30 per cent have a monthly income of less than 15 rupees, and the lowest 10 per cent have one of less than 10 rupees. The population explosion with such a pathetic per capita income can easily explain the educational crisis.

This crisis is both quantitative and qualitative. There is great wastage in educational efforts. A large number of the students who enter the first primary class do not reach the fifth standard (although eight out of every ten children between the ages of six and eleven now go to school), and only thirty-three out of the one-hundred reach the fifth class after being admitted to the first primary. A large number of students fail in higher and higher secondary schools each year. In 1961, for instance, out of 1,000,000 students, 550,000 failed, leaving a pass percentage of only about 49. In one state (Punjab) the 1964 secondary schools

8. This section was written by Uday Shankar.

pass percentage was as low as 33. The situation among candidates for the bachelor of arts, bachelor of science, and bachelor of commerce degrees was no better: the failures also ranged from 50 to 54 per cent; and out of those who pass, 70 per cent were low achievers. Such large failures are mostly due to the fact that a large number of the students—as many as one-third of those in college—have no aim, and 55 per cent of the so-called educated are dissatisfied with their jobs.

Only 29 per cent of the population are literate; this figure is expected to rise to 34.2 per cent by 1971. The number of illiterates between the ages of fifteen and forty-five was 150,000,000 in 1961–1962 and will go up to 158,000,000 by 1971. Literacy has not kept pace with the increase in population. From 1951 to 1961 the percentage of literacy increased from 17 to 24 per cent, but the population increased from 357,000,000 to 439,000,000. The literacy rate among females and in the rural areas is still more depressing. In 1961 the over-all literacy rate was 24 per cent; but for males it was 34.4 per cent, while for females it was only 12.9 per cent. In urban areas the rate of literacy was 41 per cent, as opposed to 19 per cent in rural areas. Among the so-called literates, the number of those well educated was very low: 92 per cent had only middle school qualifications.

Although 46 per cent of the population are of school-going age, about 70,000,000 students are in schools—a figure that will be double by 1985 and may be nearly 170,000,000 by the end of the century. There are more than 2,000,000 teachers, but not many are qualified. In lower primary schools 51 per cent of the teachers are trained, and in the higher primary schools 60 per cent are trained. In secondary schools, too, the percentage of trained teachers is only 60 per cent. Although the figures differ from state to state—ranging from 18 per cent in Assam to about 92 per cent in Madras—there is unquestioningly a large backlog of untrained teachers.

For educational development, the status and economic condition of the teachers has to be commensurate with their social position and has to be almost the same as other employees. But

the salaries of the teachers at all levels in India are pathetically
low as can be seen from the figures below:

TABLE 10.   AVERAGE ANNUAL SALARIES OF TEACHERS IN
INDIA

		1965–1966
1.	University Department	$6,500
2.	College of Arts and Science	4,000
3.	Professional Colleges	6,410
4.	Secondary Schools	1,959
5.	Middle Schools	1,278
6.	Primary Schools	1,046
7.	Preprimary Schools	1,083
8.	Vocational Schools	2,887
	All Teachers	1,476

Cost-of-living index of working class   165
National income per capita
  (at current prices, 1966–1967)   424

Although the recently established education commission has
suggested higher salary scales for teachers of all categories, it
only hoped that various state governments and universities would
find the means to implement its suggestions. The economic structure of the country cannot affect positively the economic status
of teachers who, feeling dissatisfied, do not do their jobs as well
as possible. This creates a vicious circle which has been playing
havoc with the educational standards in the country.

About 10,000,000 literate people in India are still out of jobs,
and the percentage of highly educated men in most callings is
extremely low. For instance, the total number of workers employed in India in 1961 can be divided according to their level
of education as follows:

Below Matriculation	183,551,000
Matriculated	3,262,000
Intermediate	756,000
Degree-Holder	1,147,000
Total	188,716,000

The percentage of graduates in fields such as agriculture, mining, manufacturing, construction, trade and commerce, transportation, communications, and services of all types ranged from 0.10 per cent to 3.9 per cent; the intermediate ranged from 0.10 per cent to 2.70 per cent; and matriculates ranged from 0.33 per cent to 10.5 per cent. The state of the various professions manned by such low percentages of educated personnel can be easily imagined. It is no wonder that production in various fields is inadequate to meet the requirements of the increasing population.

This population explosion coupled with the lack of production has caused prices to rise, so that it is almost impossible for people of ordinary means to make ends meet. In such a situation, when means are limited, neither is educational expansion possible nor are high standards practicable.

Apart from this, there is a demand for white collar jobs in India. The educated think first of finding employment in an office. This situation has led to a rush to schools and colleges, where students are admitted indiscriminately. As a result, a large number of students entering schools and colleges do not have much aptitude for academic work.

Another factor that causes low educational standards and adds to the number of the educated unemployed is the indiscriminate founding of schools with no regard for whether there will be jobs available for the graduates. For instance, it is estimated that about 8,000 graduate engineers are unemployed. To remedy the situation, there should be strict population control. In the second place, production, both agricultural and industrial, must increase to improve the economy of each country. In the third place, the expansion of educational institutions must be planned, with more stress on quality rather than on quantity. For the present, enrollment in schools should not be stressed, since it is useless to send children to school when a large number of them drop out. Fourth, admission to educational institutions should be restricted and should be based on proper selection so that only those with the capacity and aptitude receive higher education. In the fifth place, the system of education—at present bookish, rigid, and not oriented to local needs—should be made more flexible. Rural and agricultural areas should have schools stressing the vocational requirements of the area and not the ordinary schools of the towns and cities. In the last analysis, educational facilities should be provided with a view toward manpower requirements for the various jobs, and students should not be allowed to follow courses of study without having any idea whether they will later find employment. The crisis in education is both quantitative and qualitative.

LATIN AMERICA

GABRIEL BETANCUR-MEJIA

The history of education in Latin America is marked by milestones. One of these, ten years ago, was the second meeting of ministers of education and the regional conference of the United Nations Educational, Scientific, and Cultural Organization, both of which were held in Lima in 1956. These were important gatherings because they showed a new attitude on the part of national and international authorities and established, for the first time, targets for educational effort.

At the ministers' meeting, set up by the Organization of American States, the ideas of incorporating the over-all method in educational planning and of associating educational programming with the process of economic and social development were proposed. At the UNESCO meeting the major project for the extension and improvement of primary education in Latin America was formulated.

These innovations pointed out one of the most significant aspects of the existing critical situation: the necessity of strengthening leadership in education. People of high quality were needed: people able to present solutions to the problems created by the mass demand for education and able to integrate these demands with the development process. At that time there were practically no specialists in educational planning, although economic planning was already fully developed.

The results of the past ten years, although not fully satisfactory, justify some optimism about the future. With only one exception, all Latin America has incorporated planning into its departments and ministries of education, making possible a systematic analysis of major educational problems and of the causes of the educational crisis. The new awareness has served to rationalize the goals of the educational administration and to bring clarity to the formulation of educational targets and of methods to achieve them. In a few cases there have been abuses, and governments have sought to give a false picture of the development of education by means of a copious display of statistics.

The UNESCO major project has been a basic element in the quantitative extension of primary education in Latin America and in the training and improvement of teachers. An excellent evaluation of its results is available.

In 1961 the Punta del Este Charter was adopted: in it Latin America formally expressed its decision to effect structural changes in order to accelerate its development and raise the standard of living of its population. As part of establishing economic and social targets for the over-all development of Latin America, the conference approved ambitious targets for all levels of instruction, acknowledging also the economic productivity of education. As a consequence, the Science and Culture Committee of the Organization of American States made, for the first time, a comprehensive study of the outlook for educational development in Latin America.

Finally, in 1962 in Santiago, Chile, the Conference on Education and Economic and Social Development was held with the objective of achieving optimum utilization of manpower.

STATISTICAL REVIEW OF THE PAST DECADE

The efforts of the last ten years have been quite large and the results satisfactory in absolute terms; they are still insufficient, however, compared with the growth of the population.

A rapid increase of population has taken place in the area in recent years. During the years 1958 to 1964 the average annual rate of population growth was 2.7 per cent. In that same period while basic educational facilities were at a low point, the population growth increased the potential enrollment in primary education. For that reason all the efforts put forth have not yet resulted in adequate educational training. For example, from 1956 to 1965 the enrollment at all levels of schooling increased by 15,000,000— a 60 per cent increase compared with a population increase of 28 per cent during that same period. However, there was no great rise in the upper educational levels of the population, because of the characteristics of the demographic pyramid of Latin America. The educational effort was centered on a predominantly young population, the majority of which was in the early years of primary school. While elementary schools showed an average annual increase of 50 per 1,000 from 1956 to 1966, the increase in secondary schooling was barely 1 per 1,000 in annual average; and at the university level, according to unpublished data supplied by the OAS Division of Educational Statistics, the increase was only 1 student per 10,000 population each year. These increases are much lower than the increased manpower requirements of the working force. The lack of balance with the relatively rapid increase of enrollments indicates that there is still a critically insufficient quantity of education, especially at high school and university levels, to meet social demands and economic necessities.

Great progress has been made in the fight against illiteracy, although, according to census data for the years 1950 to 1960, the actual number of illiterates increased by 2,353,152. The case of Colombia is illustrative in this connection: there illiteracy was reduced from 37.2 per cent to 27 per cent in the period between the censuses of 1951 and 1964. It is probable that since 1960, with the intensification of the fight against illiteracy, there has been further improvement. Moreover, the expansion of primary education, which continues to advance, will help to close the door to illiteracy. Valid experiments have been conducted that demonstrate the possibility of totally eliminating illiteracy in the school-age part of the population.

Approximately 60,000,000 persons over fifteen years of age have never received any systematic schooling. Of the active population, they have the least occupational skill and the lowest capacity for social integration. They are also poor consumers, and they reduce the size of a market much in need of expansion. Slight developments in adult education have not made it possible to fill that deficiency.

Completion-of-schooling rates have improved in the last ten years. Nevertheless, the level attained is still so low that only one-fourth of the pupils of compulsory school age complete primary schooling. It is probable that with stricter educational standards that number would be still further reduced.

As a matter of fact, according to available figures, the percentage of those who completed primary schooling for the area rose from 25.1 for the 1957–1962 cohort to 26.5 for the 1960–1965 cohort. As is true of all general figures for Latin America, there is a wide range of variation, and the average value conceals great divergences among countries and even among regions of the same country. In 1954–1958 in Colombia, for example, a primary school completion rate of 32.4 per cent was recorded in the cities and one of only 0.5 per cent in the rural areas. Secondary school completion rates for the last ten years fluctuated between 15 and 40 per cent according to country.

Data concerning completion of courses at university level is incomplete, but isolated information from some countries suggests that the completion rate is the highest at this level. The highly selective character of the students at that level in Latin America undoubtedly has its influence.

Another problem, which is both pedagogical and economic is repetition of courses. It is difficult to establish averages, but it can nevertheless be said that the rate is as much as 20 per cent in the countries with the lowest average repeater rate in the primary schools. This means that for at least one-fifth of the elementary school students a one-year course is being financed twice. To that must be added all the educational consequences.

According to data supplied by United Nations Educational and Social Council for the conference of ministers of education and ministers responsible for economic planning held at Buenos Aires in 1966, the number of primary teachers increased considerably from 1957 to 1965, rising from about 630,000 to nearly 1,000,000. This increase is only about 100,000 short of the target proposed at Lima in 1956.

The percentage of teachers holding university degrees also increased decidedly, from 47 per cent of the total in 1957 to 63 per cent in 1966. It is important to point out, however, that in many countries a substantial number of graduate teachers are engaged in activities other than education, because they are more lucrative. On the other hand, a large number of those who have graduated are still at unsatisfactory levels of teacher training.

The public expenditure for education, in proportion to the gross national product, has practically doubled. The actual increase was from 1.40 per cent in 1960 to 2.50 per cent in 1965—still below the 4 per cent laid down as a norm at the Santiago conference in 1962. As is the case with other indicators, the differences among countries are great. Moreover, ratios between the increase in school enrollment and the growth of the gross national product are not always sufficiently illuminating. Much depends on the level at which each country started and to which it gave priority.

QUALITATIVE ASPECTS

As regards structural changes, proper attention is not given to the organization of plans and study programs. The ways of selecting course contents, the margins for choice, and the determination of the sequences of courses have so far received as little attention as the formulation of objectives and of guidelines for evaluation. Equally little attention has been given to the methodology of teaching and to other professional problems such as apprenticeship instruction and the sociological, psychological, organizational, and planning aspects.

Pedagogical research, if there is any, is certainly in an incipient stage. Opportunities to study the varied research procedures are lacking. There are even fewer possibilities of installing the schemes already planned by educational centers and institutions for scientific and technological research.

There is no doubt that a great deal of action could result from research. Proof of this is to be found in a few studies on definite problems such as dropout, functional illiteracy, and completion of schooling, and other studies that have been carried out in different countries. Even when these studies were of limited scope, they provided easy guidance to immediate improvements, even with the human and financial resources already available.

The efforts that have been made to exploit the advantages of technology have been inadequate. Whether from lack of adequate resources or from lack of properly interested and qualified personnel, the use that has been made of technology is hardly worth mentioning.

Furthermore, supervision of the various aspects of each country's own system has not proved efficient enough. This inefficiency may be the real cause of the many negative aspects linked with high rates of repeating, dropouts, and inadequate utilization of classrooms.

In the final analysis, modern instruction in the sciences and technologies, with corresponding research, is confined exclusively to a few highly developed centers which can by no means expect to cover the general requirements of the population.

PRESENT SITUATION

The current situation is decidedly better than that of ten years ago, because educational levels were at a very low point when the population began its recent rapid growth. However, a few figures and statistical conclusions stand out and serve to alert us to the still critical situation.

An examination of the figures on the rural population and agricultural training confirms the fact that in general, with the possible exception of Uruguay and Venezuela, the amount of agricultural instruction is seriously insufficient to the requirements of the rural population. It is true that there is a persistent trend in Latin American societies toward urbanization and industrialization. Nevertheless, they have an ever greater need for an increase in agricultural productivity and livestock raising for food. The process of change through agrarian reforms and improved technological working methods is of basic importance. Both processes require education, one for social integration and the other for production.

In the countries with the greatest number of students in secondary-level agricultural training, there are no more than 10 students per 10,000 inhabitants; and for most of the countries it is less than 3 students per 10,000. Even though 46 per cent of the economically active population of Latin America is engaged in agriculture, stock raising, or fishing, a very small number of pupils are being trained for these activities.

The availability of a school is only one of the factors involved in a child's attendance at school. Another factor is perhaps more important than the existence of school facilities: that is, the opportunity to take advantage of the services rendered. In Latin America the possibility of attending and completing school is determined by economic inequalities; by geographic factors such as distance from the school, climate, rough terrain; by productive activities peculiar to the locality; and by educational factors, such as inadequately differentiated and poorly localized instruction. These factors have greater repercussions in rural areas and affect the girls more than the boys. Thus, increased school attendance depends to a great extent on a general change in the social structure, which is slow in coming about.

The limitations due to the poor training of teachers are serious. Only two-thirds of all the teachers have degrees, even admitting insufficient levels. A large majority of the nongraduates teach in the poorer rural areas. It is estimated that only 30 per cent of Latin American teachers at the high school level have special preparation to teach. This problem is of particular significance because most Latin American leaders and public officials are products of that stage of schooling. It will be difficult to improve the social process in a system whose leaders are mostly educated by inadequately trained teachers and, in many cases, by hearsay and anecdote.

The low teachers' salaries in Latin America and the absence of other incentives account for these deficiencies. The demand for education exceeds public pressure for educational progress. While the community constantly calls for a better system of education and better teachers, it still directs its best students toward other pursuits which provide greater remuneration and social prestige and faster upward mobility.

Although education has become a large social and economic enterprise in Latin America, it is not administered with the most modern techniques available. The administration prunes flexibility and spirit from an effort that is constantly acquiring greater vocational obligations. Almost religiously, and paradoxically, it is forcing the teacher to transform himself into a petty civil servant.

The document prepared by the Economic Commission on Latin America for the conference of ministers of education and ministers responsible for economic planning in Latin America and the Caribbean, held at Buenos Aires in 1966, stated that as of 1965 probably less than 1 per cent of Latin America's active population fall into the category of "professionals"—even if this term is understood loosely. Those classified as "technical" do not amount to 3 per cent; more than two-thirds are primary teachers and accountants; of a total of some 54,000,000 workmen and artisans, fewer than 10 per cent can be considered skilled, and 35,000,000 have no qualifications at all. Among agricultural workers, scarcely 0.1 per cent are in professional or technical posts, while nearly 80 per cent are unskilled laborers.

If it were possible to analyze the correspondence between vocational training and actual occupation, the results would show obvious distortions, such as the fact that most education is received by the least dynamic sector. Unfortunately no accurate general data are available. The educational distribution of human resources as described may indicate the circular process of Latin American social development. A low educational level does not provide the human resources required for economic development, and slow economic growth limits, in turn, the material resources that can be appropriated for education. As one Latin American statesman has said, "We are poor because we are poor."

It is true that evident progress has been made through the new vocational training services—such as Servico Nacional de Aprendizagem Industrial (SENA) in Brazil, Servicio Nacional de Aprendizaje (SENA) in Colombia, and Instituto Nacional de Aprendizaje (INA) in Costa Rica. But on the whole education is not training the type of human being capable of breaking the vicious circle. Alas, the Latin American countries do not have all the time they would like to have to solve their problems.

THE CRISIS AND THE FUTURE

Educational development in Latin America in recent years shows a great effort, especially a quantitative effort, but one that has not succeeded in overcoming the disparity between social aspirations for education and the results obtained by the educational systems.

The social structure and the economic institutions, for their part, have continued a development that, although of irregular rhythm, has been sufficiently rapid to establish the educational demand for human resources. But it is difficult to fulfill this demand in sufficient quantity and with adequate quality. This situation has been largely due to the unrelated way in which the two sectors have evolved. The lack of coordination is especially obvious in the failure to agree on targets and to share information on the results of experiments.

The different rhythms of development of social and economic institutions and their failure to communicate with each other are also responsible for the fact that the small amount of education offered has not been the most appropriate, at least in attitude and content, to promote an accelerated and well-balanced progress for the countries of Latin America. In many of the countries that have achieved most rapid growth, that very growth has brought about wastage, accentuating further inequalities and injustices. This incompetence of Latin American education is immediately visible in the majority of the population and expresses itself in illiteracy, low levels of schooling, and structural defects in some sectors of authority.

In recent years the educational services have followed, in general, the traditional rules regarding educational organization, administration, and content and the function of the curriculum. This is to say that the crisis reveals the great gap between the extent of the problems and the capacity to deal with them on the part of those who are directing the system. In fact, Latin America has tried to meet the increased demand for education almost entirely by traditional media—a classroom and a teacher.

It has been estimated that by the year 1980 the population of Latin America will be 350,000,000 million—which will exceed by 80,000,000 the population forecast for all of North America. In comparing the gross birth rate of the area with those of other parts of the world, we find that the rate is 45 per 1,000 inhabitants compared with a rate of 15 and 20, respectively, for Europe and the United States. Owing to the decline in the death rate, the actual rate of population growth of Latin America is more than double the world average and more than three times the European average.

Aside from the constitution of the population pyramid of countries in the course of development, a series of social and cultural factors produce an unbalanced circular relation between economic development and population growth. The critical state of the educational system can be considered one of the components of that circular relation.

The Pan-American Federation of Colleges of Medicine has empirically proved, for example, that illiteracy aids high fertility because it encourages early and fertile marriages and little responsibility or ambition concerning the future of the offspring. In its turn, the increase of the population requires a quantitative and qualitative increase of educational services.

In economic and educational terms, the annual increase of young males between the ages of five and fourteen is 10 per 1,000 of economically active persons. In other words, every 1,000 workers must sustain the enlargement of educational facilities and the construction of new facilities in order to provide room for ten more pupils each year. These figures are eloquent in themselves, but they take on greater significance compared with England, for example, which has a much lower birth rate and where the number of new school pupils per thousand workers is only one a year, or exactly ten times lower than the Latin American rate.

Thus, the high birth rate brings pressure to bear on the governments to increase the actual school facilities of the country at all levels. This is a partial cause of the disequilibrium between the quantitative and the qualitative development of the educational system.

The Economic Commission on Latin America prepared a study for the Regional Seminar on Investments in Latin America, held in December 1966 at Santiago, Chile, in which it was determined that university facilities would have to show a 70 per cent expansion by 1980; a 35 per cent expansion would be needed in secondary education; more than triple in the current facilities for technical instruction; and double in primary education. Considering the population growth already referred to up to 1980, the total number of pupils and students who will attend the educational institutions will amount to nearly 81,000,000 compared with slightly less than 40,000,000 in 1965.

The answer to these requirements may be found in realistic policies implemented through highly operative educational development plans and zealously worked out budgets of capital investment and expenditure. The economists were alarmed by the size of the future expenditure for education. In the same document put out by the Economic Commission, there were warnings— which should not be disregarded—that it was doubtful whether sufficient funds could be assigned to cover the quantitative expansion of the educational services unless there were a great spontaneous effort to improve the output of the educational systems.

Each country, region, or group of countries must accurately determine, from the standpoint of both content and purpose, the volume and the form of general education that it should provide for its population. This volume should be expressed as an educational "ration," measurable in time and specified in quality norms. The period of time devoted to each level could be different for different countries, because of definite needs, economic possibilities, or special methodologies which a particular country might be in a position to utilize.

Education should be adjusted to the requirements of economic and social development in due proportion to the quantity and the quality of human resources, with special emphasis on new social usages and attitudes. For example, planners should take fully into account the significance of such developments as agrarian reform, city planning, industrialization, and changes in productive effort, which are part of the real situation in all countries.

No study has been made of the capacity of society to absorb education but Latin Americans believe that individuals are able to absorb more general education than technical or highly specialized education; and that would seem to be a more purposeful or functional education for our societies.

It is necessary to undertake with full consciousness the training of leaders by special education designed to promote the process of change. This implies that especially intense treatment should be given to secondary and higher education.

All these problems have created much concern about the educational future of Latin America. It remains to summarize, then, as guidelines for thought, questions through which adequate solutions may be sought:

1. Can Latin America guarantee a good primary education to its coming generations in spite of its rapid population growth?

2. What measures should be taken so that the educational output really corresponds to the requirements of social progress?

3. What quantitative measures will enable more and better education to be provided with the same amount of resources?

4. What measures could be taken to enable the administrative structures responsible for the educational system to ensure the maximum output?

5. From the standpoint of quality, what must be done in regard to teachers, curricula, methods, and the like?

6. How shall special ethnic, cultural, and economic characteristics be studied with a view to the development of the appropriate educational programs and methods leading to the achievement of greater productivity?

7. Could mass education methods supplement or replace systematic education at a lesser cost, and could they accomplish at least equal results?

1.   Further sources of interest are:

Rudolph P. Atcon, *The Latin American University* (Bogota: ECO Revista de la Cultura de Occidente, 1966).

Charles Christian Hauch, *The Current Situation in Latin American Education* (Washington, D.C.: U.S. Gov't. Printing Office, 1963).

Robert James Havighurst and Joao Roberto Moreira, *Society and Education in Brazil* (Pittsburgh: University of Pittsburgh Press, 1965).

Seymour Martin Lipset and Aldo Solari, *Elites in Latin America* (New York: Oxford University Press, 1967).

Martin H. Sable, *A Guide to Latin American Studies*, 2 Vols. (Los Angeles: University of California, 1967).

"Topical Review of Research on Education in Latin America," *Latin American Research Review*, Vol. III, Number 1 (Fall 1967), whole issue.

EUROPE—IN SEARCH OF NEW FORMS
OF EDUCATION

PHILIP J. IDENBURG

Europe is a continent of diversity. An attempt to give a picture of the dynamic development of education in this continent consequently runs the danger of losing itself in a confused mass of data. We have therefore chosen a central theme to elucidate a number of other essential aspects: the transformation in the position of and the function of work and the worker. A shift is taking place in the groups of activities of the working population: less agriculture, more industry, and, above all, more people in services. We are on our way to the "service society." The national figures show characteristics of this trend (see Table 11).

With the changes in production and consumption, the requirements for knowledge and intelligence become more stringent. In the agricultural sector in the Netherlands, for instance, there are no more than 12 white collar workers, only a few of whom are university graduates, per 1,000 agriculturists. In industry there are 190 white collar workers, 5 of whom are university graduates, per 1,000 employed persons. In the service sector, however, the number of white collar workers is considerably higher. In economic services, such as commerce, transport, banking, and insurance, the figure is 450 per 1,000 workers, 7 of whom are university graduates. In the fast-growing noneconomic services, such as the civil service, education, and the free professions, the number of white collar workers is 610 per 1,000 workers, 65 of whom are graduates.[1] The change in the composition of the working population stimulates the need for intellectual training.

TABLE 11.   WORKING POPULATION ACCORDING TO
BRANCHES OF ACTIVITY[2]

Countries	Years	Agriculture*	Industry†	Services‡
Belgium	1955	9	46	46
	1962	8	48	45
England and Wales	1956	5	51	45
	1960	4	49	47
France	1954	27	37	37
	1962	21	39	41
German Federal Republic	1955	19	47	35
	1962	13	48	39
Italy	1955	37	34	29
	1962	28	41	32
Netherlands	1955	12	40	48
	1960	11	42	47
U.S.S.R.	1955	43	31	26
	1959	39	35	28

* Including forestry and fishing.
† Including mining and construction.
‡ Including transport and communication.

Around 1900 in industry in the Netherlands there were about 15 staff employees per 100 workers, and in 1960 there were 57, nearly four times as many. A striking reduction is taking place in the percentage of workers and an increase in that of staff employees.

From worker to staff employee is mentally and socially a big

1.   Philip J. Idenburg, *Schets van het Nederlandse Schoolwezen* (2nd impression; Groningen: Wolters, 1964), p. 235.
2.   From R. Poignant, *L'Enseignement dans les Pays du Marché Commun* (Paris: Institut Pédagogique National, 1965), p. 34. Figures are rounded off.

step. Collective social efforts no longer count so much in the new way of life; personal happiness and the well-being of one's own family are in the forefront. Social status becomes important, and climbing the social ladder is something to aim at. New consumption habits come into being. Leisure time activities change.

At the lowest level, mechanization and automation are rendering a number of unskilled persons superfluous. Large groups of workers who did simple work are being replaced by better-qualified ones operating ingenious machines. Their work is sometimes supervision; sometimes they are performing a few specialized actions; but almost always their task makes an appeal to their sense of responsibility, since the machine is extremely expensive and its working affects the smooth running of the entire organization. What was traditionally a moral requirement—attention, the unceasing devotion to duty—now follows from the factual relation of the things themselves. It should be remarked that while the jeremiads about our modern society repeatedly invoke the specter of mass man, in the factory where he has existed, mass man seems to be increasingly on the retreat. For it is precisely where many perform uniform work that the greatest possibilities for switching to mechanization and automation lie.

Less uniformity seems to be the result of modern technical development. The variety in functions gives the worker, as it were, his face back and thus brings him closer to the staff employee.

Besides the structural changes, the prosperity of the working population has increased considerably in recent decades. The whole process has moved the rungs on the social ladder closer together. The social barrier that separated workers and non-workers in Western Europe has not been removed, but it is being bridged by numerous factors.

All of these facts are reflected in the reorganization of education. The starting point of this development was the same in all the countries of Europe: the school system of the traditional community, built up in accordance with class distinctions. In

the Middle Ages there were schools to prepare young people
for more advanced studies, but there was no such thing as popular education. Education for the masses is, among other things,
the fruit of the Reformation and of the Enlightenment. Formerly,
distinction was everywhere apparent between the education of
the elite and that of the people. This situation continued when
senior classes were added to the ordinary primary school in
England, and when the *Volksschuloberstufe* was added in Germany and the *cours complémentaire* in France, all three of which
extended education for the masses to eight years.

Class distinctions likewise manifested themselves when forms
of training between advanced and primary education proved
necessary for the middle groups. Besides long, general, continued
education, a shortened form came into being, not as the initial
phase of the long education but as a separate stream in schools
with a second-rate position.

A third time, too, the contrast between the classes manifested
itself: in the way in which vocational training was introduced
in the various countries. In this process there was an obvious
contrast between two cultures—the technical and the humanistic:
the first was characterized by the acquisition of manual skills,
and the other, by the acquisition of wide general education.

The period after the Second World War was typified by a real
educational explosion and by energetic efforts to democratize
education and to remove the barriers in the way of a homo-
geneous school system. The demographic factor made a major
contribution to the educational explosion. For our subject, however, the extension of the period of actual schooling is decisive;
it was here that the socio-economic revolution previously mentioned particularly manifested itself.

Comparative figures make clear the growth of the school population as a result of this greater participation. The percentage
of a given age group of the population receiving full-time day
education has been chosen as an indicator, thus eliminating the
demographic dimension. The figures show only the degree of

educational provision. Data of this kind are among the few that are internationally comparable. Table 12 shows school attendance of boys and girls of fourteen or fifteen and of seventeen years of age for the years around 1950 and around 1960. It should also be noted that technical education in the German Federal Republic, given primarily by means of an apprentice system with supplementary *part-time* scholastic education, has not been counted.

In the years since 1960 the intensity of education has increased further. So tempestuous a growth of educational provisions gives rise to serious difficulties. The problems of training the necessary teachers and erecting the necessary buildings, both resulting

TABLE 12. PERCENTAGE OF FULL-TIME STUDENTS PER AGE GROUP AND YEAR[3]

Countries	Age	First period (around 1950)	Second period (around 1960)	Growth %
Belgium	14	64	81	27
	17	26	39	51
England and Wales	15	30	42	41
	17	7	12	82
France	14	50	68	36
	17	14	30	117
German Federal Republic	15	35	44	27
	17	13	16	30
Italy	14	31	63	101
	17	9	24	160
Netherlands	14	70	83	18
	17	21	34	58

from the effect of the postwar birth "bulge," have been particularly severe and still are at the higher levels of the educational system. A number of aspects of the educational explosion have

3. *Ibid.*, p. 28. See Poignant for the specific years.

made themselves felt as a result of the socio-economic changes in the school system. The resulting impact has affected the administrative structure, the administrative functioning, the pedagogic structure, and the pedagogic functioning.

THE ADMINISTRATIVE STRUCTURE

The administrative structure of the school system can be defined as the distribution of the management of a school system among persons and institutions with varying competences and the relation existing between these persons and their institutions. The idea that schools could be operated by the church or by parents disappears in the face of the facts. Education has become a matter of public interest of the first order, and the public power is the authority that must be responsible for it. It may be demanded of a democratic state in the Western sense that in providing education it respect the viewpoints of the church and consider the interests of parents. Forms of coalescence of public authority and of private self-management may be useful. (Fruitful experience has been gained with this system in the Netherlands, for instance.) However, one can no longer deny the state the central, dominant place in education.

In the period after the Second World War, France, for instance, was faced with a major political problem which seriously hampered the administration of the country before de Gaulle. Nowhere was education divided by a sharper schism. On the one hand were the proponents of the public school, *l'école laïque*, an agency of the French state which is likewise characterized as *laïque* in its very constitution. On the other hand was the church, with an extensive school system that it had to maintain entirely out of its own resources.

Financially this setup was untenable, and it became more unbearable from day to day as a result of the additional influx of pupils. In the period from 1951 to 1959 France, after a scholastic struggle that had lasted eighty years, adopted the course of partially subsidizing private education. The schools enter into a contractual relation with the state, under which the more the authorities pay, the more say they have. Force of circumstances has made itself felt here more strongly than principle. Education can no longer be a private affair; it is a concern of the people as a whole. We see this situation in other European countries: the financing of schools has become entirely dependent on political forces.

ADMINISTRATIVE FUNCTIONING

Administrative functioning is the way in which the persons and institutions charged with management perform their duties. As a public concern, the school system must be developed according to plan. Consequently in all the countries of Europe there is interest in the Organization for Economic Cooperation and Development, which is working toward a well-considered educational development policy firmly based on quantitative data. People are discovering that without such a policy things get out of hand. First steps in this direction are being taken everywhere. Only a detailed investigation could reveal how much progress has been made and how far each minister of education and his civil servants have, in fact, allowed their policy to be governed by a well-coordinated and well-considered system of statistics regarding schools, pupils, teachers, and finances. It would seem that France is the most advanced on this point, although it has not managed to prevent shortcomings.

Agencies are also necessary for regional educational planning. Except for the British county education authorities, however, there are no such agencies; and the lack of forms of educational administration that are less centralized than the State and less decentralized than the small local units is felt acutely.

THE PEDAGOGIC STRUCTURE

The pedagogic structure of the school system is the manner in which the educational tasks are divided among schools of differing level and character, and the relations among these schools. The modernization of society has clashed violently with the traditional pedagogic structure.

Without question the ordinary primary school (we must unfortunately pass over preschool education) can lay the foundations for the culture of the masses. The worker of today needs more than manual skill: he is expected to think. Much depends on his concentration and perseverance. He must be aware of his place in a greater whole and must understand the art of working with others. He must have training that enables him to change his job later. In addition, he must be able to spend his leisure time profitably and to occupy a worthy place in the social and political life of the people. Elementary education does not suffice for that. In England and France the schools once called elementary and *élémentaire* respectively are now called primary school and *école primaire*, indicating that some form of secondary education should follow. Ordinary primary education is becoming basic education and is changing from final to initial education.

But what then?

This question is engaging every country in Europe. It has become the central problem of the organization of education. A unanimous answer is beginning to emerge: "After the basic school the orientation phase follows." It is the outcome of a relatively recent development. The way to elite education is not automatically open. The door that gives access to it stands ajar, but in order to be admitted the pupil must be able to identify himself by a certain level of knowledge and ability. With the Education Act of 1944, England and Wales instituted a well-thought-out examination system, under which pupils are examined at the age of eleven by intelligence tests and papers in arithmetic and English. These are weighed against report marks and the headmaster's appraisal. The intention is to determine in this way the right school for continued education. The system was regarded as an important step toward the democratic organization of education, but it has proved after the event to be instead the tail end of the old phase. It belongs to a stratified society with care-fully guarded frontier posts from school level to school level. England is now experiencing the drawbacks of a too early lead. In reaction, the idea of the comprehensive school is gaining ground.

In 1947, some years after the English Education Act, France published an important educational report, the report of the Langevin-Wallon Committee, *La Réforme de l'enseignement*. This document sounded the beginning of a new era. It begins by stating a number of principles. "The cultural level of the na-tion," says the committee, "must be raised not so much by selection methods, which again and again segregate the most gifted ones and remove them from the people, but by making culture easily accessible to less privileged groups." In addition the committee replaces the selection principle with the requirement "that every child, in the course of his school career, is observed objectively and individually" in order to guide his development as well as possible. The committee's answer to the question, "What next after basic school?" is that a period of basic education is followed by a four-year *cycle d'orientation*, a period of orientation. During the first two years of this period, education is uniform (with application of an active teaching method) and then varied in part, so as to determine the aptitudes and the interests of the pupils. The idea is that the school system will adjust to the development of the pupils and not to the national class structure. These four years form a separate school—that is to say, an inter-mediate school. Not until the fifteenth year does a variety of courses begin, as required by the differences in the pupils' apti-tudes and the differing needs of society.

The Langevin-Wallon Plan, by proposing the period of orienta-tion, introduced an idea that now concerns all the countries of Europe. The German *Rahmenplan* provides the period of orienta-tion in the two-year *Förderstufe* following the four-year *Grund-schule*. The pupils who display obvious talent for the *Gymnasium* have, however, already left after the first four years, and the rest move on to different types of school after six years. The *Förderstufe*, however, comes too soon to determine a pupil's talents adequately.

France is moving gradually in the direction of the intermediate school: the *collège d'enseignement secondaire*, a common school, but with different sections that correspond to the old-type separate schools at this level. The most adequate realization of the orientation idea is found in Italy and Sweden. In Italy the *scuola media* was introduced in 1962. All pupils move there after five years of basic education, and they remain three years. It gives general education without premature differentiation between general and vocational education. It is a school for orientation and guidance in the choice of further study or of a profession, because the pupils are introduced to a fixed part of the curriculum as well as to optional subjects that enable them to try out their talents. It is meant to be a progressive school, where modern teaching methods are used.

Also in 1962, after much research and experiment, a common school with nine classes was introduced in Sweden. The first six school years are undifferentiated. In the seventh and eighth years a number of optional subjects are offered, among which the pupils are free to choose. In the ninth year the curriculum fans out into many sections. Only after the common school— that is, after the pupils have reached the age of sixteen—do schools for continued education of various types follow. That is the modern trend: putting off the choice as long as possible, with no school differentiation before the pupils are fifteen or sixteen. Elsewhere, too, experiments are being made in this direction.

These changes should be viewed against the background of the shifting cultural and socio-economic situation and the changed policy. The Swedish Minister Erlander defended the common school as follows:

A reform work which is intended to bridge the old gaps between social classes must see to it that the school system appears to all groups in society as a unitary construction, within which there are available and open ways for all young people and where each growing individual, independent of his social starting point in life, will have the opportunity to learn how he can best utilize his potentialities for his future tasks. Such a goal cannot be compatible with an overt or disguised parallel school system. A differentiation into separate schools should according to my conviction not take place until it is necessary with regard to vocational choice.[4]

The new conception of society and the corresponding structure of education necessarily lead to changed ideas in pedagogy and didactics. The fact that the old contrast between primary and secondary education is losing its meaning immediately compels a revision of the content of primary education. It is regrettable that so little thought is given to these facts in Europe. These neglects contrast badly with the merits of more forward-looking documents such as the *Report on New Forms of Education for Five-Year-Olds to Thirteen- and Fourteen-Year-Olds* by the Netherlands Teachers' Association.[5]

The report advocates longitudinal planning of the subject matter, so that the subjects are divided among the successive kinds of school according to the intellectual development and the capacities of the pupils and according to the educational objectives of the school. As the report rightly says, "An exclusively structural renewal while outmoded content and inappropriate working methods are maintained does not yield any improvement."

Within continued education, too, gaps are being bridged: for example, between general education and vocational education and between humanistic and technical thinking. From the moment when a profession is regarded as more than just a combination of technical actions, and when the man and citizen is discovered to transcend the professional, all aspects are under

4. Torsten Husén, *Problems of Differentiation in Swedish Compulsory Schooling* (Stockholm: Svenska Bokförlaget, 1962), p. 30.

5. (Amsterdam, 1965).

simultaneous consideration. Professional training absorbs large parts of general education. Conversely, general education acquires elements of preparing for a profession. In this way, the humanistic and the technical ways of thought draw ever closer in one school syllabus: increasingly it is realized that a humanistic education that passes over the scientific and technical revolutions of our days is out of touch with reality, and that a technical education that neglects the fruits of humanistic thought lacks an important part of the development of the human mind.

Everywhere the trend is toward a society where national frontiers are beginning to lose their significance. Hence the universally growing attention to the teaching of modern languages. There is likewise a general tendency toward combining subjects into larger units, such as "social studies" and "nature study." The interdependence that is felt so strongly in the practice of science is reflected in the structure of curricula.

And yet one cannot speak of radical changes. Tradition still weighs heavily on the education that follows the basic school. Academic secondary schools are the heirs of the Latin school of past centuries. Literary studies still preponderate, and the teaching of Latin, which has powerful defenders, even now stands in the way of a new look for secondary education in many cases. Ursula Springer has pointed out that the administrators and educators responsible for the organization and progress of the school systems have often been products and defenders of classical and literary studies. Rarely does a scientist or a mathematician hold a responsible position at a ministry of education.[6]

In regard to orienting pupils to society, the Soviet Russian school system is in a class by itself. Since 1958 it has aimed at

6. Ursula S. Springer, *Recent Curriculum Developments at the Middle Level of French, West German and Italian Schools* (New York: 1967); the mimeographed manuscript is to be published by the Center for Education in Industrial Nations and Teachers College Press, Teachers College, Columbia University in 1969. I have generalized her remarks on the countries mentioned.

directing education toward the world of labor.[7] This point of view was again brought to the fore by Khrushchev in a speech in April 1958:

The most important thing in this matter is to set forth a precept and to have this precept be sacred to all members of our society. All children entering school must prepare themselves for useful labor, for participation in building communist society.

All work, whether in a factory or on a collective farm, whether in an industrial enterprise, on a state farm or in an office—honest work, useful to society—is sacred and is a need of every person who lives in society and enjoys its blessings. . . .[8]

Since then the Soviet unified school has endeavored to ensure that its pupils are informed of the principal branches of production, made conversant with the social aspects of production in the Soviet Union, familiarized with technical skills, and involved in productive work. West of the Communist countries this radical setup has no parallel. But it is true that more than ever before curricula are open to the requirements of modern life. In contrast with its former one-sided intellectual and educational objectives, general education is coming to devote attention to preparation for a future profession. In West Germany the top classes of the *Volksschule* are seriously engaged in *Arbeitslehre*, *Werkunterricht*, and *Betriebsbesichtigungen*. At the corresponding level in France there are sections for career preparation. All the countries of Europe are trying to make their pupils aware of their responsibility toward society and to teach them something about their obligations as citizens. As a result of the lengthening of compulsory schooling, teaching is extended to pupils of limited talents who would formerly have exchanged school for working life, and new sections of the population are being given a sense of

7. I am ignoring earlier experiments with polytechnical schools.
8. Quoted in George Z. F. Bereday and R. V. Rapacz, "Khrushchev's Proposals for Soviet Education," *Teachers College Record*, 60, no. 3, December 1958, p. 140.

conscious citizenship. However, civic education is not without its problems. The teachers are not very well prepared to give it, and, partly as a result, the appeal that it makes to the pupils is insufficient.

The contrast between primary education for the masses and continued education for the elite, on the one hand, and between general and technical education, on the other, as discussed above, have made themselves felt in the training of teachers. Traditionally the forms of training were separate. Elementary school teachers were old products of the elementary schools. They were prepared for their tasks in separate training institutions. Secondary school teachers, on the other hand, went to a university, earned their degrees, and then returned to the types of school from which they had come. The specialized teachers of the technical and vocational schools were trained themselves in these schools.

The revision of the pedagogic structure is making itself felt in the traditional setup in more ways than one. There is a tendency to upgrade the training of primary teachers. In France the *baccalauréat* is becoming an integral part of the training program for primary school teachers in the *école normale*, before they go on to strictly professional studies. In the German Federal Republic *Pädagogische Akademien* are being created for this category of teacher, and the British Institutes of Education are attached to the universities. The creation of intermediate schools leads in many countries to an intermediate category of teachers. In general, the dividing line between the various groups of teachers is becoming much less clearly defined.[9] More attention is being paid to the professional training of future secondary school teachers, for instance in the British Institutes of Education and the French *Centres pédagogiques régionaux*. And yet the socio-economic contrasts within the ranks of the teachers are still great, and it will be a long time before all who teach will be

9. J. Majault, *Teacher Training* (Strasbourg: 1965), p. 207.

able to consider themselves brother-in-arms in one and the same profession.

Finally, a few words about higher education, which the United Nations Educational, Scientific, and Cultural Organization defines as institutions where: (1) the basic entrance requirement is completion of secondary education, (2) the usual entrance age is about eighteen years, and (3) the courses lead to a diploma. The following are approximate figures on the influx into this branch of education. According to the UNESCO survey, participation in higher education, excluding the Soviet Union, increased on the average from 996,946 in the years 1945–1949 to 1,449, 251 in the years 1955–1959—that is, by an average of 5 per cent a year. In the Soviet Union it increased from an average of 945,940 in 1945–1949 to 2,082,600 in 1955–1959—that is, by 12 per cent a year.[10] All this points to a vigorous growth, which inspired UNESCO to the following view:

In very broad terms the last fifty years of the nineteenth century were years when primary education was expanded very greatly in an increasing number of countries—until by the end of the century, in the most industrially developed States it had become free and universal. The first fifty years of the twentieth century saw a similar advance of secondary education so that in a few of the richer countries it, also, has now become universal and free. At the same time progress was made in higher education also, but since 1950 the speed of advance has quickened enormously.[11]

Will there be universal higher education in Europe in the year 2000? It does not seem probable. Seldom do more than 6 to 10 per cent of eighteen- or nineteen-year-olds enter higher education in Europe.

Meanwhile the role of higher education inside the pedagogic structure of education is beginning to change. Its concept is being broadened. Just as secondary education was expanded beyond

10. World Survey of Education, *Higher Education*, Vol. IV (Paris: UNESCO, 1966), p. 66.
11. *Ibid.*, p. 74.

the traditional selective and academic schooling to include multifarious types of schools and programs of a less theoretical and abstract nature, so higher education is proceeding to include forms of training that were formerly regarded as of lower rank.[12] Teacher-training institutions, schools of social work, and also higher technological and commercial institutes have made their appearance in tertiary education.

Within this framework the universities form a category unto themselves. The population increase and the development of secondary education have been responsible for a large influx into the universities. But other factors—such as the lowering of standards of admission, the foundation of new and geographically better distributed institutions, and the diversification of studies— have also contributed to their growth. In the Soviet Union university education was also expanded by means of correspondence courses.

The universities, together with the classical *Gymnasia*, are aware that they are threatened in their essence by the changes taking place. In the case of the *Gymnasia*, this threat is a consequence of the modernization of the subject matter; in the case of the universities it is, among other things, a product of democratization, which has brought unprecedentedly large numbers of young people knocking at their gates. Traditionally the university is an institution where an elite devotes itself to study in isolation. The professors enjoy almost total freedom. They are expected to engage in both teaching and research. The new development is making the universities teach enormous numbers of students, many of whom are the first generation in higher education and regard their study solely as preparation for a senior profession. The professors and their numerous assistants are finding that their work consists increasingly of teaching and examining. Like secondary school teachers, they are required to

12. A. F. Kleinberger, *The Expansion of Higher Education* (Paper delivered at the conference of the Comparative Education Society, Ghent, 1967).

exercise their teaching skills. They no longer have time for research. The autonomy that was once the privilege of the professors can no longer be maintained as the size of the faculties grows. Recruiting sufficient numbers of additional staff of good quality is becoming difficult, above all because of the competition of industry, research institutes, and the social services. The problem is aggravated by the deficiency in facilities and the paucity of entrants for postgraduate studies. It was not without reason that Sir Walter Moberley entitled his book that appeared in Britain as early as 1949 *The Crisis in the University*.

PEDAGOGIC FUNCTIONING

Pedagogic functioning refers to the working of the pedagogic structure in practice.

One of the questions now being widely discussed in Europe is the extent to which the makeup of the school population reflects the idea of equality of opportunity. The scattered data make it clear that the largest numbers of children attending long secondary education and higher education come from the highest social groups; the middle class is second; and the workers and farmers are at the bottom of the list. It is mainly the middle class whose share is increasing.

A second aspect of secondary and higher education that demands attention is that of the "return" of the courses. Statistics show that a substantial proportion of students fail to be promoted to the next class and fail to earn a diploma. An important percentage incur delays of one or more years during their studies, while long secondary education and the universities may display a wastage amounting to 40 per cent or 50 per cent of the intake. The longer the length of training, the larger the number of dropouts. The conviction is gaining ground that strict selection must change to planned differentiation, so that larger numbers of students can complete their training with some kind of positive results. But various branches of education in Europe are not responsive to such ideas.

Finally we come to the question of the school system as an agent of industrialization. Here the Common Market is lagging behind in the training of executives.[13] A comparison of the Common Market, the United States, and the Soviet Union gives the following approximate figures on graduates at the first level of higher education (see Table 13). Even if the students enrolled in higher professional education for teachers and technicians were included in the European figures, the differences between the three regions would still be much to the disadvantage of the Common Market.

TABLE 13. NUMBER OF UNIVERSITY GRADUATES (FIRST LEVEL) IN THREE LARGE ECONOMIC REGIONS

Region	Population (in millions)	Graduates	Graduates in percentage of the age groups (23 and 24 years of age)
Common Market	180	101,000	40
United States*	190	450,000	196
U.S.S.R.	223	331,000	82

* The bachelors' degrees are not entirely on the same level as the European first degrees; as a result the American figures are too high for this comparison.

CONCLUSION

Several aspects of European education could not be discussed adequately here. The demographic influences have been deliberately left out. It was not possible to go into financial aspects of schooling. Neither the future nor the necessary new approaches and innovations have been discussed.

What is disturbing about the impressive evolution of education in Europe is that so much action has to be taken on the basis of

13. R. Poignant, *L'Enseignement dans les Pays du Marché Commun* (Paris: Institut Pédagogique National, 1965), p. 259. The English translation will be published by the Center for Education in Industrial Nations and Teachers College Press, Teachers College, Columbia University, in 1969.

so little knowledge. Practically every other field of life is becoming more scientific. But in education, traditions and intuition still prevail. Let us, therefore, present in conclusion the following ten priorities for study.

1. We ought to know what objectives education should have in this rapidly evolving society: not objectives in vague terms—there are more than enough of those—but definitions of expected behavior verifiable by exact methods.

2. We ought to know how such objectives, given the psychic development of the pupils, should be worked out giving due consideration to the planning of the subject matter.

3. We ought to know how the educational teaching process takes place through classroom activities, and what role can be played by the new technological aids, such as closed circuit television, teaching machines, and computer-assisted instruction. We ought to have the didactic knowledge to use these technical means in a scientific manner.

4. We ought to develop aids and achievement tests to measure objectively the results of teaching.

5. We ought to know how to organize schools: how to divide the pupils into groups, to differentiate the curricula, and to manage the schools.

6. We ought to increase our understanding of the relation between the achievements of the pupils, on the one hand, and the influence of their environment and the combination of environment and school, on the other hand.

7. We ought to know how to make the results of research find acceptance and take root in the world of education, and how to tackle the problem of innovation.

8. We ought to prepare for changes in the structure of the school system by means of experiments, and we ought to evaluate the results of those experiments scientifically.

9. We ought to know how the administration of the school system should be organized from top to bottom. In this connec-

tion educational statistics on the functioning of the school system would have to play a greater part than they so far have.

10. We ought to gain a better understanding of the technique of educational planning, notably its manpower aspects, and also of the manner in which assumed social requirements must be translated into educational terms.

EDUCATION IN THE UNITED STATES: PAST ACCOMPLISHMENTS AND PRESENT PROBLEMS

CLARK KERR

Few nations in history have relied so fully and for so long on education for solutions to so many problems as has the United States. And yet today, after more than three centuries of devotion to education, the American people face their most serious educational crisis. This crisis is not universal in its impact, for much is done effectively and even superbly. It is, rather, a crisis comprised of inadequacies—some minor and some major—in specific aspects of the educational performance. The failures of today are related, in part, to unique features of the American scene; but, in part also, they are indicative of difficulties to be faced by any highly developed industrial society.

Formal education in the United States now absorbs a little over 6 per cent of the gross national product. Over the past decade, resources put into education have risen proportionately by more than one-half, from 4.2 to 6.7 per cent of the gross national product—the highest percentage of the gross national product in any major industrial nation. The increase by over one-half in a single decade is the most substantial of any similarly short period in American history. It reflects both the high priority placed on educational effort and the great rise after World War II in the number of persons of school age.

The daily lives of more than one-quarter of the American people are involved in formal education. School and college enrollments total 55,000,000, out of a population of 200,000,-000. Teachers number 2,500,000. Beyond formal education lies an enormous amount of organized training in industry, government, the military, the churches; and related to education is the creation of new knowledge and the general dissemination of information. Fritz Machlup has estimated that the production and distribution of knowledge—in all of its many forms—accounts for 25 per cent of the national income, and that this form of activity is growing at twice the rate of the economy as a whole.[1]

This brief review will be concerned, first, with the historic relations of formal education to American development and, second, with the problems now confronting education in its relation to a rapidly changing society.

HISTORICAL REVIEW

Historically six major purposes have been served by education.

1. Individual Aspirations

Immigrants to the United States came largely from countries that, at the time of the immigration, confined educational opportunities to members of the aristocracy and the upper middle class. One of the reasons for immigration was to secure opportunities for personal advancement, and this included access to education. Education was an important aspect of the "pursuit of happiness." Schools were started as soon as the original colonies were settled. As the population moved westward, new schools were begun as each new community was founded.

This populist, egalitarian approach rejected the older elitist view of education from the very founding of the new nation. Universal access to education was first assured at the primary level and then at the secondary level. Now in the middle of the

1. Fritz Machlup, *The Production and Distribution of Knowledge in the United States* (Princeton: Princeton University Press, 1962), pp. 362, 374.

twentieth century it is in the process of being assured at the early levels of higher education. Tuition-free junior colleges are open to all high school graduates in California, the state with the most fully developed community college movement; and junior colleges are now the most rapidly expanding segment of education in the United States. In 1900 there were eight; today there are over eight hundred. They carry open access, as a matter of right, through fourteen years of formal education. At the national level nearly one-half of all high school graduates enter an institution of postsecondary instruction. In California, with its widespread community colleges, the percentage is nearly three-quarters.

This irresistible and massive wave of individual aspirations has been the most elemental force affecting education in America. Education to ever higher levels has taken on aspects of a social right. It is also a highly valued consumers' good in a high-consumption society. Nor is this historical process yet at an end. It is not clear what may be the ultimate level of general aspirations for available years of education, and how these years may be spread throughout the average lifetime. This ever rising tide of educational aspiration and attainment is one of the great triumphs of the human spirit.

2. Religious Convictions

Religious institutions, in order to perpetuate their religions and to express the ideals of their religions, have given great leadership to educational development. Many of the early primary and secondary schools were founded by Protestant religious groups. Until the Civil War most of the colleges, including the first, Harvard, were started by one or another of the Protestant denominations. Since the Civil War the Catholics have been the more active in establishing their own parochial schools and colleges. Ten per cent of all elementary and secondary students are in Catholic schools today. And 10 per cent of the colleges, with a little less than 10 per cent of all enrollments, are Catholic.

The impact of religion on education, while historically most significant, is now fading. Many institutions, once religious in their leadership and with a religious emphasis in their curricula, have now become fully secular, particularly the originally Protestant ones; even Catholic colleges are beginning to move toward lay boards and even some lay administrative leadership.

Few new institutions are being started by religiously oriented groups. The initiative has passed to the public sector, and increasingly public funds are being sought and also being supplied for support of institutions still essentially religious in their orientation. This creates constitutional and political problems in a nation dedicated to separating church and state, but the two systems of education—religious and secular—are going through an historic process of closer accommodation.

3. Political Participation

The founding fathers of the American democracy were convinced that an educated electorate was a prerequisite for political health. To Jefferson, the ownership of land and a degree of education for all the people were the bases on which a democracy could be built, and this theme of education for democratic participation has continued throughout the history of the United States. The educational expectation of citizens has moved from literacy to a primary education and now to a secondary education. As society becomes more complex, the standard expectation may rise yet higher. School-leaving age has generally been raised to sixteen, and in some states to eighteen, largely on the grounds of the educational requirements for citizenship participation.

4. Economic Growth

Benjamin Franklin was the first prominent American to emphasize the practical contributions of education to agriculture, commerce, and industry. He opposed the classical education of the day in favor of useful knowledge. A century later that view gave rise to the land grant university movement, which placed higher education at the service of the total economy and all elements of the population. Technical high schools and vocational specializations in the community colleges carry on this theme.

Economic growth is a complex phenomenon, and its requirements vary from one stage of development and one situation to another. The postwar economic miracle in Western Europe has been based primarily on large-scale injections of new labor and new capital, using technology already developed. It is not certain that the educational quality of labor on the average, rose substantially in Western Europe during this period, and in some cases it may have dropped. The United States has had less access to vast new inputs of labor and capital investment on a percentage basis. It has had to rely more heavily on other sources of growth. A recent study by Denison shows education was a major source of growth. For the period from 1955 to 1962, Denison claims, more than one-fifth of the increase in national income per person employed is explained by higher educational levels. "Advances in knowledge," related particularly to higher education, added about another one-fourth.[2] Facing the future, the United States must rely increasingly on greater skill and better technology as sources of economic growth, and both are based on education.

Job content is rising rapidly in the American and the Canadian economies. From 1940–1944 to 1960–1961, jobs in the top three (out of five) content levels rose from 45 to 59 per cent of the employed labor force in the United States and from 40 to 57 per cent in Canada.[3] Job families classified as "research and design,"

2. Edward F. Denison, assisted by Jean-Pierre Poullier, *Why Growth Rates Differ: Postwar Experience in Nine Western Countries* (Brookings Institute, 1967), p. 299.

3. J. G. Scoville, "Job Content of the Canadian Economy 1941–1961," *Special Labour Force Studies, No. 3* (Dominion Bureau of Statistics, April 1967), p. 11.

"health," "clerical," and "inspection" each rose in size three times or more than the average. There is, of course, no precise way to relate rising job content to higher educational requirements.

Whatever the exact measure, education has increasingly been shown to be a basic and important element in carrying nations to higher levels of economic output, as Benjamin Franklin intuitively sensed two centuries ago.

5. *Absorption of Immigrants*

The United States received waves of immigrants, from changing locations and in changing volume, up to World War I. The problem of absorbing these new people into the American system of life as it had been developed by the earlier English and German settlers became an insistent issue beginning with the vast migration of the Irish in the 1840's. The assimilation problem continued as the source of later immigrants moved to Eastern and Southern Europe. The schools were relied upon to provide literacy training for the first generation and full or nearly full Americanization for the second generation. This burden of amalgamation of different language and cultural stocks was carried with great success.

6. *National Power and Regional Advantage*

Beginning with World War II, there has been an increasing correlation between the quality of the educational system and both national power and regional development, particularly through science and technology based on science. The United States has moved into a clear first place in numbers of leading scientists. From 1901 to 1918, 5 per cent of the Nobel Prize awards went to Americans; from 1946 to date, the percentage is 40.

Within the nation certain regions, particularly the Boston

metropolitan area and the State of California, have used the quality of their educational systems, and especially of their front-rank universities, to attract modern, scientifically related industry. The competition is now being intensified, above all by the Middle West and Texas.

Thus education has served many purposes and has been the basis for many accomplishments in the United States. It has reflected the uncommon aspirations of the common man, the religious convictions of a more religious people, the historic effort of making America safe for democracy, the combination of greater skill and dexterity in the people with greater technological effectiveness in the capital, the absorption of many people from many backgrounds into a single culture, and the requirements of national and regional influence in a scientific age. Over three centuries the emphasis has shifted. Religious and democratic concerns have been less in the forefront, and greater attention has been given to serving economic growth and national and regional power: the spiritual and the political have been joined by the material and the national. Two concerns have maintained a more steady course: the rising aspirations of individuals for the benefits that education can bring, and the need for a mechanism to introduce unassimilated groups into fuller partnership in American society—this latter concern is at the moment most intense.

CURRENT PROBLEMS

The major problems currently confronting the educational system of the United States fall into six general areas.

1. Reducing Discrimination

About 15 per cent of the students in America are in groups many of whose members are subject to gross discrimination and neglect. These disadvantaged minorities are comprised mainly of

Negro, Puerto Rican, and Mexican-American youth, with other smaller groups such as the American Indian. On the whole, students of Oriental origins are now subject to little or no discrimination. Most information is available on the Negroes, but the problems of other disadvantaged minorities are almost as intense, although geographically less widespread.

The Supreme Court in 1954 ruled that "separate" schools are not "equal" under the Constitution. The great national effort to end discrimination dates from that historic ruling. Over-all progress since 1954 has thus far been minor, although quite spectacular in some specific situations. Today, two-thirds of all Negro students are still in public primary and secondary schools that are 90 to 100 per cent Negro in composition. These schools are generally inferior to schools predominantly composed of white children.

Progress in the South is offset by retrogression in the North. The Civil Rights Commission in July 1967 reported that "the percentage of Negro children attending desegregated schools in the Southern States in 1966–1967 increased substantially over the previous school year," and noted a "spirit of acceptance and understanding that would have seemed impossible . . . a few short years ago."[4] Excellent progress has been made in the border states; slower progress is occurring in the South, where there is a trend to establish private schools to escape desegregation in the public schools; and very slow progress is being made in the Deep South.

Segregation in the North is increasing somewhat, not as a matter of policy but as a matter of fact. The heart of the problem is in the central metropolitan areas. There the problem is "growing."[5] In smaller communities a policy of desegregation can be more easily implemented. Schools historically have been combined, or they can be combined effectively, since the total popu-

4. United States Commission on Civil Rights, *Southern School Desegregation* (July 1967), p. iii.
5. United States Commission on Civil Rights, *Racial Isolation in the Public Schools* (February 1967), p. 13.

lation lives within a small geographical area. The big city, on the other hand, tends to be divided into very populous neighborhoods and to be surrounded by its suburbs. In fifteen large metropolitan areas, the central city schools are 80 per cent nonwhite, and the suburban schools are heavily white.[6] The white students are enrolled mostly in white neighborhood schools, serving neighborhoods that are socially segregated, and in white suburban schools and white private schools. The central city schools are left to the nonwhites. The most intractable problems are in the big cities across the nation and the small communities in the Deep South: the nature of the great city itself and the historic racial prejudice of the southern small town and rural community are the highest barriers to equality of opportunity.

In higher education there is less prejudice to overcome—in fact, there is usually much good will; but for reasons, largely, of inadequate academic preparation and financing, Negroes have not penetrated far into the college and university system. The proportion of Negroes attending college is less than half the proportion of Negroes in the population as a whole; and half of those who do go attend segregated Negro colleges. Those enrolled in nonsegregated institutions are largely in junior colleges, municipal colleges, and state colleges (where they are enrolled in highly vocational curricula) and to a much lesser extent in the universities.

Inadequate preparation in primary, secondary, and tertiary school affects opportunities in the labor market now that education is so important to so many jobs. The result is lower personal income and more unemployment.

Efforts to create equal opportunity in the public schools begin with changing the policies of segregation where they have existed. Areas where segregation is a matter of policy are being reduced quite rapidly. There are fewer and fewer such areas, and more and more they are confined to the Deep South. The problem of policy is being overcome; the problem of fact is more

6. *Ibid.*, p. 3.

difficult. Two main efforts are now being undertaken: (1) transporting students from one district to another to obtain racial integration; and (2) building larger consolidated schools which cover wider areas of the city—even the proposed creation of great educational parks. Neither solution stops the escape into the suburbs and thus into a different administrative unit or into private schools. The traditional American system of local control of schools and the acceptance of private as well as public initiative get in the way of solving America's greatest dilemma: the contrast between principle and practice in achieving equality of opportunity.

The problem goes beyond the schools. When schools have been integrated, the "performance of Negro children in integrated schools indicates positive effects of integration, though rather small ones," according to the Coleman study;[7] and, in fact, the statistics show the positive effects to be very small. Behind the schools lie cultural deprivation and lack of inspiration in the home and the neighborhood; and ahead of the schools lies discrimination, fortunately diminishing, in employment. Lack of equal opportunity is a problem of the schools, but also of the city, the factory, the trade union, American society itself. For all these reasons Negro students in the metropolitan Northeast are from 1.6 to 2 years behind white students at grade six, from 2.4 to 2.8 years behind at grade nine, and from 3.3 to 5.2 years behind at grade twelve.[8]

The United States is faced with a new form of migration, not from outside its borders, but from within. This attempted internal migration is by people who have long been contained within American society but have not been a full part of it. They want to be a part. The very success of other groups already absorbed into the American way of life makes all the greater

7. James S. Coleman, *Equality of Educational Opportunity* (Washington, D.C.: U.S. Department of Health, Education, and Welfare, 1966), p. 29.

8. *Ibid.*, p. 274–275. The lower figure at each grade results from measurements of verbal ability; the higher, from measurements of mathematical achievement.

the deprivation of those still left outside. American ideals promise those still deprived that they can be a full part of American
life, but there is still a long way to go, and the problems are
more difficult than they once appeared when the Supreme Court
decided that "separate" was not "equal."

2. Correcting Imbalances

Two major shifts in emphasis are urgently needed in the
United States. The first is a vast expansion of the community
college movement to cover the entire nation. Parents and students
increasingly desire access on a fully open basis to fourteen years
of schooling. Also, the labor market can make good use of the
added technical skills.

The second shift is in the direction of the health sciences.
Higher standards of living and the new Medicare program,
longer life spans, and the improvement in the potentialities of
health care itself have greatly increased the demand for health
services. This requires many more doctors and dentists and
health technicians than are being produced.

Currently there is also a deficit in the number of persons with
the Ph.D. degree, but this lack apparently will be eliminated
within the next five years or so; the facilities already largely
exist to make this possible.[9]

Also, there are always shifts going on at the higher education
level to reflect the changing potentialities of different fields and
the needs of society. For example, resources are now being
shifted into modern biology, the creative arts, oceanography,
and the study of the problems of urban civilization, of adaptation
of the educational system, and of the new generation of youth.

3. Accepting New Assignments

Formal education in the United States has been aimed at

9. Allan M. Carter, "The Supply and Demand for College Teachers,"
Journal of Human Resources, Vol. 1, Summer 1966, pp. 22–38 (see particularly pp. 35–37).

graduation and degrees. It is now being extended in at least two new directions. First, a more active labor market policy calls for formal education at crucial points after the normal time of leaving school. The nation is committed to full employment and rapid economic growth. Inadequate or inappropriate skills stand in the way of these goals. There are at least three points in a working life where further education increasingly needs to be introduced: to turn long-term unemployment into opportunities for guidance and training, to modernize and raise to higher levels the skills of employed persons to match the requirements of new technology and new methods of operation, and to prepare the older person for a second career to extend the period of his working life. If 1 per cent of the labor force were in full-time formal education programs at any one time—and this may not be very far off—then the load on the educational system would be raised by this amount.

Second, a new emphasis on the quality of life requires more opportunities for citizens to study the creative arts, languages and literature, geography and history, and many other subjects related to the use of greater leisure time and income. The schools become cultural centers for the entire population.

The community colleges are particularly well suited to serve a more active labor market policy and the new interest in the quality of life.

4. Improving Effectiveness

A nation committed, as is the United States, to wide dispersion of educational opportunity is also committed to an eternal and intense problem of effectiveness, as compared to a society following a more elitist approach. The heavy dropout rate is the most important issue in this area: at the high school level it is 30 per cent, and at the college level, 40 per cent. The high school dropout rate is particularly serious, since most semiskilled and skilled jobs now require a high school degree, and only 5 per cent of jobs in 1970, it is now estimated, will be unskilled. The 30 per cent dropout rate from high school far exceeds the 5 per cent level for unskilled jobs; and 10 per cent of the new entrants into the labor market now have only an eighth-grade education or less.

Regardless of years of attendance and degrees earned, graduates of many schools—from primary to tertiary—have received educations of inferior quality. Also, some subjects, like mathematics, have been poorly taught in the United States, according to the highest international standards. By way of contrast, science education, particularly since Sputnik, has been substantially improved in the high schools; and most high schools have now adopted the system of ability-grouping to assist students to develop to their maximum level.

5. *Financing the Educational System*

Enrollments in schools, will rise somewhat faster than the gross national product over the next decade. Ten years from now it will take somewhat more of the gross national product to meet the enrollment pressure, particularly in higher education. But large tasks remain beyond adjusting to numbers. Over the past decade the percentage of the gross national product devoted to education has risen by one-half. Another increase in the next decade by one-fifth—or to about 8 per cent—will be necessary to meet the clear needs of assuring equality of opportunity, adjusting imbalances, serving new demands, and improving effectiveness.

Education is handicapped in two ways in trying to meet the new challenges. First, it now relies heavily on the cities and the states for financial support, and their sources of income rise generally with the gross national product and not ahead of it. Second, education is not subject to any substantial and discernible increase in productivity; thus, expansion must come mostly from new money rather than from more effective use of present funds, although the pressure for more effective use of funds will rise with the pressure for the funds themselves.

The segment of education in greatest need of additional financial support over the next decade will be higher education. The great wave of postwar births has passed through the primary and secondary schools and is now in the colleges. And graduate study is expanding rapidly. Consequently expenditures will need to rise much more rapidly at the tertiary level than at the primary and secondary levels.

The major source of new funding must be the federal government because its revenues rise faster than the gross national product. It has entered the field of financial support of education and has raised its contribution from a traditional zero to 10 per cent of the total over the past few years. But the federal government has other great demands on its resources; and internal competition for additional expenditures will be against such high priority projects as rebuilding the cities and preserving and renovating the quality of natural resources.

6. Shifting the Locus of Influence and Formal Support

Traditionally initiative in starting and governing educational institutions has been in the hands of private groups and of local and state governmental units—30,000 local school boards in fifty states. Initiative in recent years has been taken by the federal government—in desegregation, in improving the teaching of languages, in strengthening scientific research, in studying the educational process, and in many other ways. The federal government has come to supply a minority of the funds but a majority of the initiative. The external push of the federal government has been far more effective than the internal initiative of the educational establishment. The educational establishment has lost at least as much of its self-determination by default as by the usurpation of others. This has raised problems of local autonomy, of the swiftness of change required of a reluctant educational establishment, of uniformity against diversity, of egalitarian tendencies as against preservation of a margin for excellence; but the local autonomy too often has been poorly used, the new developments too often have been long overdue, the diversity too often has been in the direction of low quality, and the federal agencies have found ways to reward excellence as well as sheer numbers. However, the problems remain as problems to be watched.

Of these six problem areas, four are inherently subject to reasonable, relatively early solutions—the correcting of imbalances, the addition of new functions, the financing of the total endeavor, and the adjustment to a new element of government; but two will be troublesome for a substantial period of time—the provision of equality of opportunity throughout the nation and the general raising of effectiveness to more fully acceptable standards. These two problems are related to each other in many ways.

Beyond the problems currently most troubling the educational system in the United States lie others as yet more dimly seen. One such problem is the role to be played by education. Education has long been the servant of society—of an aristocracy or the church or the state or the industrial system. As it becomes a larger endeavor in society and a more important one, to what extent might it become, and should it become, an independent or partially independent force changing a society unconsciously or even against its conscious will? This was not possible when education was both less central and served a more singleminded purpose. In the modern world, with all its complexities and with all its dynamic change, more opportunities exist for education to become a force in its own right. Then education might lead rather than follow, might challenge as well as respond, might help set the pace rather than always lag behind, might change as well as be changed.

APPENDIX

"ENLARGING" EDUCATION: RECOMMENDATIONS

These Essays on world education were designed to stimulate an international group of educators assembled in Williamsburg in November 1967 to map out new roads for advances in education. Their work was expressed in a series of observations and recommendations, the edited version of which follows.

INTERNATIONAL COOPERATION*

The last third of this century should be designated the Age of the Development Generation. The year 1970 should be designated International Education Year to draw attention, near the beginning of this period, to the long-term importance of education in the balanced development and modernization of the planet. It should be recognized now by all—and not by governments alone—that world educational needs require continuous, patient, and expanding effort, in men, money, and resources on the part of nations; and in international cooperation for the remainder of this century. This will involve hard work by all concerned; a readiness to learn, adapt, evaluate and adjust programs and techniques, and to eradicate waste of resources; and a commitment

* Contributed by Heiman G. Quik, Ladislav Cerych, Prem N. Kirpal, Robert Gardiner, and F. Champion Ward.

312

to build a peaceful world community based on international understanding, social justice, and progress toward a more abundant life for all.

The fact that the educational systems of developing nations are short of virtually everything does not justify a piecemeal approach to helping them. There will always be room for differences of opinion about what the priorities should be, but there can never be reasonable doubt that there *should* be priorities. Significant examples of these are educational planning, diffusion of innovations, curriculum development, teacher preparation, textbooks, and libraries, a two-way movement of faculty members and of selected categories of students, educational research, strengthening the teaching of science and technology, inter-university links, education for international understanding.

Some mechanism for continuing work on problems of world education should be established. It is therefore recommended that a standing committee be set up to consider the establishment of a nongovernmental International Development Advisory Group on Education. Its functions might be to study, on a continuing basis, the major problems of developmental education and to formulate strategies for their solution; to recommend to governments, to regional and world bodies concerned with such problems, and to the world academic community, the strategies necessary for solution of the fundamental problems of world education; to encourage establishment of affiliated organizations in individual countries and regions. Membership should be composed of a limited number of persons experienced in developmental and educational problems drawn from the more and less developed countries; with a permanent secretariat. Support should come preferably from the private sector. As an illustration of its activities, the agency might: conduct and support required researches in problems of development education; conduct symposia and conferences; establish recommended strategies and priorities for deployment of resources; maintain continuing advisory liaison with national governments, regional educational and development groups, and professional disciplines. All of these activities should be complementary to—not duplications of—the work of the existing agencies or organizations.

There is now a sad insufficiency of aid. There is also the need for better utilization of existing aid. In the field of education the spending of money, if it is to be done wisely and with some sense of vision, is very difficult. This aspect of the aid program needs to be considerably strengthened. Whatever resources are available, they should be applied to strategic plans and to priorities well thought out. There must be better preparation in the recipient countries for the receiving of aid and greater knowledge and awareness on the part of the donor countries. Unless this is accomplished, the present waste, which is considerable, will go on. There is also a necessity to harmonize and rationalize the different sources of foreign aid. Foreign aid today is diversified and comes from many sources. All these programs and these operations often act in isolation. It is difficult to get the best results out of such a haphazard process.

Educational assistance must be disentangled from the morass of total aid. Aid programs operate in a totality, and seldom is there any effort to isolate the different kinds of aid. Education has a distinctive character. It is related to the making of man and not to the making of machines, and it needs to be isolated from other aid processes in order to make a greater impression on the imagination of the people.

There is also need for greater efficiency in processing aid. Sophistication is necessary on the part, not only of the donor country, but also of recipient countries. Problems and areas of aid must be carefully identified. There is need for more multilateral aid, both in giving and in receiving. Bilateral aid is considerable; it has its duties and has benefited the recipient countries, but there must be more coordination between donor countries and receiving countries.

We need a world plan for education: a pooling of efforts and possibilities. This would take time but would lead us to some kind of world program to match the crisis in education and to overcome it. An essential of such a world plan should be the greater deployment of resources. Resources are insignificant compared to the needs at present, and still they are not best used. In this context it is necessary to work for the involvement, not only of the top leaders in education, but of the masses of the people. The aid-giving process should not be confined to the policies pursued by bureaucrats but should go down to all sectors of society and should be based upon a deeper involvement of the peoples of the world.

The present average amount of international assistance, estimated at one billion dollars, should be doubled within the next five years. As an immediate practical measure, sufficient funds should be made available to the International Development Association and other appropriate international organizations in order that they might continue to provide much-needed credits for educational purposes in developing countries. But there must be a strategy of international cooperation, devised and shared by all the parties, and based on a long-term view. Its object should be to get the maximum effect from external assistance by concentrating that assistance on the most critical needs—as they appear in the context of rational educational development plans—which recipient countries are least likely to be able to meet with their own resources.

International meetings and agencies are acts of reaffirmation of a conviction that prompted the creation of the United Nations Educational, Scientific, and Cultural Organization: that the pursuit of knowledge, science, and culture is as much a national as an international concern. When we talk about education, we think in terms of preparing our children to be aware of the needs of our communities and also to be in a position to contribute to satisfying these needs. This applies also in the international society. We have, all of us, in our various communities, to prepare to live in one community. In some of the affluent, heterogeneous societies, through several social institutions, especially in the welfare state, needs are now met as a matter of obligation of the community; and we talk about aid in that spirit. We live in one economy. Some parts of the economy may not be flourishing. We live in one society with people whose needs they cannot satisfy themselves directly. Therefore we cannot use rationalizations: we are independent, but . . . ; we are all equal, but . . . ; we would like to see our resources developed, but . . . ; we would like to give aid, but. . . . Such rationalizations do not make for open-hearted international cooperation.

The dual facts of international education are first that when educational development actually occurs, it does so within countries, not among several. We are rather forcibly reminded of this whenever we get too high-falutin' about the international aspects of the matter. Secondly all national systems have common educational aims and compulsions. The need to man their economies and to increase the equalization of opportunity for individuals constitutes the major pressure on all systems at present and seems almost independent of the explicit ideological or political commitment of any one nation. Also if we are to survive into the next century we must make sure that at least some members of the rising generation in each country become, not national citizens, but citizens of the world. One of the particular parts of this world plan for education ought to take us beyond merely exchanging persons, displaying our ways of life to each other, and providing unilateral technical assistance: in the end it is necessary to accomplish an actual sharing of values and concepts of diverse cultural origins. We need to develop, therefore, a considerably widened, if not universalized, reservoir of exemplars from which the content of courses of study in our schools and colleges anywhere may be drawn.

EDUCATIONAL AIMS*

The aims of education in any country must be determined only by the country itself.

* Contributed by C. Edward Beeby and Paul Woodring.

Within a pluralistic society there are diverse aims for education which, at any particular stage of development, may be in some measure mutually incompatible. In many developing countries the resources are markedly inadequate for achieving all the aims at the same time.

Education must provide for the fullest possible development of the individual *and* for the collective needs of society. The following aims should be a part of the ultimate educational policy of every country: the ultimate achievement of universal literacy; the educating of individuals capable of making wise, independent decisions; preparing men and women to make a full contribution to the economic and social life of the community; preparing individuals for life in a world society, with a full appreciation of their individual responsibilities and the responsibilities of their country to fellow men throughout the world.

The increasing gap between the educational opportunity in countries at different levels of economic development forces each to plan the aims and policies of its education system. Specifically each must provide for the consideration at the highest level of the views and interests of all the elements in society likely to be affected by the decisions, and must be prepared to cooperate with other countries in furthering general educational development. All school systems have a responsibility to contribute as much as they can to world peace by inculcating both international understanding and an awareness of the need for peaceful means of solving conflicts.

National ministries of education, in conjunction with the United Nations Educational, Scientific, and Cultural Organization, must give greater attention to and provide more funds for: the development of textbooks and other teaching materials that contain more than a national perspective; the joint planning of courses concerned with the history and literature of the world and with the growth of agencies of international cooperation; the greater use in school and university curricula of works of art and ideas drawn from more than one national or regional culture; the increase of planned international exchange of students and teachers, and the establishment of means of facilitating the transfer of students to schools and universities in different countries; the extension of cooperative enterprises among students from different lands; and the promotion of international cooperation among educational institutions at all levels.

To accelerate the modernization of educational systems and practices, it is necessary to establish an international clearing house of educational content, methods, and organization with the following functions: to identify significant innovations in educational practice designed to make schooling more relevant to the needs of a rapidly changing world; to cooperate in the evaluation of such innovations; and to suggest and stimulate experiments in content, methods, and organization to supplement those innovations in such a way as to provide a systematic basis for the dissemination of information and advice on improvements in educational practice.

INFORMATION ABOUT THE EDUCATIONAL SYSTEM *

It is necessary to assess facts, not only about the educational system, but also about the larger social and economic context in which education is operating, particularly when the system is about to change, as it now is in all countries. Many educators, particularly at the secondary school and university levels, tend to see their part of the educational system as a sort of metaphysical entity that is, or ought to be, unaffected by the changing of society.

Isolation in some respects exists between education as an institution and society at large. A striking outcome of this isolation is the conviction of some educators that education is their business and that outside groups or agencies should not meddle in their affairs. This is also reflected in the fact that, until recently,

* Contributed by Torsten Husén, Keith E. G. Taylor, and William G. Walker.

education and research have been confined to their own frames of reference, in terms of their own values, and that there has been resistance to using a disciplinary approach in trying to solve the problems that education and research are supposed to tackle.

What each country needs, in order to plan for or improve its educational system, is a set of simple statistical data pertaining to its demography, population movements, birth rate, economy, etc. This fact-finding is a continuous business and therefore requires a permanent unit, or bureau of statistics. Educational planning is virtually impossible without certain basic information about some quantitative aspects both of education itself and of the society it is supposed to serve.

Successful planning, particularly if it is properly carried out as a regular part of policy-making, must also consider the qualitative aspects of education. The emphasis on certain types of quantity is a temptation to favor it at the cost of quality. Too many comparative statistics of enrollment tend to camouflage a rather hollow educational reality. This is particularly the case when a country tries to expand its educational system very rapidly at both the primary and the secondary levels.

There is need for a more exact knowledge of the outcome of school instruction. To know how well or how badly the system works at a particular level, the country must have evaluation machinery. Policy decisions about school structure, introduction of new programs, and requirements for teacher certification ought to be guided scientifically by scientifically valid evaluations. This also leads toward recommendations that educational research should be more closely and continuously tied up with educational policy and the development of curricular methods and materials. Precise and relevant information produced by research is, in both of these connections, essential to meeting the international crisis in education.

The countries of the world can be regarded as one big educational laboratory where experiments with different practices are carried on. Children at school at different ages are put into systems of differing structure; they need curricula of different types. One can therefore bring an educational system into better perspective by comparing it with other systems and, particularly, by relating the outcomes of the system to input factors which vary so widely from country to country.

There is need to evaluate educational projects that are carried out as part of technical assistance. This type of evaluation has not been used to the fullest extent. One part of an evaluation with an international perspective could be appraisal by examiners from abroad. Initiative has recently been taken to set up regional educational research organizations, whereby countries in a given region of the world can pool their efforts to focus on their particular problems.

The responsibility of the mass media to increase efforts in reporting educational topics should be stressed. Another aspect is the need to open up channels of dissemination, particularly among countries, to establish some sort of international currency. In order to achieve a maximum of semantic consensus, a mutually accepted terminology would help promote understanding; an internationally viable terminology would be of great value.

It is important for the public to know what is happening in education and to participate in it. In centrally directed countries this idea is often overlooked. The planning takes place at the top; attempts are made to carry out plans; and there is no discourse between the leaders and the population, or between the leaders and the people who are supposed to carry out these plans. The mass media should make a great effort to know, not just the high spots, but the whole of education—the day-to-day problems, the plans, the aims and objectives—and to help pass it out to the public.

Although dissemination is also the role of the educational administration and planning in some countries, the people who are expected to do it are already burdened with their other administrative jobs. It is important that the administration not only hand out information but also be sensitive to what is coming back from the people. In most countries the ministers or bureaus of education should have a special area for publicity or for personal or public relations.

Planners and policy-makers must have available accurate, simple, standardized, and meaningful data for interpretation within each nation and at international levels. Research must be concerned with more than purely factual, quantitative data; the outputs of the educational process must be assessed in qualitative, operational, behavioral terms.

EDUCATIONAL STRUCTURES *

During the years when children receive education in common subjects and citizenship, it is best that they be trained under the common roof.

Education of adolescents should begin at the end of the primary school, and it should be deliberately diversified to provide versatility and easy absorption into adult life.

Every human has a social right to a specified number of years of education; and after a minimum number of years in compulsory schooling, the balance of these years should be available to him in an "education bank" full-time or part-time at any age he wishes to pursue it.

A system of higher education should be greatly diversified, and a deliberate program of differentiation of function should be maintained to assure each country of several types of institution of higher education—not bad copies of universities—serving different purposes.

A system of certification of practitioners in major professions including that of teachers should be extended to include recertification at regular intervals to maintain high levels of competence.

Classroom teachers should be trained as experimenters in research, and their day-to-day solutions of important educational problems should be collected in an "education record" to form the body of data of pedagogical knowledge.

* Contributed by George Z. F. Bereday and Jean Capelle.

DEMOCRATIZATION [*]

The basic conditions for democratization of any educational system must be: a national commitment to develop education open to the largest possible segment of the country; a full mobilization of manpower to support and participate in education; a realistic inventory and commitment of resources; and determination that educational requirements promote the balance between social needs and rising personal aspirations.

Expanding and democratizing education may not be achieved in the absence of an integrated program of social development. The expansion of educational investment by national governments is all too often a way of evading crucial decisions about priorities in a development policy. Political decisions must be taken before any educational decisions.

Preliminary to establishing educational priorities, educational decisions on democratization require the application of technical methods to analyses and inventories: inventories of manpower resources and requirements—analyses of the educational systems in terms of input, output, and process, and job analyses to establish training requirements for educational support; the recognition and definition of cultural impact upon education, including wanted and unwanted inputs, and the utilization of cultural materials; the recognition of the role and application of communication in education development, including the extensions of interpersonal communications, which are produced by education, and the use of mass communications as part of the educational process; and the formation of such institutions as may be required for the support of educational development and the logical expansion of the system.

Political means—for example, the establishment of a "mobilization for education" and the development of national commitment to education—should be used, but there are limitations on the

---

[*] Contributed by Frank Bowles and A. H. Halsey.

direct impact of education, stemming from anthropological and historical factors. Such factors must be acknowleged as basic to educational planning.

The concept of national service should be introduced for students in secondary and higher education to serve as technicians, teachers, community workers, rural workers, youth leaders, and in other occupations supportive of national development. Such service must be preceded by specific training programs and properly planned and supervised.

Work-study programs (sandwich courses) for students in secondary and higher education must be developed to improve training and recruitment for the labor force, as a method of guidance for students, and as a step toward breaking down prejudice toward certain forms of labor. The development of positive selection and guidance through educational diversity must be undertaken in place of negative selection and rejection within narrow programs.

There must be continuing search for unrecognized and untapped educational resources.

There is a directly political meaning in the application of educational opportunities to improvement of status for minority groups.

The continued extension of the concept of multilateral aid—in addition to bilateral aid—must be directed toward the social infrastructure of developing countries, especially education, through appropriate agencies such as the World Bank.

EDUCATIONAL RESOURCES AND PRODUCTIVITY*

Over the last ten years much work has been done by national and international agencies in the field of educational planning within the general context of development. It has covered such vital points as the optimum allocation of resources to education as

* Contributed by Friedrich Edding, Barbara Ward Jackson, Raymond Poignant, and Carlos Malpica Faustor.

a whole and to its various sectors, the balance between centralization and decentralization, the provision of relevant statistics,
and methods of evaluating planning performance. Strong new
efforts should be made by competent agencies, national and
international, to pool this experience, study its results, and
remedy its deficiencies. The agencies should coordinate their
activities in this field and disseminate the results to decision-
makers at all levels of government.

It should be the aim of international economic assistance to
strengthen the sense of the international community as helping
itself and to mitigate the equivocal relation of donor and client.
In the field of economic assistance to educational development,
a new effort should be made to use international channels for
the planning and dissemination of aid. Where bilateral assistance
continues, the effort should be made to secure coordination between national donors so as to avoid confusion, overlapping, and
even contradiction in local national plans.

In developed and developing countries alike, the largest
potential source of frontier finance for education lies in the nations' arms budgets. Political and strategic arguments are used
to justify the maintenance and increase of massive instruments
of "overkill" in the developed sector. Also, the rationale of "national security" lies behind a general competitiveness in arma-
ments, though this decreases security with each upward twist
of the military spiral. Both national security and planetary survival would look more certain if a steady percentage of the
$150,000,000,000 spent annually in the developed world on arms
(4, 5, even 6 per cent of the gross national product in many
countries) were transferred to the works of learning and peace.

In many countries, developed and developing alike, there can
be no large immediate increase in educational spending out of
direct taxation. In the countries where large inequalities of income coexist with low, corrupt, or insufficient tax-gathering, the
argument has little merit and is one more reminder of the political nature of the central decisions made in educational strategy.

However, where the pressure is genuine, alternatives have to be sought in providing tax revenue for education. Parents unwilling to pay for any increase in general income taxes may tax themselves more radically for local schools which are in close contact with local news and local government.

The growth of expenditures for education is related to the techniques of financing. This aspect is not at all secondary in importance. Many countries tend more and more to finance education by means of the state's budget. The advantages of this system, which is general among European countries, are obvious from many angles: free education, equal developments in education both in amount and in quality in the various areas of the country thanks to the financial loans made possible by means of the state's budget, etc. Its major drawback, at least for those states whose economic organization is totally or partially liberal, are the limits that the state's financial system may encounter. Even now countries in the process of development, particularly most of the African French-speaking countries, and certain Latin American and Central American countries have taken a leaf from the book of the industrialized countries and have headed along the path of centralized financing at state level. It must be remembered, however, that, among the industrialized countries themselves, this financing technique has only been adopted in recent years, and that it constitutes the present-day ending of a long period of evolution which began with the nearly complete financing of education by families and local communities. It appears that the path of exclusively centralized financing is dangerous for all the countries that stand a chance of actually running into the stone wall of the limits of the state's financial system.

The best solution, at least for those countries that do not yet enjoy a high level of income, seems to us to be the diversification of sources of financing: (1) Financing by the state in relatively large proportions constitutes, in any case, a necessity for the development of certain levels of education, notably higher education, and for ensuring the transfer payments that will guarantee equal development of education in the various areas of the country. (2) Financing by means of taxing the local communities themselves must also play an important role. In fact, in many countries this type of financing appears to be more readily accepted by the population, especially if certain local taxes are specifically earmarked for the development of schooling. (3) In most countries private financing must not be excluded in principle, whether it is, for example, a special contribution of business for professional training, or whether it is a contingent contribution by families (in various forms and according to their ability to contribute).

Many school systems do not take advantage of the availability of long-term and short-term credit. The use of mortgages and other forms of loans to finance school systems permits the cost to be spread over periods that represent more realistically the time needed for education to generate more resourcs in the community. Governments and school authorities should examine these alternatives.

Various forms of benevolent or insurance funds to which employers, workers, and government all contribute, can help to finance the strategy of education and retraining as a lifelong process. Insofar as such schemes of insurance are in effect a tax of low visibility, they can be useful in communities where taxation has reached the limit of the citizen's readiness to pay. Governments should consider the establishment of such funds for the financing of continued education.

Since the graduate from higher education has received a direct enhancement of his lifelong earning capacity, it is reasonable to demand some return to the community for the resources— often very scarce resources—that have made this education possible. Student loans, repayable once earnings begin, offer a method recommended to éducational authorities. Care should, incidentally, be taken to remit the cost of repayment in the event of graduates' marrying.

The principle of the land grant college is recommended, by which parts of the national domain are designated as a capital base for the educational institution.

A critical problem of resources is raised by the general tendency of skilled and educated people to move from areas of lesser development to more developed centers: village to town, developing nations to developed states, Europeans to the United States. In general terms, the ultimate answer lies in creating counter poles of attraction: more development in the countryside, lively regional frontiers in the developing countries, a dynamic technological community in Europe, a general distribution around the world of major centers of scientific and artistic creating. But the facts needed for detailed recommendations on policy are not available, and impartial and authoritative studies of the issues should be undertaken by appropriate public and private agencies. This careful appraisal is all the more necessary in that the extremes of state direction on the one hand and entirely unimpeded personal inspiration on the other do not solve the delicate and opposite problems of human freedom and social responsibility that are involved.

Certain countries—notably Iran and Turkey—have used military training as a means, not only of educating servicemen, but also of involving them in rural development. Where such training exists (though the introduction of universal military training in order to secure these advantages is not advocated), its possible educational value should be seized.

The provision of better technological aids, the introduction of systems management to schools and whole educational establishments, the involvement of teachers in the planning of education, and their awareness of education as an instrument of development and nation-building can all have the effect of enhancing teachers' self-respect and projecting their image as members of a dynamic, modernizing profession.

It is in the countryside that the vast revolution of modernizing agriculture is needed. If no changes occur in outlook and response, such a revolution will not happen. There is a lamentable shortage of effective ideas for meeting this vast challenge of informal education. Pilot projects in experimental regions are urgently needed. The World Bank and other interested agencies should designate a region for an experiment in large-scale environmental change, where marketing, productivity, extension, community development, cooperatives and other needed transformations can go forward with sufficient resources and enough feedback to evolve an effective strategy in this vital field.

When the investments in materials for production represent 10 to 13 per cent of the gross national product, and the expenditures for private consumption 60 to 65 per cent, it is not unreasonable to think that expenditures for education, including the training of adults whose role in the educational system must be enlarged, could accordingly reach 8 to 9 per cent of the gross national product, or even more by the middle or the end of the 1970's. The educational expenditures of the United States, after having grown from 3.4 per cent of the gross national product in 1950 to 6.3 per cent in 1966, will reach 8 per cent in 1970.

Free education is rightly considered an important element of social progress and a deciding factor in making education democratic. The solution to the question of free education is reasonable and democratic when all or nearly all the age groups have access to given levels of education. This solution is less reasonable and certainly less democratic when only a minority of the age groups has access to it, and when, furthermore, this minority is made up essentially of children of social groups who are themselves minorities in society. In most of the countries of Western Europe where, within the limits of an average registration rate of 6 to 13 per cent, 45 to 60 per cent of children of those in the upper ranks have access to higher education as opposed to 1, 2, or 3 per cent for the children of manual laborers. Under these conditions it may be said that free higher education is not necessarily in accord with the real concept of democracy, and that, on the contrary, it is only an additional privilege generously bestowed on social groups that are already favored. Consequently, under such circumstances, it is not at all unthinkable or undemocratic, if financial straits really require it, to consider family or individual participation in certain educational expenditures—after, of course, every measure has been taken to guarantee freedom of education to all poor students. Some of the richest industrialized countries resort to such solutions.

A choice has to be made between a new increase in expenditures for education and certain forms of private consumption: this is done by families that impose on themselves additional burdens in the form of private lessons, trips abroad by their children to practice a foreign language, and so forth. This selection process, which takes place spontaneously within certain family budgets, may also be made, in the framework of a continuous economic increase, on a national scale.

The solution to problems of education in less favored countries implies an increase in transfer of funds from the rich countries to the poor ones. The example of the Soviet Union shows how effective has been the transfer of resources from the west to the east of the Urals, for the economic and social development of the central Asiatic republics and especially for the equalization of the development of education in all parts of the Soviet Union. The world must become organized to increase the size and effectiveness of these transfers of funds, particularly on behalf of education. The solution should certainly be sought by means of a development of multilateral assistance.

It is indispensable to increase the resources allocated to education, and at the same time it is necessary to try to utilize them better. On the one hand, the resources devoted to education, although increased, will remain scarce. Misuse of these resources must be completely forbidden. On the other hand, the improvement of "productivity" of education will often constitute for political, economic, and financial authorities a sort of prerequisite for the massive increase of resources. In this area two complementary methods of attack must be distinguished.

Increase of the internal effectiveness of the educational system is first. Knowledge (of Latin, mathematics, etc.) as well as desirable behavior must be more quickly and more completely acquired by students. The schools face the entire gigantic problem of the struggle against examination failures, repetition of courses, waste, etc.: that is, the need for improvement in the quality of the educational system. They need rationalization of the educational structure, employment of new teaching methods, improved training of teachers with a view particularly to qualifying them in the use of new teaching methods, and the rationalization of construction of facilities and of purchase and allocation of school and university equipment in connection with the introduction of new methods and techniques of teaching.

Increase of the "external effectiveness" of the educational system is second. It means the application of knowledge and behavior learned at school to the needs of modern society. Individual needs (development of the individual), social needs (more complete participation of the individual in social life), and economic needs (integration of graduates of the educational system into the active population) are the governing factors. Proper adaptation of the training of youth and adults for the job requires quantitative and qualitative forecasting of the needs of labor at all levels of the professional hierarchy. Some people argue that it is impossible to forecast the changes in production techniques and its consequences on the structure of professional qualifications. Forecasting, even though imperfect, is nevertheless necessary. The real difficulty to overcome is that of adequately combining various means of study in order to make the best possible forecasts.

It is necessary to draw careful and realistic conclusions regarding plans and programs for training youth and adults as well as for guiding the students in choosing their special fields.

The pupils and students may be guided by various means: information and advice to families and students through specialized services, scholarships, *numerus clausus*, etc. These should

be used concurrently, and the relative proportions to be used—
that is, the degree of "flexibility" or "rigidity" in guidance—
depends on the social, economic, and political situation of each
country.

The time factor has been one of the essential elements, one
of the basic dimensions of the crisis faced by education in the
world today. One must relate the two concepts of productivity
and resources to the concept of over-all education. An educational system receives a number of inputs, changes them as a
result of a number of procedures or technologies, modifies them,
and then produces what we might call output, which is allegedly
aimed at achieving a number of desirable and final objectives.
Resources are but a factor in this equation: they are parts of a
much more complete and complex whole which must be considered in all its dimensions before specific measures can be
proposed.

The problems of education in the world will not be solved
by increasing the traditional inputs, which increase traditional
practices en masse and thus multiply the same output that we
have been producing in the attempt to reach objectives that we
had proposed to ourselves some time ago. This is a poor conception of education, which unfortunately has been practiced a great
deal in the world. It has led many people to believe that the solution to educational problems consists simply in providing more
resources. What is worse, it has convinced many people that if
sufficient resources are not provided, it is not worth while to seek
a solution. The same could be said of an analysis of productivity.
Improvements that have been asked of us in educational technology are not necessarily aimed at increasing inputs or increasing the yield we customarily have given to society. This would
lead solely to a sterile, futile task of trying to improve constantly
what we probably should not try to improve. These limited views
must be overcome.

External productivity and analysis of that productivity could
be described as a quest for a relation between what the educa-

tional system produces and what the objectives of development require. There is broad agreement in this field, that analysis should be done, but those devoted to the planning of educational development must confess that they are not quite certain how to obtain this relation, as manifested in an equation, or how to translate it into meaningful, workable programs. However, all work toward such a goal with enthusiasm, using or sometimes abusing the faith that everybody has in education today.

Educators are the last to realize that there is a growing wave of dissatisfaction in the world because of the lack of effective education. This dissatisfaction may be due less to the fact that education is working in a worse way, and more to the fact that more and more is expected of education. For instance, in the case of resources and educational systems, systems inputs are mainly monetary in nature, but development has stopped because of lack of human resources. On the monetary side we have already mentioned the considerable increase in budgetary appropriations, but we should not forget that there are important things that money cannot create and money cannot buy. History has shown that faith and the decision of the people have been at the base of the greatest social changes and transformations of the smallest countries. We see the philanthropy of the poor practiced, and this is something that cannot remain outside the educational task. It is a source of great moral strength: those that have least are those that get most, through constant efforts to get those that have most to give more.

If educators are not able to develop the universal fraternity of mankind through education, then we should hardly expect this fraternity to be reached by following other paths. We must improve the morality of relations among countries and peoples, and education provides us the key to achieve this. The basis of the joint effort we are starting here must be the principle that we can all give, that we must all give. This does not seem to be a new thing, but in practice it would be a new element. We are living in an era where it is more common to take than to give;

but we must also agree on another principle: that we cannot give willynilly, because people as persons have a dignity of their own.

With regard to productivity, valid criticisms have been lodged —namely, that educational systems are archaic and conservative. There are so many countries in the world where the educational system does not open doors but rather builds dead end streets. These systems are not aimed at elevating man but rather at thwarting the growth of men and children. The actions of teachers are limited to the four walls of the classroom. The students devote their time to many things, but perhaps it should be asked if they could not carry a greater social burden from the time they are in the school, in the classroom.

Some agencies, such as the World Bank and the United Nations Development Program, should consider whether they could conduct, in a region or a specific area, experiments designed to test whether the changing environment can be used as an instrument of education. In an area where normal development is probably the critical factor in the provision of enough food for the human race by the 1980's, we could see the development of cooperatives, the introduction of better land tenure, the infrastructure of the market system with its roads and power, and all the informal methods of education being used together to give some kind of model of hope for people whose formal education is not yet possible, yet whose acceptance of innovation is essential for the future.

For the first time in human history it does seem possible for economies not only to grow but to grow steadily and predictably. If it is true that in the Atlantic world, in the Soviet Union, in Japan, in the other developed parts of the world, we can hope for rates of growth of 3 to 4 per cent a year, it is quite clear that the entire perspective of all our use of resources has completely changed: this might be the biggest innovation we face. Apparently we are prepared to accept something of this innovation in the single sphere of defense. The amount of resources available to education involve a political decision, one that will be taken against this background of present and growing resources. If in fact we accept the principle of the transfer of resources among regions, from town to country, only a political limitation of our imagination makes it impossible to envisage the transfer across the wider frontiers in order to achieve a community of man. Here rhetoric runs so far ahead of fact that it is difficult to get this kind of subject on the agenda of realism. But educators must train the human imagination to soar; behind the political will is the presence of the human vision.

MANAGEMENT*

The crisis of education lies in the disparity between expectations and achievements. While this is no doubt true, it is in itself but a symptom of deeper causes, among which there is a group that might be roughly classed as the lack of relevance of educational systems to the needs of contemporary and future society.

Education is frequently reproached as being backward-looking, as preparing the young for the world of yesterday, as lacking a vital connection with society's goals. While these may be exaggerations, there is enough truth in the accusations to necessitate a close look at educational obsolescence, to identify its causes and take steps to increase relevance.

Until recently the main task of education has been considered the transmission to new generations of the traditions of society and the accumulated experience and information of the race. In a relatively static situation this has meant that the teacher had but to communicate his own knowledge and experience, acquired in turn from his own teachers. In a world dominated by change, with the reservoir of human knowledge swelling spectacularly within the lifetime of the teacher and even within the education cycle of the pupil, with growing aspirations, trans-

* Contributed by Alexander King, Henry Chauncey, Arthur Tremblay, and Richardo Diez-Hochleitner.

formed societies and completely new types of employment, the knowledge and attitudes of the past have become inadequate.

How then can education change so as to find a new relevance for society and its individuals? The very nature of the educational system insulates it from change. Its cycle is very long, and accepted reforms may take as much as twenty years to reach their full effect. It possesses a built-in inertia, in that teachers, unless continually refreshed with new knowledge (which proves difficult in practice), are inevitably presenting material that is at least a generation old. One has only to realize that children in school today, assimilating obsolete facts and attitudes, will be teaching those who will reach their full activity in the middle of the next century. This situation, tolerable until recently, is just not good enough for present needs. What is required is a dynamic transformation of the system which will enable it to cultivate adjustment to change and make innovation possible—but this is very difficult to achieve.

Educational policy and management lie at the heart of the matter. Unless management is constructed deliberately in directions that will favor reform, and accepts innovation as a major task, it inevitably becomes obstructive to change. This is true for organizations in general, not just for education. The first requirements are probably to increase the professional competence and consciousness of educational management and to reform its structures so as to permit this loose and complex system to maintain close and fruitful contact with other areas of activity and policy. Educational administration can too easily become isolated from parallel systems of management elsewhere and from the impressive development of its techniques; it can also be too remote from world trends in other fields, thus becoming insensitive to the changing nature of the functions of education.

Too rigid management can become isolated from the realities of the schoolroom. Educational managers and policy-makers should thus be selected and trained for greater professional competence and flexibility, so that they are able to understand the problems of the politician, the economist, and the sociologist and to enter into dialogue with them in such a way that, not only can education be made more responsive to the needs of society, but other fields of national policy can the better appreciate what education has to contribute to the attainment of national goals.

It would be unwise for education to attempt a slavish imitation of management structures and methods which have been devised for other types of organization. Nevertheless, recent developments in management have led to the establishment of principles and techniques that are of wide application and could, with suitable modifications, be adapted to the special features of educational systems. Much is already being done in this direction. There is, for instance, a trend to organize the line structure of education according to functional categories such as curriculum development, school building, examinations, guidance, etc., and not only in accordance with the classical divisions of education—primary, secondary, etc.

Of great importance also is the development of staff functions in educational management. There is already a trend in this direction, but it requires considerable strengthening. Great care must be taken—in educational as in other organizations—that staff activities are organized so as to exert influence at all levels down the line and not just at the top. Otherwise the assimilation of new iedas can be greatly impeded.

One of the most striking innovations in educational management is the increasing importance of the planning function, for which many central ministries have now created special staff units. This is very welcome; it is important, however, to ensure that "the plan" is not just a piece of paper to frame or file away, but that planning becomes a lively and dynamic process responsive to changing needs and possibilities, broad in its conceptional basis, and fed with all the necessary data.

The existence of a plan, however progressive, is not sufficient to ensure innovation throughout the system. There is need to establish deliberate and conscious mechanisms for innovation at all levels—the minister and senior policy-makers, local authorities, the universities, and the schools. With regard to innovation at the center, we propose the establishment of a unit that would be headed by an outstanding educational leader close to the minister of education and charged with the task of cultivating the innovative spirit throughout the system. Such a unit might or might not be part of the planning mechanism. It would seek out opportunities for experiment, channel selected and significant results from the growing world body of research to the points of decision-making, stimulate pilot schemes of reform and evaluate their results, cultivate and examine critically advances in educational technology, arrange for the setting up of "extension services" to speed up the application of new methods and systems, and generally be responsible for the responsiveness and relevance of education of each nation.

Such an innovation staff would have to exert its influence at all levels and not just at the top. It would no doubt find it useful to establish interdisciplinary task forces, which would include representatives of the various line functions, to help in the rapid penetration of its work.

Educational change cannot simply be dictated at the top and then come into automatic operation in the schools. There is need for understanding, participation, and willingness throughout the system and especially within the schools and in the teacher-training colleges where attitudes are created that can favor or oppose innovation for many years to come. Some informal machinery of contact between the various types of education is needed, on a professional but non-trade union basis, to make possible really informed debate on educational developments involving every category of educator. Pilot and demonstration experiments in education should as far as possible be distributed throughout the regular system, rather than segregated within experimental schools. As the latter are predisposed to change, they are not always representative of normal conditions and do not provide the participation of typical teachers in new approaches. Legislation that permits the choice of particular schools or particular classes for particular experiments would meet the need.   •

If highly professional managers of education are to be forthcoming, a new approach must be taken to their recruitment and training. Certainly a high proportion of such people should be teachers, selected rather early in their careers as showing special aptitude for managerial activities and responsibilities. Such picked candidates must then be given a substantial and modern training in administrative procedures, management principles, and techniques of operational research and systems analysis, as well as instruction in economic and other matters necessary for the understanding of the perspectives of their future work. A proportion of the managers should, however, consist of bright young professionals already experienced in other sectors.

The training of managers requires special consideration. Eventually each country should establish an administrative staff college that combines a thorough knowledge of educational practice with the most up-to-date approach to management problems. If possible such colleges should not be isolated institutions but should work closely with or be part of new facilities for management education in general, since education could benefit greatly from awareness of management problems and development trends.

It will not be possible for all countries to establish such colleges immediately; among other difficulties, suitable teaching staffs will be hard to find. Initially, therefore, the international organizations and especially the regional organizations, such as the Organization for Economic Cooperation and Development and the Organization of American States, could give a great impetus by establishing regional courses or schools to provide countries with a demonstration of the type of instruction required, and by aiming mainly to produce the teachers of the national management.

In all environments, planning begins as the work of experts:

sociologists, economists, demographers. It takes place also inside or outside the administrative structures of the educational system. The result is educational plans for development that have all the purity and quality of architectural blueprints. There would be no problem if the planning of school development included nothing but technical and scientific details. We all know, however, that it goes far beyond technology: it involves all the values of a society and occurs within a process of over-all social transformation, as both a cause and an effect of it. Indeed, when the planning is done exclusively by experts, the experts themselves choose new directions that society is to take. In any case, planning cannot avoid choices that commit the entire social order, so that when the experts' plans are carried out, they sometimes come up against insurmountable resistance from both the educational system and society as a whole. This is the problem: the deadlock where technical planning leads. One must find ways of avoiding this impasse by setting up mechanisms to allow wider participation by all the groups involved: participation not only in the execution but also in the planning; participation built on the various levels of the central, regional, and local administrations; participation of the teachers and even the students (where the students have acquired a sufficient level of maturity to make a positive contribution); participation of socioeconomic groups, not just educational professionals.

This cooperative planning effort, which commits and involves the consumers of the educational system as well as the agents and the authorities, should take place within planning committees on regional and local levels. These committees must participate in planning development as well as executing it. These committees must be given technical information in order to force the experts to translate their academic conclusions into everyday layman's language. The latter would be allowed, then, to formulate the choices and the options that all planning implies.

Such cooperative planning is slower and more laborious than technical planning. It leads to projects that perhaps are not as cohesive or as scientifically rigorous as purely technical plans, and that therefore are less satisfying to the intellect; but they have the great advantage of being better or more deeply rooted in the environment for which they are destined. They correspond better to the aspirations and values of the society, as this society itself defines and perceives them. The desire for innovation is seen as the society itself wants to use innovation. In this respect the blueprints for a transformation process conceived by cooperative planners are much more difficult to visualize, because sometimes they are not examined carefully enough to suit the experts.

Although it is true that integral educational planning began ten years ago precisely in the northern hemisphere, modern educational administration, infused with these same principles and practices, is our greatest challenge at the present time. The idea of integrating educational planning was conceived with a view to proposing rational and concrete action based on a systematic study of the over-all educational process and its socio-economic relations.

The time has come to see to it that the whole administrative-educational apparatus participates in the planning process, that this process is not limited to the mere technical responsibility of a technical body. But it is going to require a firm will and positive political decision to eliminate incompetence and ignorance from educational management and to undertake a policy of professionalization and continuity.

Educational management should now be mobilized toward a readaptation of its structures and procedures more in accordance with the functions assigned to education, and thus be able to reject the artificial and traditional compartmentalization of archaic educational systems. However, this functional agility will depend on the professional competence of each manager and on duly institutionalized mutual cooperation.

The training of educational managers or administrators will have to receive renewed attention, so that it may be better related to the needs of the present and the future—beginning with the in-service training of executives and supervisors. Provision must be made, not only for teaching procedures, but also for the study of techniques and the contents of our educational enterprises, based on the results of serious preliminary investigation.

International action cannot give too much importance or too much assistance to this enormous and noble undertaking. It has already begun with the initial effort of the United Nations Educational, Scientific, and Cultural Organization in establishing regional centers and the international center, the International Institute for Education and Planning. No matter how sophisticated the developed countries are, they can learn a great deal from the efforts and solutions of the less developed ones. In this, as in other human undertakings, international cooperation is a two-way street.

Management in education must itself become an educational effort, a quest for knowledge and practice in the exercise of freedom; and we must all continually study and search for realistic, efficacious new solutions which will be in keeping with the needs of our world and the means within our reach.

In summation, education must be related more clearly to other elements of national policy. While this is essential at a national level, it is also important at regional and local levels, where complex problems require a combined attack from many policy angles. Also principles and structures evolved in other fields can, with advantage and after modification, be assimilated by educational structures. There is, furthermore, a need, to coordinate people and ideas from different parts of the educational system. This should be established outside the bureaucracy. Individual teachers, in particular, should be encouraged to engage in innovations.

CONTENT AND METHODS OF SCHOOLING[*]

If education is failing, it is educators who have failed: some of us because we have defended the indefensible, and some of us

[*] Contributed by John Vaizey and Wilbur Schramm.

because we have fought battles we have not yet won. For better or worse, the world, if it survives, is in a continuous process of technological change. The most able and creative minds polarize into two groups: those who accept this world, and those who absolutely reject it. We need both groups in our schools. If we just accept technology, it will destroy us. We must use it for life. Democracy means that individuals count and have to be given the means to be counted. It was to the credit of the liberal generations in the developed world that they got Mark Hopkins and his friend off the log and into the schoolhouse. It is our generation's task to get them, not only into the schoolhouse, but also into meaningful life, where they are not alienated from the world's culture by this schoolhouse.

What must be done is as follows: first, the individual student is our concern, rather than the teacher. That means that education must be custom-built for the student. It is wrong to talk about teaching: we ought to talk about learning. Among the two-thirds of the world's population that goes to school, many are already so handicapped by social, economic, and psychological misfortunes that they cannot learn. They must have more than the others and must be specially cared for in the curriculum. Some will join education in infancy already handicapped; others will not join until they are grown, but the principle applies to both groups. Note that this requires the educational system to deal with the individual and not with the group. Each need must be specifically met.

If the motivation to become a lifelong learner is to be sustained, the curriculum must be relevant. The teacher's attitude is crucial. If he is alert, sensitive, and civilized, he is a model. Otherwise he is death. We know that teacher education and re-education is at the heart of our problem. If the schools of medicine were as badly endowed financially and intellectually as some schools of education, doctors would still be using leeches. Surely a great cooperative, innovative effort is necessary in which the universities as a whole and all their major disciplines enter into a discourse with all the teachers. The educational system too often has not been a sounding board for this discourse. Tell the universities that they are in education. Their leaders are the leaders of education. It is their job to innovate. Modern teaching techniques, at their best, release teachers from boring and repetitive chores to be free to stimulate, to guide, and to think about what they are doing. Only skilled and resilient teachers can really use these new techniques. But, of course, to think about how you teach is to think technologically, for technology means to think about how to use resources in different ways to achieve a given end. Many good teachers reject many of the values that seem to them implicit in this world.

Whether we talk about rich urban schools or about poor rural schools, we always get back to three key concepts: (1) What people learn has to be immediately relevant to their needs, but at the same time it has to enable them to change their environment. We must educate for discontent. (2) The fact is that to do this, the teachers have to be strong enough and well educated enough to help their pupils by every means open to them. (3) To be strong and well educated, the teachers have to have confidence that all the resources of our culture, which is an innovative culture, are available to them. The educational system is not equipped to innovate, except by accident, unless these concepts are fulfilled in practice.

Individualized learning is desirable. Segregated education is not. If the new media can lead to true individualization so that those whose needs are greatest can get most, then they will be truly liberating. But if they are used to enforce the existing structure, they will merely weld the manacles more firmly on our wrists. Equally, student-centered education should be vocational in the sense that each student's education should culminate in the entry of a fully qualified adult into the world of work. We need a highly diversified secondary and higher educational system. We reject narrow vocationalism. We welcome broad education, plus very specific training. Lastly, since education is so

intimately associated with the culture and with the world of
work, it must be, in essence, lifelong. This poses a profound
challenge to the content of education, to its style, and to its
methods. We await a Piaget of the adult.

We know that educational attainment is determined mainly
by socio-economic factors. We know, therefore, that if we care
to give education to all, we have to work directly on these factors. We know, too, that if we offer a segregated education, we
will reinforce socio-economic differences. We know, therefore,
that if we want a common culture, we need, to some degree and
at some stage, a common curriculum. Likewise, we also know
that a curriculum designed for purposes other than the expressed
needs of the individual student causes failure and dropout. To
escape from this dilemma we must devote much effort to the
individualization of the learning process.

Still, we leave open the question of how to find out what is
to be taught. The social sciences have only a few fairly imprecise
things to tell us at this stage; clearly manpower-forecasting can
only tell us generally what society will need in the future.
Further, though social demand is a useful concept, it tells us
little or nothing of what we ought to teach. Parents demand,
almost by definition, what is past. The task is to find the right
values for the future. The renovation and the invention of educational content seem to be an interdisciplinary matter and a matter for the continuous involvement of society as a whole. The
isolation of education that has culminated in the special discipline of the educator, is part of the disintegration of the modern
world. Our cultures lies shattered about us. We have to pick up
the pieces. We have to say that to be interdisciplinary is to lose
caste, but to save our souls. And institutions must be devised
for this work: not only local, regional, and national bodies to
attack concrete problems of curricula and teaching methods (they
are very important), but more important still is the widest involvement of society, and especially of the universities and professional institutions, in the problems of the schools.

The problem is not tools—we have excellent tools. As a matter of fact, hardware is far in front of our software. We have over five hundred well-done experiments that would say to us that these tools can be used either effectively or ineffectively. They can be used to share the best teaching, to take burdens off the shoulders of the teachers, to carry educational opportunities where they would otherwise never reach. It is we who are lagging. We have not found out what we should about where and when and how these new tools may most effectively be used. Between the overselling and the overcaution of the conservative educator, we need chiefly a flow of information and experiment aimed at finding the most realistic possible base for our decisions on the use of these new opportunities.

RESEARCH TO IMPROVE EDUCATION[*]

Educational research should be closely and continuously tied to the making of educational policy and the development of curricular methods and materials. Precise and relevant information produced by research is essential to meeting the international crisis in education. For example, research should be used actively to determine educational priorities at particular stages of economic, social, and political development. Structures of educational agencies should foster interaction between research and operations.

Much greater use of research should be made, both in analyzing educational aims and in evaluating the outcomes of education. Aims should be formulated and outcomes assessed in terms of specific behaviors and capabilities.

Funds should be provided for cooperative, multinational research projects. These funds should be sufficient to cover the planning of programs and the dissemination of findings, as well as the actual research operations.

Educational research should more readily utilize interdisci-

[*] Contributed by Torsten Husén and Arthur A. Lumsdaine.

plinary contributions. Research should consider the *social and political impacts* of educational policies and programs, as well as their economic consequences. More research is needed on the effects of educational policies and practices on the development of international cooperation and the changing attitudes that lead to international conflict.

In line with the recommendation of the United Nations Educational, Scientific, and Cultural Organization for projects at the national level, international educational projects should reserve at least 2 per cent of the operational costs for research and evaluation.

EDUCATIONAL TECHNOLOGY*

A center to gather information and experience on the use of new educational media and technologies should be established somewhere in the world, with appropriate publications and easy availability for usage. Insofar as possible, this should be a center of centers: many nations or regions will want to have their own information centers.

A demonstration project, adequately financed for a period of five to ten years, should be established in each of three developing regions—Latin America, Africa, and Asia. These projects should not be limited to one technology but should grow out of an examination of needs of the region to be served and an adaptation of many technologies in the most imaginative way to those needs. Research should be built into each project from the beginning to test out different methods and applications, and a continuing training program should accompany it to prepare people at all levels for the introduction of suitable new technologies throughout the region.

The potentiality of communications satellites for education and development should be thoroughly explored. The full impact of such satellites will not come for some years, but their potential

* Contributed by Hans Leussink and John E. Vaizey.

contribution to the distribution of knowledge is so great that studies of their usefulness should begin as soon as possible. One country or region should study fully the possible uses to it of a communications satellite; if this preliminary study indicated feasibility, a pilot project should be financed for the use of such a satellite, with adequate testing and opportunities for observation and training built in.

There is an urgent need for developing countries or regions to establish demonstration and training centers of their own, aided when necessary by international organizations or bilaterally, to familiarize their teachers and others with modern technologies of education. Recognizing that education is broadly defined, they should deal with education outside as well as inside school.

The methods of systems analysis must be used to modernize school systems to meet the current demand upon them with the new technologies that are available. Multidisciplinary task forces would be useful in bringing the methods of systems analysis to planning schools for the modern world.

School systems should be made to realize that the new technologies will not diminish existing costs but, if used well, can make a qualitative contribution and help to extend educational opportunities. For example, they can share the best teaching more widely and help to reach children and adults who otherwise could not be taught, or at least could not be taught expertly. Unit costs can be reduced if new technologies like radio and television are not limited to in-school use, but are offered for full educational service: to children and adults, in school and out of school.

To use the new technologies adequately, it will be necessary to have an extensive program of in-service training for everyone concerned with the system: classroom teachers, studio teachers, writers and seekers of material, and administrators.

School systems should try to minimize resistance to new technologies by effecting a maximum involvement with them. This

may be done in many ways: by including some of these skills—
for example, computer programming—in the curriculum, by giving teachers full opportunity to plan for and become well
acquainted with the new techniques, etc.

NONFORMAL EDUCATION [*]

In a world where nothing is certain except change itself, no
term for learning short of a lifetime has much relevance. Education conceived as schooling, or something for children, or mere
preparation for living, falls far short of man's needs or capacities
for growth. By lifelong learning we mean an attitude to human
growth and a process that starts in the family and nursery school,
that comprehends all the stages of schooling and all of the nonformal experiences by which children and adults grow in
perception and understanding. The concept of permanent education, of the "seamless web of learning," is as old as man himself
but is now endowed with fresh urgency and meaning. For
educational planning: how can you plan for parts of a system
unless you have a concept of the whole? For teacher recruitment
and training: how can teachers of children prepare their students
with the appetite and skills of learning, and how find and prepare
teachers of the millions of men and women who have kept alive
their zest for intellectual adventure? For research: what methods
and materials and organization and management are needed
when the educational enterprise is seen as a great enlarging
continuity? For formal and informal education: both are im-
plicated, in all their dimensions. For curriculum: perhaps an
education planned for a lifetime may have some hope of dealing
with the complexities and wonder associated with the human
condition. Educational authorities must be used everywhere to
adopt a concept that will bring wholeness and coherence to
learning, and all present educational practices must be re-
assessed in the light of this concept.

[*] Contributed by Bertrand Schwartz and J. Roby Kidd.

Many have said that education is far too important to leave it exclusively to the educationists. Highest on the list of those who need to be concerned about and involved in education are the students, young or old. The students should participate in the organization and provision of education by identifying needs, by allocating resources, and, as they become more skilled, by becoming increasingly responsible for the management of their own learning experience. We know that children can be helped increasingly to be proficient in the art of learning, and so can older youths and adults. The process of involvement should go on in both formal and nonformal education. There should be participation by the learners in the planning of educational materials (books, broadcasts, films, etc.) as far as possible and, at least by older students, in the management of schools, libraries, and other agencies. In rural areas this means the development of *animateurs* and village leaders to give continuity and impact to a program. Educational planners, educational administrators, and teachers of all kinds should understand the need and the value of participation by the learner and develop skills in working with students.

Formal schooling is planned and offered usually by government departments. Responsibility is assigned by law and is discharged with the support of tax funds. Nonformal education should be offered under many auspices—government, church, business, farm, labor union, and hundreds of other organizations. Rarely is responsibility assigned—for planning, for research and assessment, for finance, for maintenance of standards, for innovations. The result far too often is duplication of effort or gaps and shortcomings, a curriculum that is a patchwork instead of a sequence of planned experiences, that involves inadequate or wasteful use of resources. In many countries the enthusiasm that comes from private voluntary effort is prized, and any initiative by students or by an organization is to be valued and increased. A rational plan is needed for all education, a plan in which clear responsibilities for education—under government or private auspices—are assumed and recognized. In addition to planning, some coordination of activities in regions and local communities is essential if scarce resources are to be fully utilized.

The World Literacy Campaign, which has been developed under the leadership of the United Nations Educational, Scientific, and Cultural Organization, should be urged upon all governments and international agencies. Adult education should be considered and organized everywhere as part of the regular provision of education. In particular, all governments and international agencies should undertake its implementation: by universities, teacher-training institutions, documentation, curriculum, and research.

Growing participation in formal educational systems serves to increase the desire for education—a desire that the formal system may fall far short of satisfying. This disparity between educational desire and its satisfaction looms as a worldwide problem; therefore more support, recognition, and refinement should be given to nonformal education as the opportunity afforded school leavers and adults to pursue continuous educational experience for the improvement of personal, occupational, and community goals. Further, additional forms of educational achievement, certification, and credit evaluation should be devised, in order that learners may move forward both to the satisfaction of personal goals and to recognition by the achievement standards of formal education.

Nonformal education is rooted in the experience and participation of people, and the capacity for accommodating to changes grows in importance in all parts of the educational process. Nonformal education should be characterized by aims, knowledge, and techniques that stress the interrelation of personal, community, and occupational lives. Research into matters of adult learning and motivation should be rapidly expanded.

The field of nonformal education is yet to be crystallized into an extensive and worldwide profession; meanwhile the advocacy of the field as a natural part of the educational system is very deficient. Imperative attention must therefore be given to establishing more and larger programs of graduate work and faculty research in colleges and universities in that field. Professional associations of specialists in adult education should be strengthened, both by each country and in the world as a whole.

TEACHERS *

It is rather meaningless to divorce the subject of the supply and utilization of teachers from the consideration of available resources. From the qualitative point of view, obviously there will always be a dearth of good teachers. But what is a good teacher? In the last century during the French Third Republic, a lay teacher was in fact the ambassador of a certain concept of government and of the republic, and he did much more than just stand in front of a blackboard. It may well be that the teacher of today or tomorrow should be an agent of change, an agent of modernization, constantly on the alert for new ideas: that is, he ought to be, not only a catalyst, but also a person who can accept constant transformation of the society itself. If he does not see that as his mission when he takes over his first job after regular training in a teachers' school, (or after passing through a crash training program), he might as well be pronounced "dead on arrival." His job, as far as we are concerned, should consist of much more than just inculcating dead knowledge but should embrace the transformation of rural life, the animation of community life, the organization of literacy, educational research work and the prompting and participating in administrative reorganization. Such a mission in itself might well provide the kind of high motivation that is absent among the young people who enter or want to enter the teaching profession.

To maintain this spirit, however, we are aware that other

* Contributed by Silvain Lourié, Necat Erder, R. Freeman Butts, and Alex A. Kwapong.

incentives ought to be available; one of them is the possibility
of constant promotion within the system. This promotion may be
based on qualifications gained through participation in permanent refresher in-training programs, which may well be taught
through radio, television, or correspondence courses. At the same
time we ought to avoid the automatic transfers of teachers from
one level to the next. Another essential is to devise, as objectively
as possible, means of evaluating and testing the performance of
teachers to ensure selection of those deserving to go on to the
higher echelons of the profession, either within their educational
level or in the next. How to ensure this mobility and promotion
through testing or evaluation based exclusively on professional
criteria gives rise to the embarrassing question of what to do
with the old school supervisors who control the new teachers.

As far as the quantity of supply of teachers is concerned, it
appears rather obvious that, given the magnitude of the demand
for increased enrollment and of the costs of hiring additional
teachers, the solution certainly does not lie in recruitment of more
civil servants. There is a need for mass solutions, for it is an
illusion to think that you can stop, or even apply brakes to,
enrollment-growth ambitions. Yet if we try to meet these ambitions with the traditional modes of hiring more teachers who
want more pay and claim more retirement rights, it is obvious
that we shall, in spite of the optimistic perspective opened to us,
run into insoluable difficulties. The solutions, therefore, for
quantitative growth of education call for such devices as unpaid
work through certain global voluntary movements, be they
civilian or military. Secondary students could be mobilized for
some months of the year, or the compulsory military service
could be transformed into a teaching service.

Obviously solutions to the massive demand also lie in the application of new techniques, as long as we accept the fact that
these new techniques, while they ought to be mastered and
controlled by the teaching profession, may well alter the very
nature of the profession and transform pseudo teachers into

technicians as they propel the better teachers into real centers of intellectual development and growth.

Another solution appears to lie in the direction of new methods in the training and upgrading of teachers, which ought to be an investment in quality for the future. While we must accept the pressure for quantitative growth, we ought not at any time to give up the ambition to respect and to develop the nucleus of quality teaching.

This leads us straight into the training problem. Teacher-training schools must be in the hands of specially selected and well-trained personnel, for they have the multiplier effect both in time, over generations, and in space, over people.

Another consideration in the training program is how to inculcate in the teachers and in the trainers of teachers the moving vision of an ever dynamic education and society. How can we inculcate the appreciation of the transformation of society as a constant, permanent process? This transformation will affect the content and the structure of the educational system at one time or another. So we come back again to the need for injecting into teaching-training schools appreciation and respect for new techniques. The teacher should understand that the living educational system should be his permanent school of education, his permanent teacher-training program, and that the deadly disease he must plan to ward off is "professional sclerosis." Teacher training must also be seen as a central process, linking the various specialized teacher-training programs and schools with colleges, universities, and institutes of education in a homogenous entity. There ought to be no more academic dead ends.

One of the consequences of this necessity is that universities should accept their responsibility in the promotion and constant adaptation of education through research and training. Teacher-training institutions should test whatever method is most applicable to the requirements within which they have to work. In one case it may be to shorten the duration of the formal training period, to sandwich it between practice in the field and a return to the institution. In other cases it may be different. What we wish to impress upon educators is the constant need to question the structures and dimensions of the training operation itself.

Teacher-training centers should be located in rural areas or should at least participate in a regional development process. This will call for a better liaison between educators and those responsible for agricultural marketing, agricultural production, and industrialization programs.

From the point of view of manpower resources, most of the ideas about teachers and teaching resource requirements reflect two illusions that should be abandoned. The first is the illusion of quality. Assumptions about the standards and quality of our teachers are usually based on the possibilities and requirements of a smaller system of education. When we increase the teaching body at the pace we are now, it is statistically necessary that the talent basis for the stock of teachers be modified. It is a statistical and genetic problem of talent distribution in society.

The second illusion is that of quantity and is closely linked with that of quality. Education is an intensive industry which wants to utilize highly skilled manpower. It is, in this sense, an uneconomic and expensive industry. So educational claims for manpower, when compared with the lists of claims of other sectors, do and will appear unreasonable. It would be difficult for countries to meet the demand for educational manpower at the levels expected now.

For these two reasons the crisis in education in relation to teachers is a structural problem, and the solution should be a structural solution. In this case innovation in the area of teacher training and in the technology of teaching (innovation is equally important in both areas) is not a luxury but a necessity. It is of greater importance for the underdeveloped countries than for the developed countries. One warning for the underdeveloped countries: Unless they develop these new technologies, they will be faced with the situation in which their technologies are determined from the outside, and they will have to import all their equipment; in many cases this solution does not fit their economic interests or resource possibilities. Thus innovation in underdeveloped countries should be considered only within the framework of their own special problems.

Salaries and status of teachers should be radically improved and linked with the built-in, on-going in-service training programs designed to provide promotion for the teachers and to avoid wastage and "dead end" frustration. We must make every effort to improve the salaries of teachers as a major inducement to recruitment and utilization of teachers; it is especially important to supplement the salaries of those teachers who successfully engage in further training.

Teachers should be made agents of change and development, and the scope of their function should be broadened, especially in developing countries. The training of teachers has to be adapted to this enlarged view of their functions. Teacher training should be a constantly changing process with constant opportunities for review and experimentaion. It is strongly recommended that the recurrent costs of teacher-training institutions at all levels in the developing countries should be considered as capital investment costs, and these costs should be financed for a reasonable period by the international agencies.

Fundamental solution of the problems of teacher supply and utilization requires the reform, reconstitution, and rationalization of institutions of teacher education, the rapid upgrading of the competence and motivation of teachers in service, and the development of the teaching skills required for modernization. All the resources of modern technology should be used in this rationalization. The first step should be the appointment of national commissions (including representatives of government, education, and universities, and with the aid of international assistance) to review the problems and propose steps for implementation. Since there is a world crisis in education, there should be a world plan for enlarging the supply and enriching the quality of the world's teachers.

The highest priority of teacher education is broadening the perspective and scope of the teacher's function as an agent of national development and modernization. The academic road to the improvement of teachers must be made more flexible and diversified in order to open the academic dead ends that now keep many of the world's teachers from higher intellectual, academic, and professional achievement. The role of universities in the education of teachers for all levels of the formal and the nonformal education systems should be enlarged and strengthened. A possible solution here is the establishment of many institutes of education.

STUDENTS[*]

The vitality of the process of education springs from the capacity to be transformed by learning or teaching. Someone whose nature will not be affected by new discoveries of the spirit or the heart cannot learn. Only those learn by being taught or by teaching for whom the transformation comes from within.

It is true of the student as of the teacher that one must talk, not only about his necessary participation within the school environment in the process of the acquisition of knowledge, but also about his participation in life outside that environment; because essentially one is a teacher or a student, not only during certain hours of the day in certain buildings, but also as a citizen leading an individual life.

The teacher who lectures is addressing himself, not to the students, but to a given concept, a dead concept. The student who is learning by rote does not see education as a responsibility, a right, or an obligation; thus he is denatured and becomes deadened. The pressure of the ever greater numbers aspiring to education is now increasing in the rural areas. What do we know of all these aspirants to knowledge? What do we know of their fears, their ambitions, their dreams, as they pass from a tradi-

[*]   Contributed by Silvain Lourié and Senteza Kajubi.

tional world to a new dynamic structure of a modernizing society? Do we know how to deal with social injustice in this school environment, which stresses abstraction and verbal competence?

We must develop psychological studies of the student in the school and family environment. We have to study the organization of guidance services, based on a greater knowledge of the young people and the possibilities society can offer them.

A second point is the importance of setting up preschool education on a large scale precisely to give children who at the outset suffer the considerable handicap of having had no access to an educational environment, a chance to catch up with the others. It must be noted, however, that we have no right to advocate any particular structure without saying that it would be possible in the developing countries only if it were established on a voluntary basis, because we cannot imagine that already scanty resources could be increased to meet this additional need.

Another important point is implicit in the answer to the following question: what can we do with all the students for whom primary education is the end, who are ready to work, yet who are not yet able to do productive work? We should talk about a second chance for those children to retrain themselves before they go into the workaday world. We must at least modernize the world's schools, so that these people can participate in a technical or a commercial world, and so that the teachers will inaugurate teaching programs that will instruct these students with as much dignity as the students who follow academic endeavors.

There is also the great problem of student agitation and dissatisfaction. This unrest will only be solved in the last analysis through renewed interest and access to centers of education corresponding to the concerns of the students as citizens of the modern world. This implies, of course, structural changes and great changes in teachers' attitudes. It is on this level particularly that we must encourage real participation of the students in the life of the institutions they attend; and this participation must be accompanied by increasing awareness of responsibility.

Recently the great English poet Auden said that schools should teach children to choose. Whether he is in a developing or a developed country, the student is an object of solicitation and requests. Society is trying to appeal to him in different ways; and since the school must teach the student to want to belong to that modern world, perhaps it can also teach him to acquire the mental stability he will need to make a proper choice of the direction his existence will take.

Manpower plans inform us that if developing countries want to transform their economies into modern ones, they must plan on 50 per cent of the children of primary school age and 4 per cent of those of secondary school age going to school. The parent in an African village in Uganda, Kenya, Tanzania, or Ghana does not understand this principle. Every parent wants his child to be among the 50 per cent, and later among the 4 per cent, who will go to school, and is content as long as it is the other man's child who remains out of school. This is the nature of the crisis that concerns us. We have to accept the fact that teachers must be produced to teach 100 per cent of the world's children.

If we accept the necessity of offering education to all children as the heart of the crisis, we have to think of means of meeting this critical necessity; we shall have to reject the manpower approach, whereby a portion of the world's human resources would be put into "cold storage" while our planners seek ways of building enough schools and producing enough teachers. We must instead think of ways of jumping into the future.

We suffer in the developing countries from not knowing enough about the children we teach. If teacher education is to meet the challenge and be improved, those whom we train as teachers must not only demand research but also accept its results, particularly in the field of how children grow and learn. Then every teacher we produce will do valuable research every day by seeing how children learn and develop in school. Teachers have often not been inspiring enough to make their students wish to accept the challenges of the future.

Students and children are the *raison d'être* of the educational system and provide its vitality. There is hence great need to study children and students in their social and cultural milieus; important research should be done in child development, especially in the developing countries. The strongest criticism of the present poor teaching and rote learning that prevails in some developing countries was made by George Bereday when he spoke of the deleterious effect of the schools on children "who come to school with bright eyes and two years later leave with glazed eyes." This effect is one of the strongest arguments for revitalizing teaching and other educational methods in the developing countries. In the case of students in high schools and universities, a determined effort should also be made to understand their aspirations and motivations and to encourage in them, in an imaginative way, a sense of responsibility and participation in the life of the educational institutions. The whole area of student life and student participation should also be investigated.